Be Reconciled with God

Be Reconciled with God

Sermons of Andrew Gray

Edited by Joel R. Beeke

REFORMATION HERITAGE BOOKS
Grand Rapids, Michigan

Be Reconciled with God
© 2019 edited by Joel R. Beeke

Reformation Heritage Books
2965 Leonard St. NE
Grand Rapids, MI 49525
616-977-0889
orders@heritagebooks.org
www.heritagebooks.org

Printed in the United States of America
20 21 22 23 24/11 10 9 8 7 6 5 4 3 2

Library of Congress Cataloging-in-Publication Data

Names: Gray, Andrew, 1633-1656, author. | Beeke, Joel R., 1952- editor.
Title: Be reconciled with God : sermons of Andrew Gray / edited by Joel R. Beeke.
Other titles: Sermons. Selections
Description: Grand Rapids : Reformation Heritage Books, 2019. | Summary: "Contains twelve rare sermons from Andrew Gray" — Provided by publisher.
Identifiers: LCCN 2019028939 (print) | LCCN 2019028940 (ebook) | ISBN 9781601787040 (hardcover) | ISBN 9781601787057 (epub)
Classification: LCC BX5330.G7 S47 2019 (print) | LCC BX5330.G7 (ebook) | DDC 252/.052—dc23
LC record available at https://lccn.loc.gov/2019028939
LC ebook record available at https://lccn.loc.gov/2019028940

For additional Reformed literature, request a free book list from Reformation Heritage Books at the above regular or email address.

CONTENTS

EDITOR'S PREFACE

It is a great privilege to introduce the publication of twelve rare sermons by Andrew Gray (1633–1656), a well-known Scots divine. Gray represents solid, experiential Reformed teaching at its prime. Compelling and practical in all his sermons and writings, this volume seeks to stimulate true Christians to renewed zeal in fearing God and having a heart for Him and His glory.

Andrew Gray was born in Lawnmarket, Edinburgh, to Sir William of Pittendrum, a merchant and staunch royalist, and Egidia Smyth. He was the fourth son and eleventh child in a family of twenty-one. As a child, he was convicted of the sin of ingratitude by unexpectedly witnessing a beggar pour out his heart to God in a field near Leith. He thought, "There is a most miserable creature, in the most destitute of all conditions, while I have everything I need, and yet I never made such an acknowledgement of my mercies as that poor creature who does not lie under one tenth of my obligations." Subsequently, he was brought by Spirit-worked faith to rest in the finished work of Jesus Christ for his distraught soul. Peace that passes understanding became his portion.

Gray felt called to the ministry already as a boy. That gave impetus to his studies at Edinburgh and St. Andrews universities which were marked, in the words of Francis Coxon, by "remarkable proficiency, both in learning and divinity." He earned a Master of Arts degree in 1651 and at age nineteen was declared a candidate for the ministry. He was ordained in the Outer High Kirk in Glasgow by the Protestors on November 3, 1653, despite the objections of Robert Baillie and other Resolutioners who opposed his appointment for political reasons (largely because he was a Protestor), and because of his weak voice, his youthfulness, and his lack of being known. Baillie's fears were put to shame, however, as the Lord enabled Gray to exercise singular preaching gifts with considerable divine approbation.

Gray's popularity as a preacher was nearly unparalleled in his day. He rendered doctrine intelligible and practical. He could say with Luther from personal experience, "Doctrine is heaven," for scriptural truths had sunk deeply into his heart and molded his life and preaching. Incessantly Gray aimed for the conscience: in conviction of sin, in believing on the only Mediator, and in requiring godliness. He spoke to the heart in comforting the newly reborn, in arresting the backslider, and in unmasking the hypocrite. William Blaikie, author of *The Preachers of Scotland*, wrote, "His knowledge of Christian experience was wonderfully extensive and minute; he knew well the joys and troubles, the helps and hindrances, the temptations and elusions of the Christian life. He had a remarkable power of probing the conscience; as James Durham remarks, 'he could make men's hair stand on end.'"

Gray left no room for the "carnal Christian" of our day; his Christianity demanded knowing Jesus as both Savior and Lord. He was skilled in separating the precious from the vile. His exhortations were weighty; his invitations, persuasive; his comforts, moving. In a word, all his preaching honed in on winning souls to Jesus Christ. "Christ," as William Tweedie has rightly noted, "was the beginning, the middle, and the end of all his sermons." Small wonder then that Gray was regarded by thousands who gladly heard him as a burning and shining light!

Happily, Gray's popularity was conjoined with humility. To illustrate, the story has been frequently told of Gray and his illustrious colleague, James Durham, walking together to church on a particular Lord's Day. These two divines were to preach that day in the vicinity of each other. Observing that the vast majority of parishioners were entering Gray's church, Durham remarked, "Brother, I perceive you are to have a thronged church today."

Gray responded, "Truly, brother, they are fools to leave you and come to me."

Durham replied, "Not so, dear brother, for none can receive such honor and success in his ministry except it be given him from heaven. I rejoice that Christ is preached and that His kingdom and interest is gaining ground, for I am content to be anything, or nothing, that Christ may be all in all."

Gray excelled in experiential and practical applications. Both in preaching and in personal life, he accentuated sanctification. Like his fellow Scot, Hugh Binning, his entire demeanor conveyed genuine piety. Another fellow Scot, George Hutcheson, spoke of him as "a spark from heaven."

That spark, however, was soon destined to return to heaven. Andrew Gray was early made ripe for heaven. He often preached of and longed for glory. When he turned twenty-two, he expressed the joyous expectation that he looked forward to meeting his blessed Master in celestial bliss before his next birthday. And he received his wish, dying six months later on February 8, 1856 at twenty-two years of age, after contracting "purple" fever. He left behind a God-fearing wife, Rachel Baille (who later married George Hutcheson), and two children, Robert (who would soon die as a child) and Rachel. Gray's body was interred in Glasgow Cathedral.

"We may safely say," Blaikie remarked, "that never in the history of our country did a man of his years make so deep a mark." Gray was used in an unusual degree by God for the conversion of souls and the spiritual arousal of believers in the twenty-seven months of ministry allotted him in this life.

Happily, most of Gray's sermons were taken down in shorthand and preserved for posterity. These were first published from a student's notes but contained numerous errors. Later, they were meticulously revised from additional sets of notes, including those remaining in the possession of Gray's wife, and issued by Robert Traill and John Stirling as short books: *The Mystery of Faith Opened* (1659); *Great and Precious Promises* (1669); *Directions and Instigations to the Duty of Prayer* (1669); *The Spiritual Warfare* (1671), etc. Gray's written sermons proved as popular as his actual preaching, not only in England, Scotland, and North America, but also on the European continent—particularly in the Netherlands where most of his works were translated into Dutch and are still being reprinted and read today. For more than a century these little works passed through numerous editions until they were collected and printed in 1813 in Glasgow as *The Works of the Reverend and Pious Mr. Andrew Gray.*

This volume went through several reprints, the most readable being an 1839 edition published by George King in Aberdeen, reprinted by Soli Deo Gloria in 1992.

Gray's gifts do not lie in the area of propounding new theological insights, but in presenting "old truth" to the heart in fresh modes. Often his summaries of a doctrine are most enlightening. For example, when proving that assurance of faith can be known, Gray points to the following phenomena: (1) the lives of biblical saints that evidenced assurance; (2) "the great scope of many scriptures, to show how Christians may attain unto assurance"; (3) "commands in Scripture for Christians to be serious in searching after assurance," most notably in 2 Peter 1:10; (4) "the blessed end of God's oath in the everlasting covenant [is] that a Christian might get assurance"; (5) "the ends of the sacraments, that our assurance may be confirmed"; and (6) the very exercises of divine graces which affirm the necessity of assurance's attainability. None of these six points are novel to Gray, but few prior to him had compiled such a succinct list.

Unlike many collections of *Works*, Gray's is thoroughly readable, from the opening series of sermons on *The Mystery of Faith* to the closing letter addressed from his deathbed to Sir Archibald Johnston. In this volume you will find no abstruse theological debates or impractical messages, but rich food for your mind, soul, and life.

For many years, I thought that all of Gray's writings were contained in the *The Works of Andrew Gray*. Later I came across an obscure reference to fifty more sermons of Gray taken down by shorthand, titled *Select Sermons*. This volume was the first on my want list for more than three decades when I finally found a copy in the bottom of a box of Dutch books that were given to me by a widow of my congregation. I immediately went to work editing them for publication under an expanded title: *Loving Christ and Fleeing Temptation: Select Sermons of Andrew Gray* (Grand Rapids: Reformation Heritage Books, 2007).

Select Sermons was first published in 1765 from handwritten manuscripts obtained by Gray's former wife from a friend in northern Scotland. A second edition was printed in 1792 by Patrick Mair in Falkirk. The 2007 edition is freshly typeset and edited from the more accurate 1792 edition. (A selection of twelve sermons from this volume was reprinted as *Twelve Select Sermons* by Westminster Standard in Gisborne, New Zealand, in 1961.)

Select Sermons includes the following:

- Five sermons on how to fight spiritual pride (2 Cor. 12:7a)
- Four on praying against temptation (2 Cor. 12:8)
- Three on God's way of answering prayer (2 Cor. 12:9)
- Three on precious remedies against Satan's devices (2 Cor. 2:11)
- Three on resisting the devil (James 4:7)
- Two on beholding Christ (Isa. 65:1)
- Two on the role of Christian diligence in obtaining assurance of faith (2 Pet. 1:10)
- Two on Christ's preciousness to believers (1 Pet. 2:7)
- Several on Communion occasions
- A variety of individual sermons

Some of the more remarkable individual sermons include "The Necessity and Excellency of Delighting in God" (Ps. 37:4), "The Mansions of Glory Prepared for Believers" (John 14:2), "The Christian's Case and Exercise in the Night of Desertion" (Song 3:1), "The Intercourses of Divine Love Between Christ and His Church" (Song 2:1–2), and "The Necessity and Advantage of Looking Unto Jesus" (Isa. 45:22).

In 2007, I was wrongly convinced that all of Gray's sermons were in print. A few years ago, Rev. M. D. Geuze, an emeritus Reformed pastor in Nunspeet, Netherlands, informed me that the Newberry Library in United States had an additional twelve sermons titled, *Sermons of Andrew Gray* (1746). With the help of Rev. F. W. Huisman, I was able to obtain a scan of this book, and am grateful to bring another dozen earnest, rich, compelling sermons to you from this young preacher. I wish to express thanks to Marjolein de Blois and Carissa Feathers for typing these sermons from a difficult-to-read text, to Misty Bourne and Ian Turner for assisting me in editing them, to Gary and Linda den Hollander for their typesetting and proofreading, and Amy Zevenbergen for the cover design.

I have chosen to title this book, *Be Reconciled with God: Sermons of Andrew Gray*, drawn from its opening, powerful sermon, "Christ's Treaty of Peace with Sinners," based on 2 Corinthians 5:20, which

concludes: "Be ye reconciled to God." Meanwhile, a Dutch transla-
tion of this book has already been published under the title, *Opdat
ik Hem kenne: Twaalf preken* (So that I Might Know Him) (Houten:
Den Hertog, 2018).

The twelve sermons contained in this book are vintage Andrew
Gray. Each of them is succinct and compelling, alluring and hum-
bling. They are packed with both simple and profound thought
communicated with almost tangible passion. How I wish we could
hear Gray in person! Since his writings are sermons taken down
in shorthand rather than treatises, we ought not expect exhaustive
treatments of each subject discussed. Nor ought we to look for pre-
cise language, as Gray never had the opportunity to edit his own
sermons. On the other hand, we may be assured that Gray's sermons
were "studied with prayer, preached with power, and backed with
success." Moreover, his profound insights, poignant statements, and
succinct summaries of various truths should not be underestimated.

Like the English Puritans and his fellow Scotsmen, when Gray
preached a text, he preached it fully. If he preached from a text that
invites sinners to come to Jesus unconditionally, his whole sermon
consisted of compelling invitations (see the first two sermons of
this book). If he preached on experiential themes, such as union
and intimate communion with Christ, his whole sermon unpacked
these riches (see the third and fourth sermons). If he preached on
texts that focus on our responsibility to sanctify ourselves before
God, his whole sermon presses us on the particular aspect of sanctification that his text stresses (see sermons five through seven). If
the text selected contained a strong emphasis on warning against
one kind of sin or another, his whole sermon conveyed a solemn,
urgent warning note to abandon that sin and flee to Christ (see sermons eight through twelve). Gray was a preacher who was on fire,
as it were, to bring his church family the whole counsel of God as
contained in the variety of texts that he selected to preach. But each
particular sermon focused like a laser beam on the text at hand. This
helped make his sermons so compelling and powerful.

Much more could be said about the precious sermons contained
in this valuable book, but I will forebear. There is no substitute
for reading Gray himself. He will warm your soul, convict you of
slothfulness, and urge you to godliness. He is always full of spirit

and life. His sermons make doctrine intelligible and practical. They powerfully speak to the mind and the conscience, comforting the regenerate and inviting the unsaved. Above all, they seek to win souls to Christ.

Gray is a rare gem—read this book prayerfully from beginning to end. By the Spirit's grace, you will be fed, allured, chastened, convicted, and compelled to flee to and rest in Christ alone for every iota of your salvation and Christian living.

—Joel R. Beeke
Puritan Reformed Theological Seminary
Grand Rapids, Michigan

Christ's Treaty of Peace with Sinners

Now then we are ambassadors for Christ, as though God did beseech you by us: we pray you in Christ's stead, be ye reconciled to God.

—2 Corinthians 5:20

We have excellent and glorious news from a far country to declare unto you today. We have excellent tidings from the court of heaven to make known to you today. They are these in short: heaven desires to be reconciled to earth, the Persons of the blessed Trinity desire to be reconciled to you. And this is the thing that we are to preach unto you, as the ambassadors of Christ, that you would be reconciled to God. The contract of marriage is delivered over unto us; it is subscribed by the hand of Christ and is delivered unto us; and He has sent it here today, that you might claim it.

What do you say to this? Will you claim this blessed contract of marriage or not? What shall we report to Christ today concerning you? Shall this be the report that I shall carry back to Christ: "I came to Thy own, and Thy own would not receive Thee"? Or shall this be the report that I shall carry back to Christ today: "This people will not have Thee to reign over them"? Or shall this be the report that shall be carried back to Christ today: "This people shall be willing in the day of thy power" (Ps. 110:3)?

I shall not say much before I come to the words, only I would say these four things unto you: first, there are five great voices or things that cry forth, "O come and be reconciled to God." Does not the transcendent beauty that is in the face of Christ cry forth, "O come and be reconciled to Him"? Is not the great voice of the everlasting gospel, "O come and be reconciled to God"? Is not the great voice of His commandments, "O come and be reconciled to God"? Is not the great voice of the law, "O come and be reconciled to God"? And is not the great voice of your necessities, "O come and be reconciled to God"? You are surrounded with these many things that cry out our text, "O come and be reconciled to God."

Second, I would say unto you that, among all the suitors that ever fought for your heart, there was never the like of Christ. I confess we cannot set Him forth unto you; but sure we are of this, that Christ exceeds all suitors in His beauty, and He exceeds all suitors in His offers, and Christ's heart is more engaged unto you than all other lovers. Now, search today whether or not you will be content to take Him, that this may be reported in heaven today, that you have subscribed to the precious contract, "Even so I take Him."

Third, I would say unto you, if once you were acquainted with the Person that desires to be reconciled unto you, you would cry forth, "O for a tongue to commend Him, and to set forth His praise! O for eyes to look upon Him that is 'white and ruddy'" (Song 5:10)! O for a heart to lodge Him in, who is the noble "King of glory" (Ps. 24:8)! And oh for hands to obey what He commands, and for feet to walk in the paths of His commandments! I will not say with some that ignorance is the mother of devotion; but sure I am that ignorance of Christ is the reason why you refuse to be reconciled to God.

Lastly, I would say unto you, would you make all the Persons of the blessed Trinity to rejoice? Would you make the Father, the first Person of the blessed Trinity, to rejoice? Would you make the Son, the second Person of the blessed Trinity, to rejoice? Would you make the Holy Ghost, the third Person of the blessed Trinity, to rejoice? Would you make all the angels in heaven to shout and sing for joy? Would you make all these blessed thousands that are round about the throne to rejoice? Then obey this command: "Be ye reconciled to God" (2 Cor. 5:20). Know you not there is more joy in heaven at the conversion of one sinner than of ninety-nine that went not astray? I may say this by the way, O people of this place, what do you know but this is the last embassage and commission from heaven that shall be delivered unto you to be reconciled unto God? What do you know but, before night, Christ shall close up the blessed treaty of peace that has been between Him and sinners?

Therefore do not delay to be reconciled to God and to give your hearts unto Him.

The apostle Paul, in the former verse, discourses most divinely to that truth that "God was in Christ reconciling the world unto himself," and that, after the blessed contract was made up between the Father and the Son, He sent down the "word of reconciliation," and has "committed" that to His ambassadors (which commission and embassage, Paul here says, he was to preach) (2 Cor. 5:19). In the words we have read in this verse we have two things about which to be confident.

First, we have the noble and divine exhortation that is given to the Corinthians, and it is this: that they should "be...reconciled to God" (v. 20) — that they should lay down the weapons of their rebellion, and go and seek quarters from God, and subject themselves unto Him. Second, we have these five considerations by which the apostle presses this divine and excellent exhortation.

The first consideration is imported in that word *now*, which relates to the former. And it is this, in short, that since all things are ready upon God's part, since the contract is written and subscribed by His hand, there is nothing remaining but for us to consent to the bargain. This is a reason we should be reconciled unto God; all things are ready upon His part. Are you ready? Are you ready to subscribe your consent?

A second consideration, by which Paul enforces this exhortation, is also in that word *now*, and it is this: the time (says he) that this blessed treaty and offer of peace is to continue with you is but for *now*, and only for a short time. Therefore, since it is so short, you should by all means endeavor to make use of the day while it is with you. We know not how soon the long shadows of the everlasting evening shall be stretched out upon us, when there shall no longer be such a desire or exhortation heard as this, "O be reconciled to God."

A third consideration is that Christ is exceedingly condescending and loving in the way of His proposing and bringing about His excellent work, our reconciliation with God. And there are two steps of Christ's condescendence in the words. First, that He sends forth "ambassadors" in His name, to desire and request "in Christ's stead," that you would be "reconciled unto God," and give your hearts unto Him. The second step of Christ's condescendence in the words is that He does "pray" and "beseech" you to be reconciled unto Himself (v. 20). There is not a preaching of the everlasting gospel except as though Christ were sitting down upon His knees, desiring you to be reconciled to Him and saying, "I beseech you, be reconciled unto Me." Oh, will some ask, "Why does not Christ come Himself to woo then? What is the reason that He comes not Himself?" I would give you these two reasons. The first reason Christ does not come Himself to suit His bride is that we would not be able to behold Him; yea, if Christ would come down and preach this text unto you, "Be ye reconciled unto [Me]," you could not hear Him speak, nor could you behold Him. He is indeed a lovely and soul-ravishing Object, whom you cannot behold nor hear.

The second reason why He comes not Himself to suit is this: in a manner we could not believe Christ were real if He came Himself. Indeed He does not come Himself, to remove many objections of misbelief. O if we saw Him preaching this doctrine unto us, and did behold His matchless and transcendent excellences shining in Him, might we not cry forth, "Will He ever take me?" When we should compare Christ's beauty and all our deformities together, we would cry, "Will He ever take me?" And when we should compare Christ's highness with our baseness, would we not cry forth, "Will He ever take me?" Therefore He has thought fit to send out ambassadors to suit and woo a bride to Himself.

A fourth consideration in the text, to enforce the exhortation, is this: refusing the ambassadors that are sent forth in Christ's stead is as great a sin before God as if you did refuse Christ Himself. For the wrongs that are done to His ambassadors He takes as done to Himself. Yea, know it—there is not a sermon that is preached unto you by Christ's ambassadors in which you refuse to consent to take Christ, but it is as great a sin and indignity done to Christ as if Christ were from this place personally preaching unto you, or as if you would say to Christ before His own blessed face, "We will not be reconciled unto Thee."

A fifth consideration from the words, to enforce this exhortation to be reconciled to God and to take Christ, is this: that Christ took exceeding much pains to bring about that glorious, that excellent, and that advantageous work of our reconciliation and peace with Him. Did He not send forth His ambassadors to invite them who are strangers, and to persuade them to come and take Him? I would say this by the way: you cannot do Christ a greater wrong than to refuse to have Him, and you cannot do Christ a greater pleasure than to take Him.

Now we shall come to speak a little to the exhortation in the close of this verse: "God did beseech you…be ye reconciled with God." In it we may take notice of four things.

First, that *it is the great request that Christ presents to sinners, and which is made known in this everlasting gospel, that you would be reconciled to God.* Second, that *Christ, in pressing this request and desire, vents exceeding much matchless condescendence.* Is not this condescendence that He, who is the Party offended, should be the first Person that should seek the agreement? Is not this condescendence that He, who never did offend us, should carry Himself to us as though He were the Party offending? This is sure: we make the fault, Christ makes the amends. It had been no wonder to have seen man desiring to be reconciled to God; but, behold, here is a mystery of infinite condescendence, that an offended God desires to be reconciled with offending man. There is this, third, in the idea that *Christ is exceeding willing that this excellent work and blessed design of our reconciliation must be brought about and accomplished.* And does not His willingness appear in this, that He desires this so much? He beseeches you to be reconciled to God. If you could ask Adam, he would say Christ is willing to be reconciled unto sinners. If you would inquire of Manasseh, he would say Christ is willing to be reconciled unto sinners. If you would ask persecuted Paul concerning this, he would say Christ is willing to be reconciled to sinners, and to be at peace with them. Lastly, this is the exhortation: that *there is much freedom of love and unspeakable grace that vents in Christ's pressing this exhortation.*

Does not freedom of love vent itself in this, that we are enemies when He desires to be reconciled unto us? For so it is imported in that word, *reconciled.* It says Christ finds us in a state of enmity when first He proposes the offers of friendship. Is not this a declaration of the freedom of Christ's love in pressing this desire? There is nothing that moves Christ to desire to be reconciled unto you but love. If so we may speak, many a sore heart has Christ had, and many a tear has He shed for these woeful refusals we have given Him.

Now, in speaking to the first thing in the exhortation—that it is Christ's great desire and request that He presents unto you, that you would be reconciled and be at peace with Him—we shall not stand long to clear it. It is clear from Job 22:21, "Acquaint now thyself with him, and be at peace." And it is clear in Song of Solomon 2:10 where there is the great voice of the gospel, "Rise up, my love, my fair one, and come away." As likewise from Isaiah 27:5, "Let him take hold of my strength, that he may make peace." Now, when we press you or desire you to be reconciled to God, it imparts these three things: First, that you would let the weapons of your rebellion fall out of your hands, and submit and subject yourself to Christ; that is to be reconciled. This is pressed in James 4:7, "Submit yourselves therefore to God." Second, it imparts this: that a Christian should give his hand unto God. This is pressed in 2 Chronicles 30:8: "But yield yourselves unto the LORD." Or, as the saying is: Give your hand unto God. You know, when parties are to be married, they join hands together; so, when we press the duty of reconciliation upon you, we implore, give your hand unto God, and desire to resign and give over yourself unto Him. The third thing imported in this exhortation is that you would give your hearts unto God, according to that exhortation in Proverbs 23:26, "My son, give me thine heart." Christ is coming to woo today; Christ is coming to suit today—are you ready? Are you ready to consent to take Him? Did you ever see or behold Him? I shall say no more of Him but this: He is "white and ruddy, the chiefest among ten thousand" (Song 5:10).

Now in speaking to this truth, that it is the great desire and request that Christ presents unto you that you would be reconciled unto Him, I would speak a little to these things.

First, I shall clear that it is Christ's desire and earnest longing to be reconciled with you. And there are these things that prove it. One, do not His many commandments that are registered in Scripture, O sinners, speak this, that Christ is willing to be reconciled unto you? There is not a command in which He desires you should return to Him, but His very heart lies in the bosom of that commandment. I shall only give you these three precious places which speak to this His willingness that you should be reconciled. The first place is Isaiah 65:1, "I am sought of them that asked not for me; I am found of them that sought me not: I said, Behold me, behold me, unto a nation that was not called by my name." As it were, you cannot do Christ a greater favor than to take a sight of Him, and behold Him. Second, "As I live, saith the Lord GOD, I have no pleasure in the death of the wicked...turn ye, turn ye from your evil ways; for why will ye die, O house of Israel?" (Ezek. 33:11). The exhortation is doubled in this verse to point out God's willingness to be reconciled to you: "Turn ye, turn ye." Lastly, "Return, return, O Shulamite; return, return" (Song 6:13). Four times the word is there, *return*, which speaks that Christ is willing to be reconciled unto us, and to take us home unto Himself. Therefore you read of these precious commandments of Christ, that He is willing to be reconciled unto us.

There is a second thing which proves He is willing, and it is this: The blessed and the precious oath of the everlasting covenant speaks His willingness to be reconciled unto us. Does not that oath in Ezekiel 33:11—"As I live, saith the Lord GOD, I have no pleasure in the death of the wicked"—preach this, that Christ is willing to be reconciled unto you? Third, there is this that proves it, to wit, the lowness of the terms upon which He has condescended to be reconciled and to be at peace with you. O you will get Christ at easy terms; you will get Christ for a look, you will get Him for a listening of the ear to hear. This is clear in Scripture, "Look unto me, and be ye saved" (Isa. 45:22). There Christ is gotten by a very look. And later in the book of Isaiah, "Incline your ear, and come unto me: hear, and your soul shall live" (Isa. 55:3). There Christ is gotten by a very hearkening and inclining your ear. And fourth, there is this that speaks Christ's willingness to be reconciled to sinners, namely, the very terms upon which He has granted to give Himself, He has promised to fulfill these upon your behalf. It is promised Christ shall be gotten by a look. "But oh," says the Christian, "how shall I get a look to Christ?" That is turned over into this promise, "They shall look upon me whom they have pierced" (Zech. 12:10). The very look, upon which you shall get Christ, is turned over into a promise. Likewise and fifth, the very hearkening of the ear, by which you shall get Christ, is turned over into a promise, "The LORD thy God will raise up unto thee a Prophet from the midst of thee, of thy brethren, like unto me; unto him ye shall hearken" (Deut. 18:15).

The many sad regrets and complaints that Christ has had, why persons will not be reconciled and be at peace with Him, prove

Christ's willingness to be reconciled to you. Who can read John 6:40 and Luke 19:41 and not cry forth, "Christ is indeed willing to be reconciled to sinners"? Yes, know that, Christ weeps more for the lack of our reconciliation than some of us ever wept ourselves. There is this sixth thing that proves Christ's willingness to be reconciled to sinners, namely, that He has prescribed the way how a Christian may win this excellent thing, peace and reconciliation with God. This is clear from Isaiah 27:5: "Let him take hold of my strength, that he may make peace with me." "I tell you the way," says Christ, "how you shall win peace. It is even this: *take hold of my strength.*" There is this seventh thing that speaks Christ's willingness to be reconciled to sinners, and it is this: that notwithstanding the many refusals He has gotten from us since first this precious gospel was preached unto us, yet He continues with this, "O be reconciled unto me. Will you take me, and embrace me?" Christ, as it were, buries in oblivion and everlasting forgetfulness all our repulses of Him. There is this eighth thing that proves Christ is willing to be reconciled unto sinners, and it is this: He will even take a sinner at the close of their time, when they have been giving the strength of their heart to vanity, and when they have been giving the strength of their life to idols. Yet Christ is willing, if at last they will take Him, to be reconciled. Oh, is not this a mystery of love in Christ, that He is content to take you after all your idols have forsaken you? Is not this a mystery of love in Christ, that He is willing to be reconciled to you when you can do no better? Now all these things say Christ is willing; Christ is willing to make the bargain. But what should I speak of these things? Does not His dying, His traveling from heaven to earth, His subjecting Himself to the curse of the law speak this, that He is willing to be reconciled unto you?

Now, second, we shall speak regarding the close of our verse that *it is Christ's desire to be reconciled unto sinners.* We shall propose some considerations to enforce this excellent thing upon you, that you would obey Christ's request.

The first consideration is this: know the Person with whom you are to be reconciled; study the matchless excellency of Him that desires to be reconciled and at peace with you. There is more oratory and rhetoric in that word, *God,* to persuade you than we, if we could speak ten thousand years, could make mention of. Is it not an excellent thing to be at peace with God? Is it not an excellent thing to be reconciled to God—to have that precious name given unto us, which was given to Abraham, "And he was called the Friend of God" (James 2:23)? O what a noble thing were this, to have this engraved upon our foreheads, that we are the friends of God! And know it, the lack of knowledge of the excellency of Him that desires to be reconciled unto us, is the great reason why we stay so long in our enmity. Cursed be the person that is at peace with his idols and is not at peace with God.

There are four sorts of things persons desire to be at peace with rather than to be at peace with God, and all these "peaces" shall certainly end in war. There are some persons that desire rather to be at peace with their conscience than to be at peace with God; if once they could win to that length to silence their conscience, and to have conscience speaking peace to them, that would be their heaven and happiness. But know that your conscience may speak peace unto you when there is no peace unto you from God. There is a second sort that would rather be at peace with the ministers with whom they speak than to be at peace with God; that is, they are more desirous to have the minister speaking peace to them than ever they were to have God speaking peace unto them. And they whose peace or war does depend upon the minister's tongue, their peace shall end in war. A third sort of persons rather desire to be at peace with persons that are Christians among whom they live than to be at peace with God; some take more pains to keep up the peace and love they have from Christians around them than to keep up a correspondence with God. I suppose there are some whose conscience may charge them with this, that the loss of peace with a Christian, the loss of love from one that is eminent in religion, did affect them more than the loss of peace with God, or the apprehension that it was gone did. I say, that peace shall end in war. A fourth sort of persons rather desire to be at peace with their idols than to be at peace with God; that peace shall one day end in a cruel war. Is it not known that there are many who by all means endeavor to have their idols and their hearts united together by the constant chain of love and desire? And shall not that peace be declared from heaven one day to be a false peace? Now, take a broad sight of Christ, and this will exceedingly press you to be reconciled to Him.

A second consideration to enforce this thing upon you, that we would be reconciled to God, is that there is a fourfold peace that attends a Christian that is at peace with God. There is a peace of *conscience* that attends that Christian when once he is brought to be reconciled to God. When he knows he is in favor with God, then the disputing and debates of his conscience are silenced; then the storms that troubled him before are now blown over and gone, and there is a sweet composedness and quiet of conscience that is to be gotten by beholding the face of Christ.

There is also a peace in our *desires* that is to be gotten by our peace with God. Before people are reconciled to God, their desires are divided among many different objects; but when once they come to be reconciled to God, then they cry forth, "One thing have I desired of the LORD" (Ps. 27:4). Before we be reconciled to God, the language of our desires is "Give, give"; but, if once we were reconciled to God, we would have a blessed peace and quiet as to these.

There is a third peace that attends the Christian that is at peace with God, and it is this: in every lot and *condition* that a reconciled person can be in, he will have peace in it; there is no condition or state of life that a reconciled person can be in but he will cry out, "I have learned, in whatsoever state I am, therewith to be content" (Phil. 4:11). A person reconciled to God, when he is under a cross, can with one eye look up to the face of a reconciled God in Christ, and cry forth, "As sorrowful, yet alway rejoicing; as poor, yet making many rich; as having nothing, and yet possessing all things" (2 Cor. 6:10). A reconciled person can get something in Christ that may afford him contentment in his darkest nights.

A fourth peace that a reconciled person has is this: he has a peace under all the *vicissitudes*, the changes, the troubles, and the anxieties that are here below. Would you know the person that is "not afraid of evil tidings"? It is the person whose "heart is fixed, trusting in the LORD" (Ps. 112:7). Would you know the person that has this motto, *semper idem*, "always the same"? It is the person that is reconciled to God.

A third consideration to enforce this, that you would be reconciled to God and obey Christ's command and desire, is this: All things are ready upon God's part; there is nothing left undone by Him. Would you know what this is, even this noble Scripture? It is the contract of marriage sent down from heaven, subscribed by the hand of Christ; and He desires you to put your names to it. It was long since "God was in Christ, reconciling the world unto himself" (2 Cor. 5:19); now He has sent out ambassadors to desire you to be reconciled unto Him.

A fourth consideration to press you to yield unto Christ's desire is this: The time that this treaty of peace is to continue and last is but for an hour, even a very short time. Therefore it is of eternal concern that while Christ has not delivered up the kingdom to His Father, while Christ is entreating you to be reconciled, you would obey the exhortation, "Agree with your adversary quickly, whilst thou art in the way with him," lest the day come that He "deliver thee to the judge," and "thou shalt by no means come out thence, till thou hast paid the uttermost farthing" (Matt. 5:25–26; cf. Luke 12:58–59). Know it and be sure of it: there is no treaty after death; there will not be such a voice heard by the souls in prison as that, "oh, be reconciled unto God." Now I would ask this question to you by the way, "Are you reconciled to God? Are you at peace with Him?" If the most part of us would answer as we should do, we would say, "I am not at peace with God." Then I say unto you, "Agree quickly with your enemy while he is in the way; do not delay that excellent work of being reconciled to God."

A fifth consideration to enforce is this: that a person that is reconciled unto God has many soul-precious and excellent advantages waiting for him. This is clear in the Scriptures: "Acquaint now thyself with [God], and be at peace" (Job 22:21a). And the argument to enforce it is this, "Thereby good shall come unto thee" (v. 21b). Not this or that particular good only, but "thereby *good* shall come unto you." It is an endless work to describe the noble dignities of a reconciled person; it is an endless work for us to tell the riches of a reconciled person. I shall only point out the advantages that flow and come to a reconciled man.

First, a man that is reconciled to God may go in with boldness to the throne of grace, and seek things from God. Would you know what is the foundation of a Christian's spiritual boldness with God? It is even the faith of this statement, "I am reconciled to Him." O there will be much freedom used between a reconciled person and a reconciled God. This is clear from Romans 5:1–2, "Being justified by faith, we have peace with God…by whom also we have access by faith into this grace." A person that is reconciled with God "sitteth alone and keepeth silence" (Lam. 3:28); a reconciled person can draw the veil back, and go boldly into the chambers of preference.

A second advantage that attends a reconciled person is this: he is the person that meets with many sweet manifestations of God, and of the love of Christ; he is the person that has manifest visits from God. This is clear from comparing these verses in Romans 5: "Being justified by faith, we have peace with God" and "the love of God is shed abroad in our hearts" (vv. 1, 5). Would you know why you do not have communion with God? It is because you lack reconciliation with Him. "Can two walk together, except they be agreed?" (Amos 3:3). It is impossible that there should be a walk of communion and fellowship with God except reconciliation go before. Christ must be a Prince of peace (Isa. 9:6) and a King of righteousness (Isa. 32:1) unto us before we can be admitted to the banqueting house and have "his banner over [us as] love" (Song 2:4).

A third advantage that attends a reconciled person is that he can walk with much holy submission and contentment under every sad dispensation that he meets with. When a reconciled person meets such a cross, he (as it were) comforts himself with this: "I am reconciled." Let all terrors call themselves as in a solemn assembly against this man, he will cry forth, "I am reconciled, and this may comfort me." Who is the person that can "glory in tribulations" (Rom. 5:3)? It is the reconciled person. Who is the person that can endure the trial of "cruel mockings" and "reproaches" (Heb. 11:36; 10:33)? It is the reconciled person. "Let them curse, but bless thou" (Ps. 109:28). A person that is reconciled, he "sitteth alone and keepeth silence" (Lam. 3:28) under all the reproaches that he meets with, and lifts up his face to God and cries out, "O blessed am I in this, that I am at peace with Thee, though I be at variance with the world!"

A fourth advantage that attends a reconciled person is that they are the persons that lie nearest the mortifications of and victory over their lusts. As long as a Christian is under debates of his saving interest [in Christ, it is] one to a hundred if such a Christian overcomes; but when once you have won to this length as to cry out, "I am my beloved's, and his desire is toward me" (Song 7:10), you will then have strength to fight and overcome.

A fifth advantage that waits upon the reconciled person is that the reconciled person has a pleasant way of going about duties that others are strangers unto! There is a mystery in the way of a reconciled person's going about duties, which these that are still disputing of their saving interest [in Christ] do not know: It is a holy and spiritual art of praying, and of communicating, and of hearing, and of reading that the reconciled person has which the rest of the world does not know. There is that advantage likewise that waits upon the reconciled person, namely, he is the person that can do duties most diligently, that can do duties most divinely, that can do duties most believingly, and that can do duties most humbly and tenderly. Would you know the constant Christian in the exercise of duties? It is the Christian that lives within sight of his reconciliation. Would you know the Christian that can pray with most humility? It is the Christian that lives within the sight of a reconciled God. Would you know the Christian that can walk most tenderly? It is the Christian that has Christ reconciled always before his eyes.

Now, there are some that may say, "Why is there so much pressing of this? Are there any that are not willing to be reconciled to God?" *I will name you seven sorts of persons that are not willing to be reconciled to God, and I would desire you to search yourselves if you be among them or not.*

First, such as will never quit their idols; these are they that are not willing to be reconciled to God, for you must vent your willingness in this, in quitting the seven abominations of your heart. The idols must be put out before Christ come in. Does not your holding fast your idols between your breasts speak that you are not willing to be reconciled to God? And are not many such here? Are there not many who "hold fast deceit" and "refuse to return" (Jer. 8:5)?

A second sort of persons that are unwilling to be reconciled to God are the persons who trust upon their own righteousness; such are mentioned in Romans 10:3: "Going about to establish their own righteousness, [they] have not submitted themselves unto the righteousness of God." As long as you come not this length to cry out, "All [my] righteousnesses are as filthy rags" (Isa. 64:6), this speaks you are not willing to be reconciled to God. Till once you come to this, to acknowledge you have nothing to commend you to Christ, you are never persons willing to be reconciled to God.

A third sort of persons that are not willing to be reconciled to God are the persons who delight in ignorance and estrangement from God, who "desire not the knowledge of [His] ways" (Job 21:14). Are there not many who never received Christ in their minds? Therefore they cannot receive Him in their hearts. Know that Christ must lodge in your life before He can lodge in your heart. Can you love Him whom you know not? Can you admit of Him when you did never understand who He is? You that delight in your ignorance, that are strangers to the deep mysteries of the knowledge of God, you are persons that declare you will not be reconciled to Him.

A fourth sort of persons that desire not to be reconciled to God are these who dwell with contentment upon their resolutions and convictions, as though that were sufficient religion. These are persons who desire not to be reconciled to God. These are some who think they cannot lack peace with God because they lack peace with their conscience. Some do suppose, because they are at variance with their conscience, therefore they are at peace with God; and they build upon that. Some think they are reconciled to God because of their resolutions and purposes. But know this: a man may win the length of convictions, a man may win the length of resolutions, and yet be a person unwilling to be reconciled to God.

A fifth sort of persons that are unwilling to be reconciled to God are these who would take Christ as a Savior but not as a King, that would take salvation from Christ but would not take commandments from Him. Hence is that word, "We will not have this man to reign over us" (Luke 19:14). It is not said, "We will not have this man to *save* us," but, "we will not have this man to *be a ruler over* us." You must take the whole Christ if at all you think to be reconciled to Him. And do not the disputings of His commandments speak this, that you are not willing to be reconciled to God? That is a remarkable word in John 15:14—"Ye are my friends, if ye do whatsoever I command you"—as if Christ had said, "You would testify your friendship to me by giving a general obedience to all my commandments."

A sixth sort of persons that desire not to be reconciled to God are those who were never convinced of their enmity. Are there not some here that never sat down one hour to mourn under the conviction of the enmity they had against God? And this preaches that you desire not to be reconciled with God.

A seventh sort of persons that desire not to be reconciled to God are those who never took pains to keep any of the impressions of God constant upon their spirits. There is a threefold impression that is communicated by God unto a hypocrite, the not keeping of which proves him to be such a one. Sometimes the Holy Ghost will engrave impressions of sorrow for sin upon a hypocrite; sometimes the Holy Ghost will engrave impressions of delight in duty upon a hypocrite; sometimes the Holy Ghost will engrave impressions of love to Jesus Christ upon a hypocrite's heart. And this is that which preaches his unwillingness to take Christ: he knows not what it is to entertain any of these three.

Now, what shall I say unto Him who sent me? Alas! There are many of us that are here, whose countenance says, "We will not be reconciled unto God." Oh, shall precious Christ go away today without one heart to embrace Him? Shall it be told upon the mountains of Israel that Christ was here today paying suit to our hearts, and there was none among us that would fall in love with Him? Have you seen Him today, and have you desired to be reconciled unto Him today? *I shall say but these five things, and close.*

The first is this: "Many are called, but few are chosen" (Matt. 22:14). I may say, without breach of charity, that there are some hundreds here today that have been invited in the name and authority of the Master of this precious gospel to be reconciled to Him; and I could wish there were one among every twenty here that has been content to take Him. May we not question this, whether we shall call Christ precious or undervalued? We must even put them both together and say, "O precious but undervalued Christ, pardon our slightings of Thee."

Second, I would say this to you: behold, behold, the day is coming when Christ, who now desires to be reconciled unto you, shall eternally denounce war against you. Yes, know it to be true: Christ must either be your friend or your foe.

There is this, third, that I would say: namely, that if all the angels in heaven, and all the saints that are around the throne, were admitted to give you their counsel, if Paul who preached this text were admitted to give you counsel of this place, it would be, "O be reconciled to God." There would not be another advice in heaven given you than this, "Be reconciled to God."

Fourth, I would say this: Do not the souls that have entered into the sweet fruition of these excellent things that attend the persons that are reconciled to God, do they not now sing, "It is good to be reconciled to God"? Does not Abel now say, "It is good to be reconciled to God"? Does not Moses now say, "It is good to be reconciled to God"? Does not David now say, "It is good to be reconciled to God"? Do not the twelve patriarchs now say, "It is good to be reconciled to God"? And do not the twelve apostles say, "It is good to be reconciled to God"? And do not all who are here who have tasted of the sweetness of reconciliation with God say, "It is good to be reconciled to God, and to be at peace with Him"?

Fifth, I would say this: There are many that are here today that may question if ever God and they were reconciled together, or if ever the covenant of reconciliation between God and them shall be made up. Oh, it is sad to die an enemy of Christ, it is sad to communicate being an enemy to Christ, and it is sad to go over the borders of time being an enemy to Christ. Oh, will you seek to be at peace with Him? Now, what shall I say? What shall I say unto Him who sent me? Shall that Scripture verse be verified of us, "I pray thee have me excused.... I cannot come" (Luke 14:19–20)? Shall some of you say, "I am building a house, I cannot come to Christ; I have married a wife, I cannot come to Christ; I have bought a plough of oxen, I cannot come to Christ; I must be taken up with my merchandise, I cannot come to Christ"? Cursed be the feet that go away from Him; you never went to more blessed a gate. We shall even leave it at your door, and let this sermon be a heap of witnesses, that here you were obsessed and invited by all the virtues that are in the face of Christ, by all the joys of heaven, and by all the love you owe to your immortal souls—you have been desired from the consideration of all these to be reconciled to God. And upon your own peril will it be if you shall not take this precious ambassage off our hand. O take Him, take Him; you never had such a blessed offer, you never saw such a blessed sight!

Christ's Invitation to the Heavy Laden

*Come unto me, all ye that labour and are heavy laden, and
I will give you rest.*
　　　　　　　　　　　　　　　—Matthew 11:28

All Christ's words are fitly spoken, and are like apples of gold in
pictures of silver and, as Solomon speaks, a divine sentence in the
mouth of the King—how sweet is it! I would in the beginning of this
exercise summon all that are here to come and wonder and stand
astonished. Old men wonder, young men wonder, old women
wonder, young women wonder at this noble sentence: "Come unto
me." It is near six thousand years since first the lost posterity of
Adam did begin to drink of this noble fountain that is opened in
the house of David, and all of them have drunk and satisfied their
thirst, and yet the fountain is as fresh and full today as it was at
the first beginning. Are not these two well met, a full Christ and
an empty sinner? Are not these two sweetly met, a spotless Christ
and a sinful one, a merciful Christ and a self-destroying sinner? In
the verse preceding our text, Christ is declaring to His disciples
that all things were delivered unto Him; and (as it were) having
received that inexhaustible fullness, the next word that He speaks is
"Come," as if He would have said, "It is my delight to communicate
unto you of that fullness I have received."

I shall say to you concerning Him, "Come you to Christ whenever you will; you shall find Christ above your faith; believe never
so much good in His hand, He shall always be above your faith.
And come to Christ whenever you will—you shall always find Him
above your hope; hope as much in Him as you will, and He shall

always overcome your hope. And come you to Christ whenever you will—He shall always overcome your desire; seek as much from Him as you will, and He will always give you more than you seek. And come to Christ whenever you will—He shall always overcome your thoughts; let your thoughts of the preciousness of Christ be elevated to never so high a pitch as when you come to Christ. Sight and faith will tell you more than ever you thought. And come to Christ whenever you will—He will overcome your necessities; though your necessities be never so much, yet there is more in Christ than will answer them all.

Now to come to the words we have read. We have these three things to be considered: First, we have a noble and precious command that is given by Christ, and it is, "Come unto me." A commandment that is gilded with love, a command that has the heart of Christ in the bosom of it, a command that is full of mysteries, a command that has endless riddles of the love of God shining in it.

Second, you have the persons that are exhorted to come, and these are all that are weary and heavy laden. Or, as the word may be rendered, all these that are under an unsupportable burden, and are weary in pursuit after their vanity; if they desire to come, let them come. The persons that are invited are most comprehensive. Is there none of you that knows your name in this text? Is not your name here in this text? Is there not a person within these doors that knows your name here? Do not they call you weary? Then I am sure they call you heavy laden. There is not a person within these doors but may be called one of these two names. Then I say, "Come."

The third thing in the words are the considerations by which Christ presses the exhortation; and we conceive that they are three. The first is in that word "me," as if Christ would have said, "If there be no other argument to persuade you to come, let the excellence of the Inviter move you," or, "Come to transcendent Me, come to beautiful Me, come to dying Me, come to crucified Me, and come to glorified Me." This is the topic and common place out of which many of our arguments can be drawn to persuade you to come. I think in that word "me," in that one word, all the rhetoric and oratory of heaven is comprehended. What can entice you to come to Him, if not that word "me"? Come to Him.

The second consideration in the words, to press people to come, is this: that He would give them rest. Is there any of you that would have rest today? Then come to Christ. And, by the way, we may take notice of these four things from this consideration: The first is this: the infinite wisdom that shines in Christ choosing of His arguments; He will make choice of that argument, to persuade you to come, that will be most effectual. What argument can persuade a weary soul to come more than this argument of rest? There is a sweet harmony between our necessities and Christ's arguments. Second, we may take notice of this from it, that there is not a necessity in a sinner, but there is something in Christ to answer it. Are you weary? There is a rest to be found in Christ. Are you heavy laden? There is rest to be found in Christ. Are you under the wrath of God? There is righteousness to be found in Christ. Do you want holiness? There is sanctification to be found in Christ. Do you want victory over your idols? There is redemption to be found in Christ. Do you want wisdom? There is wisdom to be found in Christ. Yes, I may say unto you, if you have a necessity that you cannot see anything in Christ to answer it, you may say, "There is something in Christ to answer this, though I see it not." Third, take notice of this from it: that it argues not from a mercenary or legal spirit to be persuaded to take Christ because of rest. Some persons think, "It is not good to take Christ for heaven." I say it is both good and commanded to take Christ for heaven. This is certain: when first a Christian engages with Christ, he loves Him because of His gifts; but, when he is well acquainted with Him, he loves His gifts because they are Christ's. So when a Christian first engages with Christ, he loves Christ because of heaven; but after some acquaintance with Christ, he loves heaven because Christ is there. Fourth, take notice of this: no matter how persons pursue after rest, there is no rest to be found but in Christ. O weary ones, will you come and rest upon Him who is the Rock of ages?

The third consideration in the words to press persons to come to Christ is the excellence of this rest. And we conceive it is described from three things in the words. First, the freeness of this rest is pointed out: "I will give you rest." And we conceive this word is put in to obviate that ordinary piece of pride in persons who, when they come to Christ, think they deserve something from Christ. "No," says Christ, "you deserve nothing, yet I will give you rest." Second, it is described from the matchless excellence of it: this is pointed out in that word "I"—"I will give you rest." The Giver is most matchless and excellent, and must not the gift be suitable to the Giver? As the man is, so is his gift. Third, it is described from the perfection and completeness of this rest. The word that is here rendered "rest" imports a complete, soul-satisfying rest. Alas! We may ask, "Why does Christ need arguments to persuade souls to come? Is He not Himself an argument?" Now, to speak a little of the exhortation "Come to me," I shall speak a little to these five or six things.

First, I shall make clear that *it is the duty of a Christian to come to Christ*. Is it not commanded? "Rise up, my love, my fair one, and come away" (Song 2:10). And it is commanded, "The Spirit and the bride say, Come" (Rev. 22:17). And is it not commanded, "Come; for all things are now ready" (Luke 14:17)?

Second, we shall speak a little to this: *What is imported in this duty to come*? And we conceive it imports these five things: (1) It imports that a Christian should be apprehensive of the distance between Christ and him before he comes. It is impossible for one to come to Christ before he knows there is a distance between Christ and him. (2) This is imported in it: a Christian should be active to overcome, and go the distance. This likewise is imported in that word, "come." (3) This is imported in it: a Christian should have some distinct and precious apprehensions of Christ, otherwise he cannot come. We must know Christ's willingness and His suitableness to help us before we can come. (4) This is imported in it: a Christian should turn his back upon all other things beside Christ, and he should subscribe a bill of divorce unto them. (5) Lastly, this is imported in it: a Christian should make choice of Christ for making up all his necessities, all his wants, removing all his fears, supplying and strengthening all his hopes; so that if there be any emptiness in things here below, and if there be any imperfections in yourself, you will look to Christ and say, "Here is a remedy."

Now that which, third, we shall speak to is to propose unto you some *objections that hinder persons from coming to Christ*. And I may say by the way that often we create objections that hinder persons to come to Christ. And I may also say that often we create objections ourselves and spin them out of our sinful curiosity when it is not our exercise.

The first objection of one, why he will not come to Christ, is this: "Oh," says one, "I cannot come to Christ, for I know not if He will make me welcome if I come." I would say but these four words unto you who have this objection. First, I would say this: "Be of good comfort—the Master calls you. There is not a temptation that meets you in your way but you should answer it with this: 'The Master calls me.'" Thus, when you set about the duty of closing with Christ, there come in so many temptations that say, "Oh, dare you close with Him?" Answer them with this: "The Master calls me." Second, I would say, "Did you ever know of any that came to Christ whom He did not make welcome?" I have heard of many exercises of the saints, and I am sure I never heard of this exercise of any, "I came to Christ, and He made me not welcome." And, if there had been such a thing, it had been an exercise before now. Did you ever know a Christian under that exercise to say, "I came to Christ, and He did not make me welcome"? Did you ever hear of any that brought up that bad report? Third, I would say this, "You have Christ's promise to make you welcome, therefore come." "Him that cometh to me I will in no wise cast out" (John 6:37). There is that, lastly, that I would say unto you who have this objection: "Will you try Christ; and, if He does not make you welcome, come your way again." O try Christ, whether or not He will make you welcome; and, if you perish, let your ruin be under His right hand, and even say that word Esther spoke, "If I perish, I perish" (Esth. 4:16), but "I will venture upon Christ." Yes, believe it. I would say these three words unto you: If you knew Christ, you would go though He bade you not; if there were not such a commandment in Scripture as this—"Come"—yet you would come. Yea, I would say this unto you, which may seem strange: If you were acquainted with the beauty of Christ, you would venture upon Him, though He forbade you. Third, I would say this unto you, "Venture but upon Christ, and if He kill you, let your blood be at His feet." Now, I hope this objection is removed, that Christ would not make you welcome. Will you try Him today and see whether or not He will send you away?

The second objection of some why they will not come to Christ is this: "Alas," say they, "I am not prepared to come to Him; I have not the qualifications that the Scripture requires in them who come; I am not weary, I am not heavy laden; I am a person that has not the spots of His people; I am under the pressure of many idols." I would say this to you: What divinity is this? You will not come to Christ because you are sick! Do you think any wise person would argue this: "I am sick, therefore I must not go to the Physician; I am filthy, therefore I must not go to the Fountain to wash; I am under the power of my idols, therefore I must not go to the Redeemer; I am under the power of spiritual death, therefore I must not go to the Prince of life"? I pray you, what kind of argument is this?

Then, second, I would say this unto you who have this objection: If you are matchless and chief of sinners, I hope you will say that you have the greatest need of Christ; and, if you can have no other argument to persuade you, let your very necessities gain your consent. There is this, second, that I would say unto you: "How do they call you that object this? Do they call you thirsty? Then I invite you to come. Ho, everyone who is thirsty, come ye to the waters. Or do they call you hungry? Then I invite you to come. Ho, everyone who hungers, come and eat and be full. Do they call you weary? Then I say, come to Him. If they call you heavy laden (I hope none of you will not answer to your names), then come. Yea, more, do you have a desire to come? Then come. Do you have need of Christ? Then come. Do you have a willingness to embrace Him? Then come. For any of these three are qualifications good enough, either willingness, desire, or necessity. Whoever will, let him come. I am sure the greatest sinner within these doors may know his name here. Believe it—our name is more in this text than if it had been set down by name and surname. Come ye as such a person unto Christ.

The third objection of some, why they will not come to Christ, is this: "Oh," says one, "I cannot come to Christ, for I know not the way how I should come to Christ." I would only say this: He will guide you by His counsel, if once you come to Christ. Come once this far, and He will guide the blind in the way they should walk.

The fourth objection of some, why they will not come to Christ, is this: "I cannot walk to Christ, although I know the way." I say this unto you, creep to Christ if you cannot walk to Him. He will carry you in His arms; He holds the fainting in His right hand. Say no more to Christ but this: "I desire to come, but I cannot walk," and He will carry you. If you cannot come to Christ and take a grip of Him, cast a greedy look to Christ; you may look to Him when you cannot grip Him. And believe it: it is faith to cast a look to Christ when you cannot take hold of Him.

The fifth objection of some, why they will not come to Christ, is this: "I desire to close with Christ, but I am not able to exercise faith upon Him." I will tell you these grounds why a person who desires to close with Christ yet gets not freedom actually to close with him. And, first, we go about the duty of believing upon our own strength; but we must know this, that it is He who works in us both to will and to do. After you have gotten a desire to close, you must depend upon Him for ability to close with Him.

The second ground why persons that are willing, yet are not able to close with Christ, is this: their apprehensions of Christ are not such as they ought to be. There is nothing that hinders active closing with Christ so much as the lack of suitable apprehensions of Him. The third ground of it is that the willingness you have is not deep enough. Therefore, when you have some desire to close, and cannot get freedom actually to close with Him, go back and strengthen your willingness. And fourth, this is the ground of it that Christians may be instructed more in the truth of this that faith is the gift of God: that though we desire to close, yet we cannot. However, do not quench your desires. Think about where a pursuing Christ is, and a desiring sinner is; it will not be long before they shall meet. Do you think that a seeking sinner and a seeking Christ will be long asunder? Therefore do not quench your desires to close with Christ.

The sixth objection of some about the closing with Christ is this: "I would come, but the devil will not let me." You may take in this, "But my own heart will not let me." I would remind you of that word from Isaiah 49:25 that the lawful captive shall be delivered and the prey shall be taken from the mighty. I desire no more of you but this, that you would not make the devil Christ's party, and then I hope ere long you shall be delivered. If this is the thing that indeed sticks with you, I think Christ will soon show Himself mighty to save; He will give you a proof of this, that stronger is He who is in you than he who is in the world.

The last objection of some about their coming to Christ is this: "O I would come to Christ," say they, "but I fear I will dishonor Him, after my coming, by my walk; I fear I will bring up a bad report upon Christ if I come; I fear I will turn the grace of God into wantonness if I come." I would say these words unto you: "Take therefore no thought for the morrow: for the morrow shall take thought for the things of itself. Sufficient unto the day is the evil thereof" (Matt. 6:34). Do your duty, and let alone your fears. Second, I confess, it is as suitable for a Christian to come to Christ with fear as it is to serve Him with fear, or to pray with fear; it is as suitable to believe in Him with fear.

Third, if you dishonor Christ, you may blame yourself, for you have many precious things to uphold you in the day of your straits. However, I say to that person, "O close [with Christ]: He will once present you without spot unto God." O Christians, prisoners of hope, comfort yourselves with this: Christ shall make a blessed count of you all when He shall say that word, "Of them which thou gavest me have I lost none" (John 18:9). Is there a person in hell today that can say that Christ lost them? Or is there a person in heaven today that dare say that Christ has not found them? That which, fourth, we would speak to is this: to persuade you immediately to close with Christ and without delay to come to Him.

I charge you in the name of Him whose divine sentence this is; I protest for this in the name of Him who is the noble Plant of renown, who is the eternal Wonder of angels; I desire you in the name of Him who is white and ruddy, the chief among ten thousand, "O come quickly and close with Him." Obey that command, "Go with thine adversary to the magistrate, as thou art in the way" (Luke 12:58), and, "Come; for all things are now ready" (Luke 14:17).

There are these six considerations to persuade you to come quickly to Christ. The first is this: now is the season and appointed time of coming, therefore come. Know you not that word of Solomon's, "He hath made every thing beautiful in his time" (Eccl. 3:11)? Now, this is the season of closing with Christ, therefore come. Is not this the season and appointed time? Therefore do not delay. The second consideration is this: every call and invitation of God unto you to close with Christ is no doubt the thing that should persuade you immediately to come. This is the call from heaven to you today: "O come." And what do you answer? Will you stay away?

The third consideration to persuade you to come presently is this: Every hour's delay of coming to Christ is an affront done to Him. How many persons will be here today that will affront Christ, and tread Him under foot? O shall this be reported in heaven concerning any that is here today, that the congregation of Glasgow has trodden Christ under foot? Shall this be reported concerning you? O will every one of you ask yourselves, "Shall it be I? Shall it be I who shall be the ground of that report in heaven?" The fourth consideration to persuade you to come immediately and presently to Christ is: There is not a refusal that you give to Christ but it is as a sword piercing His heart. And is there a person so cruel here today as to thrust a spear into the side of precious Christ? Is there any of you so cruel as to do this? Be sure of this, if you refuse Him, you will thrust a sword into His side. There is not a sermon you hear but it is (if so I may speak with reverence of His majesty) Christ sitting down upon His knees, beseeching you, saying, "O man, or O woman, be friends with Me." And dare you refuse Christ, when He sits down upon His knees entreating you? I think the very words that He speaks should make you to wonder. O shall Christ be sent away today not having the consent of any? There is this consideration likewise to persuade you presently to come: There is not one hour's delay of coming but it makes you more unfit to come. I say, be who you will who will not come today; you shall be more unfit tomorrow, therefore delay not the time. Are there not some of you saying, "Now I may spend ten years yet in following my idols, and then I will come"? I say unto you, "Boast not of tomorrow, for you know not what a day may bring forth." It is likely the person who delays his closing with Christ shall never get freedom to close with Him.

The last consideration to press you immediately to close with Christ is this: I hope I may say it without presumption, yet heaven is waiting for you to come. What will you answer to this desire this morning to come to Christ? One of these four things I must answer to

Christ today, and which of them shall I answer? Either I must answer this today, "I came to Glasgow, and they would not receive me"— Are you willing that this shall be the report concerning you? Would not you be sorry to have this reported of you to Christ?—or this must be the report that I must carry back: "I know not what to say of them; I have no understanding of their case; I know not whether they will come or stay away; they have taken it to advisement." O will you take it to advisement whether or not you shall come to Christ? I may say to you, you should not take it to advisement; where there is no choice, there is no deliberation at all. And therefore come, and take Christ blindly; He shall never disappoint your hope. Or this must be the report that I must carry back to Christ: "Thy people shall be willing in the day of Thy power"; "The bride has made herself ready"; "Come Lord Jesus, for they desire to come to Thee." Now, which of these shall be the report in heaven concerning you today? O will you not be persuaded to come? Will you make heaven to rejoice today? Or will you think of the matter and speak your minds? Or will you make the heart of Christ sad today?

I shall yet, to seal up this upon you, *propose these considerations further to move you to come.* The first consideration is this: All things are ready; therefore come, and stay not away. O shall Christ open the market of grace, and there be not a person coming to buy? Don't you think it is sad that Christ should go out from our church doors today, weeping as He goes, and saying, "I came unto them, and there was none that would receive Me, and there was none that would give Me his heart." All things are ready: What would you have that is not ready? The contract is ready; the contract is subscribed by the blood of Christ. Heaven is ready; preparation is ready; all things are ready but your consent. O will you put to your name? Shall this be returned to Christ? For this is indeed the contract, and not one name put to it. Are you ready? Are you ready? If you are, then come away; and if you are not, then come away; do not stay, close with Him.

A second consideration to persuade you to close is this: You shall find rest in Christ. There is a fivefold rest that you shall find in Christ. First, you shall find rest for your conscience in Christ; all the challenges that troubled you before, you shall get them answered in Christ. Is there a challenge in your conscience? O soul, if you come to Christ, you shall find an answer to it. Would you have rest in your conscience? Then come to Christ. Second, would you have rest for your desires? Then come to Christ. As long as you are strangers to Christ, your desires are divided among many different objects; but, if once you would come to Christ, your desires should be fixed and terminated upon one divine and most precious object. Third, if you will come to Christ, you shall have rest for your love. Now it is pitched upon many different objects; but, if you would once come to Christ, your love should have one most lovely and precious object. Third, if you would come to Christ, you should have rest for your hope. Often you place your hope in such a thing, in the enjoyment of which there is no satisfaction to an immortal soul; but, if once you would come to Christ, you should find a suitable Object to place your hope upon. Fifth, if you would come to Christ, you should find an eternal rest; therefore come away. I think men and angels cannot tell what this rest that is to be found in Christ is. I would even say that word unto you which that woman spoke, "Come, see a man, which told me all things that ever I did" (John 4:29). I say unto you, "Come and behold a man that will give to you everlasting rest."

A third consideration to persuade you to come to Christ is this: Is it possible for you to resist any of the precious things of Christ before you come? This is clear in that word, "I sat down under his shadow"—that is the exercise of faith, and immediately it is subjoined—"and his fruit was sweet to my taste" (Song 2:3). Heaven will be sweet after your coming to Christ, sanctification will be sweet after your coming to Christ, and duties will be sweet after your coming to Christ. There is a great fault among Christians, that I would reprove, and it is this: Many of us are much more taken up in desiring death than in desiring heaven. Let a Christian search his own bosom, and he will find ten desires for death, when he will not find one for heaven. What is the reason for this? It is because it is not so much for our hope as for our restless anxiety that we desire. And I think a desire of death, which has anxiety for its mother, has not a desire of heaven as the end of it. I never love a desire of death that has not love as the principle of it.

A fourth consideration to persuade you to come to Christ is this: Would you have your pursuit after the world exceedingly quenched? Then come to Christ. This is clear, "He that cometh to me shall never hunger; and he that believeth on me shall never thirst" (John 6:35). This is a part of the meaning of it: if you come to Christ, your desires after things here shall be much abated.

A fifth consideration to persuade you to come is this: Christ will make you welcome, and what can you get more? He will make you welcome if you come. If so I may speak, there are four times when Christ does make one welcome. First, when they come out of the estate of nature, and are translated to the kingdom of Christ, then Christ speaks that word to them, "Welcome, stranger." I say, come to Christ; He will make you welcome. Second, when a Christian is recovering from his apostatizing state and declining condition, when he begins to come home again, He will say unto him, "Welcome, O backslider; where have you been going? And why did you depart from Me? Yet welcome home again." Third, Christ makes one welcome at the feasts of love, when Christ bids His friends welcome, when He commands them to sit down, and to eat and drink abundantly. Fourth, when first they are entered into the possession of heaven, when first their feet stand within the gates of the New Jerusalem, then Christ says this, "Now welcome, My beloved; O prisoner and travelers of hope, welcome." I think there is none of you but you know there is such a thing as we call the courtesy of the city when a stranger comes to it. O who can tell the courtesy of the city that is above! Can anyone tell it? I shall say this: sight, sight, sight will be the best commentary upon many of the mysteries of heaven; sight will resolve many things that are now dark riddles. Now, if there were no more to persuade you but this, Christ will make you welcome. O come away!

A sixth consideration to provoke you to come is this: Would you make Christ to rejoice today? Then come away. Heaven will wonder at your coming to Christ, in a manner; according to that word, "Who is this that cometh out of the wilderness?" (Song 3:6). O shall this be spoken in heaven of you today, "Who are these that are now coming up out of the wilderness?" Shall angels wonder at you today? Shall Christ rejoice at you today, when He shall cry out, "Who are these coming up out of the wilderness like pillars of smoke?"

A seventh consideration to persuade you to come is this: mortification and heavenly mindedness shall attend you if you come to Christ; you shall come up like pillars of smoke.

Now, to summarize all for you, I give you this eighth consideration, which is: Come to Christ, and you shall get heaven; what do you think of that? Come to Christ, and you shall get righteousness; what do you think of that? Come to Christ, and you shall get sanctification; what do you think of that? Come to Christ, and you shall get adoption; what do you think of that? But why should I speak? Come to Christ, and you shall get Him; and, when you get Him, you get all. Come to Him, and you shall get Him. I think, if we should speak till midnight, we should be forced to close up all with this: Come to Christ, and you shall get *Him*.

Now I would ask you, "Are you ready?" O what shall I report to Christ? Believe it, I may say—heaven is waiting for your return. Now, would not you think shame to have a bad report carried to heaven concerning you? Is there none of you that will give me an answer? What shall I report concerning you, and you, and you? What shall I report concerning you? Have you nothing to say that I shall report? Shall I have to give to Christ a blank report? Is there none that will give anything to report? I shall give you permission to report yourselves, if this is your desire. O report what were your thoughts when you were invited to come.

I shall shut up all with this: *O come away*, for the day is coming when there shall not be a word heard in heaven, nor earth, but this word, "Come"; when the Spirit shall cry, "Come"; when the bride shall cry, "Come"; and when he who has a thirst shall come, and he who wills shall come, and when all the weary travelers of hope shall cry, "Come." O blessed Lord Jesus, come. O what a blessed day will it be when heaven shall cry, "Come"; when earth shall cry, "Come!" In a manner, it will be like David when he thought upon that day to summon all the hills, beasts of the field, fish of the sea, grass, hail, snow, vapor, stormy wind, old men, young men, old women, and maids: "O come, come all and help me to rejoice" (see Psalm 96). What ails you, David? What is the matter that you summon us to help you to rejoice? I tell you the matter, says he, "Let [us] rejoice before the LORD: for he cometh, for he cometh to judge the earth" (v. 13). David, when he comes to this, must call all the creatures to help him to rejoice. Now, are not these glad tidings of great joy unto you? The day is coming when there shall not be a word heard in heaven but this: "O come." I would even ask this question: What a pleasant voice shall it be when Christ shall speak that word unto you, when you are standing upon the marches of eternity, "Rise up, my love, my fair one, and come away. For, lo, the winter is past, the rain is over and gone; the flowers appear on the earth; the time of the singing of birds is come" (Song 2:10–12)? Now, may not that provoke you to come?

I would say unto you, "Believe it, all in heaven are crying unto you, come away." You have the Father, the first Person of the blessed Trinity, crying out, "O come away, and come up hither"; the Holy Spirit, the third Person, is crying out, "O come away, and come up hither." Yea, I may say, angels' advice, if they were admitted to give it to you, would be this, "O come away, and come up hither." If all your brethren and sisters who are now around the throne, if all the spirits of just men made perfect, were admitted to give you their counsel, it would be this, "Come away, and come up hither." You are surrounded about with voices that cry out, "O come away."

There are five things that cry out unto you, "O come away, come away." Does not the law cry out unto you, "O come away, come away, and take Christ"? These are the two great voices of the law, "Deny yourselves, and come to Christ." This is the very great voice of Moses, "O come away." Second, this is the very great voice of the gospel, "O come away." This is even all the gospel, "Come away, come away." Third, does not your necessity cry out, "O come away"? Is there a necessity with any person here but it cries out, "O come away, and make use of Christ"? Fourth, does not the transcendent loveliness, the matchless beauty, the overcoming comeliness that is in the face of Christ cry out, "O come away, come away"? Did you ever see Him? Do you ever see Him? The very beholding of Him put you to this: "O come away." Do not all the promises of the everlasting covenant, does not the sweetness of heaven cry out, "O come away"? Where can you look to anything but you meet with the voice in it, saying, "O come away"? And will you delay this precious summons of Christ? Now, is there a person here who shall be marked for compearance[1] in heaven today who will not answer the request of Christ? I entreat you, as you love your souls: Come away. Now, are you ready, old men, who have spent your days in vanity? Are you ready, men of sixty years old? Are you ready? O come away and embrace Him. Old women, who have spent the flower of your years, come away. Young women, are you ready? Then come away. Will you answer to your names? I shall say this: If you will come to Christ when you are eleven years old, you shall be more welcome than if you come to Christ when you are eighty years old; Christ loves young religion well. And I shall give you these three grounds why Christ loves young religion well. The first ground of it is this: Young religion is much to the commendation of Christ's grace; according to that word, "That we should be to the praise of his glory, who first trusted in Christ" (Eph. 1:12). O Glasgow, contend who shall be the first who shall come to Christ, for you shall be the person who shall get first leave to put a crown upon His head. And will you not debate for this honor and prerogative, "O shall I be the person that shall put the crown upon Christ's head?" The second ground why Christ loves young religion best is because it has the most temptations. Young persons have manifest temptations, and therefore, if they come over the belly of their temptations, He loves that well. And, third, Christ loves young religion well because it has strongest temptations to wrestle with.

Now, I shall close with this: O are you ready? Are you ready? Yes, believe it—heaven is waiting for your return. Now, what do you say? What do you say, O Glasgow? I shall say no more but this: I know not what to report, except you give it. But this also I say: I take the Father, the first Person of the Trinity to witness; I take the Son, the second Person of the Trinity to witness; I take the Holy Ghost, the third Person of the blessed Trinity to witness; I take angels to witness; I take all the saints that are round about the throne to witness; I take the rafters of this house to witness; I take the stones of the walls of this house to witness; I take your own consciences to witness, that this day you have been invited to come to Christ. Yes, know it. I shall be a witness against you, though perhaps some of us may not embrace the call and invitation, yet we may be witnesses

---

1. To formally present oneself in court as a party to a cause.

notwithstanding. I would rather that you would come away. Yes, this should be the prayer of a minister: "Give me children, or else I die." Now, will you be entreated to come away? Yes, know it— if Christ has not gained you, the devil has gained you. These two *comes* have been presented unto you today; Christ has presented His *come* unto you today, and the devil has presented his *come* unto you today; and which of them, do you think, will you obey? It shall be a dreadful "Depart!" which shall be spoken unto you if you will not come. However, to Him who is coming, who will come, and will not delay, to Him who can persuade you to come, be praise.

The Spiritual Marriage

Wherefore, my brethren, ye also are become dead to the law by the body of Christ; that ye should be married to another, even to him who is raised from the dead, that we should bring forth fruit unto God.

—Romans 7:4

I would say unto every person that is within these doors, that word which Ehud spoke to Eglon, "I have a message from God unto thee" (Judg. 3:20). And this is the thing that I am sent for today—I am come to woo today in the name of Him who is the Prince of heaven, to present this desire unto you, that you would be married to another, even to Christ Jesus, who was raised from the dead. I know not if I shall succeed this morning, but I think the matchless condescension of Christ ought to provoke you. It is condescension in Him to behold the things that are in heaven, and the things that are in earth; and how much more condescension is it in Him to love the things that are in heaven, and the things that are in earth? And it is yet more condescension in Him to dwell with the things that are in heaven, and the things that are in earth. But this is the capstone of His condescension: He desires to be married to the redeemed that are in heaven, and the redeemed that are on earth.

It is the opinion of the apostle that marriage is honorable in all things, and I am persuaded of this: that no marriage is so honorable as one's marriage to precious Christ. Young women, do you desire to marry? I have a noble Husband to present to you, the noble Plant of renown, Jesus Christ. Widows, do you desire to marry? I have a noble Husband to present to you, Jesus Christ, who was raised from the dead. I am sure it is better to marry than to burn after the pleasures of a present world. In short, this is the thing that I must speak to all of you that are within these doors: "Will you marry?" I am sure he is blessed who is called to the marriage supper of the Lamb; I am sure he is blessed who, in the day of His visitation, can get Christ in his arms and cry out, "He is mine; He is mine."

Now, to come to the words. The apostle, in Romans 4:1–7, is insisting to prove that believers are set free from the law by Jesus Christ. And he has been explaining this by a familiar resemblance and similitude in verses 2 and 3, which is, in short, this: it is lawful for a wife, when her husband is dead, to marry again. And in verse 4 he makes application of the similitude, and says to them, "Now, Romans, your first husband is dead; I entreat you, come and marry." And in the verse we have read, we have four things to be considered. First, the noble privilege and advantage believers have—they are set free from the law.

Now, brethren, you are free from the law. By this it is not to be understood that believers are freed from the commanding power of the law, but we conceive it takes in these three things: (1) Believers are dead and set free from the rigor of the law; the law is not so rigorous a master as it was before Christ had abated the rigor of it. (2) Believers are set free from the curse of the law, and are dead to that. (3) Believers are freed from the law as it is an occasion to stir up sin in us through our corruption. The law was once a stirrer-up of sin in us, through the sin that dwells in our mortal bodies; we are set free from that in the law.

The second thing in the words is the meritorious cause and fountain from whence this privilege does flow, which is set down in these words: "Ye also are become dead to the law by the body of Christ" (v. 4), that is, by the sufferings of Christ. You are dead to the law, as Hebrews 10:10 expounds it.

The third thing in the words is the noble design and end that Christ has before His eyes, in setting believers free from the law, and making them dead to it: that they should be married to another, that is, to Him who was raised from the dead. Which in short is this: that they should be married to a risen and glorified Christ, and should be content to take Him, and be married unto Him, as if Christ had said, "I have freed you from your former husband, not that you should continue in your widowhood, but that you should be married again."

The last thing in the words is the duty that is imposed upon and required of them who are married unto Christ, that they should bring forth fruit unto God. They should not be unfruitful nor barren, but should have a fruitful womb, always bringing forth fruit.

There is only one note that we shall insist upon in this; Oh, that we could persuade you to take notice of it! It is this: it is the great design of Christ in many of His works and dispensations that sinners should be married unto Him, and be content to take Him for their Husband. This is clear in the words, "Ye also are become dead to the law by the body of Christ; that ye should be married to another, even to him who is raised from the dead" (v. 4).

I tell you nine glorious dispensations of Christ, the end of all which is this: sinners should be married to Him.

First, what was the end that Christ came from heaven, from the bosom of the Father? Was it not that sinners should be married to Him? Why did He come from heaven? It was to woo a bride for Himself. Yes, know that this was the precious design of spotless Christ, when He came out of the bosom of the Father: "I go to woo a bride to Myself." And oh, what a wonder it was that He who was the only begotten of the Father, who had infinite fullness dwelling in Him, should go out of Himself to seek any proportional object for His love!

Second, was it not the great design of all the sufferings of Christ? Why was it that Christ was born of a woman? It was that you may be married unto Him. Why was it that the blessed hands of Christ were pierced? It was that you might be married to Him. Why was it that He was content to put a crown of thorns upon His head? It was even this: that you might be married unto Him. Why was it that He was content to lie in the grave three days and three nights? It was that you might be married unto Him. I say, there is not a wound that ever Christ received, there is not a reproach that ever He met with, there is not a buffeting that ever He got, but this is the language of it: "Oh, be married to Christ."

Third, is it not the great end and design of the gospel that you should be married to Christ? What is the design of the gospel? It is even this: "All things are ready: come unto the marriage"

(Matt. 22:4). We have no more to say to you but this, "Come to the
marriage, for all things are ready." The very substance of the gospel is comprehended in that one invitation, "Be married to Christ."
And I think, if this work were put by our hand, we have not much
more to do. Oh, be married to Him.

Fourth, it is the great design and end of the law that you
should be married to Christ. "The law," says the apostle, "is our
schoolmaster, to bring us to Christ. Yes, if you will consent to what
the law bids you do, it is no more but this: 'Go to Christ.'"

Fifth, is it not the great end and design of His sending a settled
ministry among His people to deliver you the gospel in one word:
"Oh, be married to Christ"? That is all we have to say. Why are we
here? It is that we should be married to Christ; if we will not take
Him, I know not for what use we are here. If you will not make
the ministry among you unprofitable, and if you will not cross the
design that Christ has in sending us, I entreat you to be married to
Him. If this were done, might not you go to your grave in peace, if
once you be content to be married to Christ?

Sixth, it is the great end and design of all the afflictions and
sad dispensations that we meet with: "Oh, be married to Christ."
There is not a cross you meet with but this is indeed the voice of it:
"Oh, come and take Christ for your Husband," and I am sure it is a
blessed bargain. Oh, will you take Him?

Seventh, it is the great end and design of Christ's discovering
to us the vanity and emptiness of all idols and created contentment
beside Him. When He writes vanity upon such an idol, the great
end design of it is this: "Oh, be married to Christ." And you would
make this use of all the discoveries of the vanity of all your idols, to
study to be married to Christ.

Eighth, what is the great end and design of Christ's leaving so
many promises upon record, so many great and excellent promises
of the everlasting covenant? Is it not that you may be persuaded to
take Him, and to marry Him? All the promises that are written in
the volume of this book, this is the great voice of them to you today:
Oh, come and take Him, and have Him!

And, lastly, what is the great end and design of all the threat-
enings that are within the Bible? What is the great end of all the
curses of the book of the covenant? Is it not that you may be chased

to Christ? Now, I say unto you, there are so many things that cry out unto you, "Come, come and be married to Christ." Oh, will you stand out against them all? Do not your necessities bid you to be married to Christ? Does not your misery bid you to be married to Him? Does not His beauty bid you come and be married to Him?

In speaking to this more fully, I shall speak a little to three or four things shortly. The first thing that I shall speak to shall be this: *to propose unto you some considerations to press you to be married to Christ.* Oh, young women, will you marry? Old women, old men, will you marry? The consideration that I shall propose unto you is this: I am persuaded Christ should outbid all other suitors. I have this to say in my Master's name, that Christ excels all that ever suited your heart, and He excels them all in these five matters: One, *He excels them all in His offers.* What will the world offer you? What will the idol that courts your heart offer you? I say, Christ outbids them all. See, whatever they can bid you, I shall bid you a thousand times more: come therefore away.

Is there any of your suitors who offers you thus, "Come and marry me, and I will give you a kingdom"? Is there any of your suitors who courts your hearts, who can give you such an offer as this: "Come and marry me, and I will give you rest"? I defy all the suitors who ever courted your heart to propose unto you such a thing. I tell you how all the suitors, except Christ, do court you: they court you as Amnon courted Tamar—they lust after your heart, and then they will hate you. But Christ is not so. Will you come and marry?

I say, Christ exceeds all the suitors who ever courted your heart in His beauty and excellency. Oh, did you ever see such a beautiful wooer as Christ is? Had you ever seen Him, you could not deny Him an answer. Did you ever see such a noble wooer as Him who is the noble Plant of renown, the Light of the higher house, the Rose of Sharon, and the Lily of the valleys, the eternal Wonder of angels, Him that makes heaven to shine? Now, did you ever see such a beautiful wooer as Christ is? Does not Christ exceed all the suitors who ever courted your heart, in His right to you? I am sure Christ has a better right to you than all the suitors who come to you to woo. Oh, will you not consent to take Him to whom you owe yourselves? Christ exceeds all the suitors who ever courted your heart, in the easiness of the offers and terms that He consents to. What does He require of you to make up the bargain but this, "O come and consent, and it is done"? There is nothing that He requires of you but that you would consent; oh, will you not consent to take Him? Christ excels all other wooers in His love and in the reality of His offers. I am persuaded there is not one wooer who loves you so much as precious Christ. Oh, will you take Him? Don't you think it is a pleasant thing for every one of us to cry out, "I am married today"?

I shall, as a second consideration to press you to be content to marry Christ, point out a little to you *the virtues of Him whom we desire you to marry*. I desire not that you should make a blind block of it; I shall point out Christ, who is the Suitor today, under these virtues:

First, I say, He who suits you today is a most excellent Person, the eternal Son of God; He is God equal with the Father: And is not that a most excellent Person? I wonder that, when Christ offers Himself to us, we cry not out, "Will ever He who is white and ruddy take me who is black as the tents of Kedar?" (see Song 1:5). I wonder that we cry not out that word, "Whom doth the King of Israel pursue?" (see 1 Sam. 24:14). I tell you, it is even after you, if you be content. Oh, how many cries has Christ given to us when we have been running away from Him! How often has He said, "Oh, return and take Me!" And yet we have run away from Him who is the eternal Son of God.

Second, we commend Him from this: that He is a most beautiful and excellent Person. He has no match. According to that word, Song of Solomon 5:10, He "is white and ruddy, the chiefest among ten thousand." And I say to you, if I could sit down and commend Christ to you till night, I may close all my discourse with these three words: (1) I might close it with that word from Hebrews 11:32, "What shall I more say? For the time would fail me." What should I say more of Christ? Time would fail me; yea, I may say, eternity would fail me in commending Him. (2) We may close with that word from Job 26:14, "Lo, these are parts of his ways: but how little a portion is heard of him?" (3) We might close it with this: oh, come and see; that would best resolve the question. Will you come and take the trial? Believe it—"the queen of Sheba shall rise up in judgment with this generation, and shall condemn it: for she came from the uttermost parts of the earth to hear the wisdom of Solomon; and, behold, a greater than Solomon is here" (Matt. 12:42).

Third, if you will come and marry Christ, you shall have an excellent dowry and higher good. What would you have? I shall read four branches of the contract unto you, and you may judge what to think of the rest by these four. The first is that all things are yours (1 Cor. 3:2–22). Is not that a noble article? I say, come and be married to Christ, and all things shall be yours. What would you have that is not within this contract? Whether Paul or Cephas, or death, or life, or things present, or things to come—all are yours, and you are Christ's. Is not that an excellent article? The second article of the contract that I shall desire you to read is, "He that overcometh shall inherit all things" (Rev. 21:7). That is indeed a step higher than the last. I say, would you inherit all things? Then come and be married to Christ. What would you seek? For Christ has all things within the contract, and the inheritance of all things. The third article of the contract that I shall declare unto you today is that which Christ shall give. He will give grace—is not that much? And He will give glory—is not that much? And "no good thing will he withhold from them that walk uprightly" (Ps. 84:11). Oh, will you come and be married to Christ? He will give grace, and He will give glory, and no good thing will He withhold from you who are content to take Him. The fourth thing of the contract that I would have you read is: "And God said, ask what I shall give thee" (1 Kings 3:5). He bids him ask what he will, and He will give it him. It is as if Christ had said, "If there be any thing that is not included in the former articles, I leave a blank in the contract for you to fill up: ask what you will, and you have it." Therefore I desire you to come and be married to Christ, this excellent Husband. And do you think you will fill up anything when you come? I doubt much if you will fill up anything. However, it speaks this: Christ is exceeding willing you should be married to Him.

Fourth, we would say this of Him who desires you to marry Him, and it is this: He is exceeding wise; in Him dwell all the treasures of wisdom and knowledge. And is not this a noble argument to persuade you?

Fifth, there is this that I would say of Him, that He is exceeding rich; and what would you have? He is honorable, He is beautiful,

He is wise, and He is rich; and are not all these exceeding excellent things to persuade you? Is not Christ Jesus rich, who has the ends of the earth for His possession? And is He not rich, who is made the Heir of all things? I say unto you, O poor wretches, come and marry this Husband. Is there a person here who does not even have a penny in your possession? I entreat you come, and be the richest man or woman in all the world today, if you will come and marry with Christ. Now, merchants, I have one piece of advice to give you, for I am sure it is one of the great devices you plot after, to be rich. O merchants, come and buy this precious Pearl, and be heirs of all things, and exceeding rich. Is not this noble advice? O merchants, will you flee from this invitation? You need bring no money with you, for I have one of the richest Jewels to sell to you today, if you will but be content to take Him; a Jewel that will eternally satisfy you. Oh, come and be married to Him. Are there not some of you reduced to great necessities? Oh, come and take Him, and you shall be the richest persons in the world today.

Sixth, we would say this to persuade you to come away: He is the loveliest Husband that ever you shall get. Oh, if Jesus Christ were known, and if His love were known, we would not be able to stay away. I tell you this: if you knew Christ, you would woo Him. I entreat you, begin to woo Christ, for this is not unsuitable.

There is this, seventh, that I would say to commend Him unto you, namely, there was never a person who saw Christ but they were constrained to be friends with Him. I defy the most desperate enemy that ever Christ had, but, if they saw Him in His beauty, they should be constrained to cry out, "What wilt thou have me to do?" I tell you what I would have you to do—come and be married to Christ. This is the thing that heaven would have you to do: Oh, come and be married to Christ. There was never one who saw Him who ever turned His enemy. The first sight that persecuting Paul got of Christ made him to cry out that word, "Lord, what wilt thou have me to do?" (Acts 9:6).

And, lastly, I would say this to commend Him: there is not a moving of the tongue in heaven that is not taken up in commending Him. Oh, what are they doing in heaven? Are they not all fixed upon precious Christ? Yea, I say, there is not a thought in heaven that is not taken up in thinking upon Christ, there is not a desire in heaven that is not taken up in desiring Christ, and there is not one moving of the foot in heaven that is not taken up in following Christ. Do not they follow the Lamb wherever He goes? And must not He then be an excellent Person? Now, are you content to marry Him?

The third consideration to press you to come and marry Christ is this: *Christ is inviting you today to come and marry Him.* It is the desire of heaven that you would come to the marriage, for all things are ready (Matt. 22:4). "Come; for all things are now ready" (Luke 14:17). I say, if there were no other thing to persuade you to come but only this, that Christ invites you, will you not come?

The fourth consideration to press you to come is this: *all things are ready.* O Glasgow, will you come away? Christ is ready. He is waiting for you. Your marriage clothes are ready. Will you come to the Man and say a marriage disposition is ready? Will you come to the marriage? Is there anything that is not ready? What can hinder you to come, that is not answered in this, that all things are ready? Perhaps one will say, "I am not ready, how then are all things ready?" I say to you, "Tell Christ in earnest that you are not ready; and then you may be ready."

The fifth consideration to press you to come and be married to Christ is this: *there is a blessedness pronounced upon the person who will come and take Christ.* "Write, blessed are they which are called unto the marriage supper of the Lamb" (Rev. 19:9). Not only the persons who take, but the persons who are called, are pronounced blessed. And, says he, do not think this is a fancy; these are faithful and true sayings of God. He who is content to take Christ is certainly blessed, be whom he will.

The sixth consideration that may provoke you to take that excellent offer that is presented unto you is this: if you take Him, and are content about the bargain, *I assure you in His name you shall never repent of it.* Are there not some of you who curse the day that ever you married such a husband? I say, come here and marry, and you shall bless the day eternally that ever you married Him. There shall not a day pass over your head but you shall say, "Blessed be the Lord, who gave me counsel and persuaded me to marry." I shall say no more but this, "Repentance shall be hid from your eyes, if you be content to take Him."

The seventh consideration that we would propose is this: Oh, come and take this noble Bridegroom and precious Husband, and *you shall have many joyful days in His company.* The children of the bride-chamber shall not mourn while the Bridegroom is with them. Would you spend your days with joy? Would you go to heaven with delight? Oh, then be married to Christ.

The last consideration that I would propose unto you is this: I have this to declare, that *the consent of the Father is given to the match, the consent of the Son is given to the match, the consent of the Holy Ghost is given to the match; all that is resting is waiting till you put it to your hand.* Has not the Father sent Christ once to die, to make up the match? "Unto us a child is born, unto us a son is given" (Isa. 9:6). And is not Christ willing? I hope none will dispute it; He woos you and invites you. And is not the Holy Ghost willing? He is content to seal the contract, if you will put it to your hand. I shall only give you a view of Christ's wooing of a soul: Christ (as it were) stands without, and He cries, "Open to Me, My sister, My spouse; oh, come and take Me." And He stands within, and He makes the soul cry out, "Lord, I am content to take Thee." So that Christ is both within doors and outside the doors: He is without, crying, "Open"; He is within, opening the door. He both suits us, and moves us to consent. Now, is not this a noble and excellent draught that is drawn of Him who is the Wooer? I tell you how Christ courts a soul: You know how the great monarchs of the world woo their queens; they send their picture by the hand of their ambassadors, to show it to the woman whom they desire to marry. I say, Christ has delivered His picture and portrait to us, to show it unto you; and what do you think of Him now? For you may read and see the beauty of Christ in His excellent words. What we can say of Him, and what all the angels in heaven can say of Him, is contained within the volume of this book. Oh, will you not fall in love with Him?

Now, second, *I shall remove seven objections of persons who are invited to come to be married,* and I shall remove them all from that excellent Scripture, Hosea 2:19: "I will betroth thee unto me for ever; yea, I will betroth thee unto me in righteousness, and in judgment, and in lovingkindness, and in mercies."

The first objection that one has against the marriage is this: "Oh," says one, "I think, though I be now content to marry Christ, yet I will break the bargain ere long, and provoke Him to give me a bill of divorcement; I would take Him today, but my heart will be taken with my lusts tomorrow. I should go out of these church doors with this, 'I shall never have another husband but Christ,' yet I am afraid I should have another before I sleep tonight." I say, consent once really to take Him, and that shall stand; according to that word, "I will betroth thee unto me for ever." Although you play the prostitute a hundred times, He will keep you in a marriage state. Your Husband shall never give you a bill of divorce. Do you not know that word which Christ said, "that he hateth putting away" (Mal. 2:16)? I say, be whom you will that will truly consent today—the marriage shall never be broken. I defy devils and your own hearts ever to break it, if once it be concluded. Is there any here who will be content to have the knot cast between Christ and your heart? Oh, for the invisible knot of love to be cast between you and Christ! I defy all the hands of men and angels to loose it.

The second objection of some as to why they will not come to be married is this: "I lack marriage clothes to put on; I want suitable apparel for such a Husband. Do you think I can go to Christ with these rags, being all polluted with my filthiness?" That is answered in the second part of that word, "I will betroth thee unto me in righteousness." I say, "Come and be married to Christ, and He will give you clothes" (see Rev. 19:7).

The third objection of some is this: "Oh, if I come and marry Christ, I commit so many wrongs, and will offend Him so much, that I am sure there will not be a peaceable day between Him and me." I say, that is answered from the third branch of our text, that He will betroth you "in judgment"; that is, He knows what we are before He marries us, and therefore He will be to us as one who knows our frame.

The fourth objection of some is this: "Alas! If I come and marry Christ, I am sure He will never continue to love me." I say, that is answered from this branch of that precious contract, "I will betroth thee unto me…in lovingkindness." Although there be nothing in you to move you to it, yet He will betroth you because He will love you, and He will keep the marriage because He delights to have it so.

The fifth objection of some as to why they will not come and be married to Christ is this: "Alas," say they, "what shall I do? How shall I look Him in the face? I grieve His Holy Spirit so much. What shall I do when I play the harlot with many lovers? What shall I do when I love a reward under every green tree?" I say, that is answered from this branch of the contract: "I will betroth thee to me…in mercies." If you offend Christ, He will pardon you.

The sixth objection of some is this: "Alas! If I be now content to take Christ and to marry Him, I am sure I will never keep my purpose; and do you think that Christ will keep His purpose? Christ consents to take me, and I consent to take Him, but what if I break the marriage? Will not Christ break it also?" I say, *no*, He will never break it; there shall not be an article in the contract, but in His own time it shall be accomplished.

"Now," says one, "I think you have indeed answered all the former objections, but there is one more. I doubt much if you will answer it, and it is this: I cannot get my heart up to the bargain." I say, that is answered from that branch of the contract, "And thou shalt know the LORD" (v. 20). That is, you shall believe on the Lord, as "knowledge" in Scripture at times refers to faith. You can't *not* consent to take Him; you have a promise that you *will* take Him, and believe and consent. Now, if you say that is not clear enough, there is a place that clarifies it: "Thou shalt call me Ishi; and shalt call me no more Baali. For I will take away the names of Baalim out of their mouth, and they shall no more be remembered by their name" (Hos. 2:16–17). Thy consent is within the bosom of the contract. I think there is a gracious and pleasant emphasis in that word, "I will betroth thee unto me"; that is, "If you will not consent to take Me, yet I will betroth thee unto Me; the work must depend upon Me." Now, how do they call you? Is not your name "Desolate," and is not your name "Forsaken"? Oh, come and take Christ, and this promise shall be fulfilled, "Thou shalt no more be termed Forsaken; neither shall thy land any more be termed Desolate: but thou shalt be called Hephzibah, and thy land Beulah: for the LORD delighteth in thee, and thy land shall be married" (Isa. 62:4). That is, thy name shall be married to the Lord, thy name shall be Hephzibah, that is, the Lord's delight. Is that not a glorious name? Oh, will you change your name? Would you not be content to be called a queen? I say, come and marry Christ, and you shall be such. I shall only allude to that word which David spoke, "Seemeth it to you a light thing to be a king's son in law?" (1 Sam. 18:23). And I say, Glasgow, do you think it is a small thing to be a daughter-in-law to the King of heaven? He has sent His Son to you, and will you not take Him?

Now, I shall only speak a little to these things, and close. *If you come and be married to Christ, there are these things that are required of you as your duty when you are married.*

First, if you take Him for your Husband, I hope you will think it suitable that you love Him. Is it not a command that wives should love their husbands? Now, if you are married to Christ, you must love Him.

The second thing that is required of you, if you are content to take Him, is this: Christ must be the covering of your eyes if you marry Him (see Gen. 20:16). Let Him be the covering of your eyes. I say, when I press that Christ should be the covering of your eyes, I press these two points: First, that you should carry about with you the mark of your married state, that you may tell everybody you are a married person. Yea, you should answer all your temptations with this: "I am married." Second, that Christ should be the covering of your eyes, it is this in short: that your eyes should be closed from beholding all other objects but Christ; He should (as it were) be a veil over your eyes, that you should not get permission to see any other thing.

Third, if you are content to come and be married to Christ, you must submit yourselves to your Husband. "Wives, submit yourselves unto your own husbands" (Eph. 5:22). There is nothing Christ bids you do but you must be content to do it.

Fourth, it is required of you that you must make a complete resignation of yourselves over unto Him, according to the Word, "The wife hath not power of her own body, but the husband" (1 Cor. 7:4). If you are content to take Christ, you must make a resignation of yourself unto Him.

Fifth, if you come and be married to Christ, you must endeavor to please your husband in all things. You should have this as the scope: how to please your precious Husband, Christ. "She that is married careth…how she may please her husband" (1 Cor. 7:34).

And lastly, if you come home to be married to Christ, you must bring forth fruit unto your husband; this is the marriage duty that is set down in the text. You must be a fruitful branch by the sides of the house, always bringing forth fruit. And I shall add this: if you come home and be married to Christ, you must reverence Him. "Let…the wife see that she reverence her husband" (Eph. 5:33). Now, are you content to be married to this excellent Husband, all of you who are here? Ask yourself if you be minded to marry. There are only five reports you can give to Christ; and which of them will you give?

First, is there any person here who will give Christ this answer, "I have married a wife, I cannot come"? Will you give this report to Christ, "I am married"? Whom have you married? "I have married the world; I cannot come." I say, "Cursed be the person who has done so." But I say unto you, will you break that marriage, and come and marry Christ?

The second report and answer that shall be given is, "The wife hath made herself ready" (Rev. 19:7). Shall this report be rendered concerning you, that "the wife hath made herself ready"? Are you indeed ready? Oh, would we not make a lie concerning you, if we should report this, "The bride has made herself ready"? Or, shall this be the answer we shall take to Him, that, when you are invited to the marriage, you will make light of it, and you will reject this precious offer (Matt. 22:5)? Oh, shall it be told that Christ came to woo you today, and there was never a person who would give Him their heart? Shall Christ go away today, not having a wife any more than before? Oh, who will be so blessed as to give Christ your heart!

Fourth, there is this report that some will give, even that which Joash returned to Amaziah, "The thistle that was in Lebanon sent to the cedar that was in Lebanon, saying, Give thy daughter to my son to wife…Glory of this, and tarry at home" (2 Kings 14:9–10). Oh, shall this be your answer? Oh, shall you desire Christ to return back?

Or, fifth, shall there be such a person here as will give this answer, "I intend to take Him upon advisement"? But should the dust of His feet advise? I entreat you, advise not, nor delay. I may say to you, "Behold, the bridegroom comes unto you, O Glasgow; go forth to meet Him." Yea, more, He is among you; will you go and see him? Is there not one who will give this noble Husband one sight? Christ is begging marriage with you upon His knees, saying to everyone who is here, "Will you take Me?" I say, if there be nothing else that can persuade you to take Him, will you take Him because he is importunate? You know it was forbidden for the priests under the law to take four sorts of women to wife (Lev. 21:14).

First, he was not to marry a widow. Yet I say, Christ is our High Priest, and He desires to marry widows. Your first husband is dead; you are widows. Will you come and marry Christ? Though He be indeed the glorious High Priest, yet He is content to marry widows; will you come away?

Second, the priests under the law were forbidden to marry divorced women. You are divorced, yet He is content to take you; will you come and take Him?

Third, they were forbidden to marry persons who were condemned. Now I say to the greatest atheist and stranger to God, I entreat you to be married to Christ. Oh, profane persons, will you take Him? Lay aside your profanity, and come away, and be content to take this glorious Husband; this glorious High Priest will be content to marry condemned persons.

Fourth, the priests under the law were forbidden to marry harlots. Now, have you not played the harlot with many lovers many times? Yet, "Return unto me…saith the LORD" (Mal. 3:7). Have you not played the harlot under every green tree? Yet, "Be married unto me," saith Christ.

Now, shall I go away and will you not marry Christ? I entreat you, think of it. Oh, if you knew this excellent One who desires you to marry, you would certainly marry, and be content to take Him. If you will be married to Christ, you shall have much communion with Him; if you will be married to Christ, you shall have much union with Him; if you will be married to Christ, you shall have much of His secrets; if you will be married to Christ, you shall have much of His love, and you shall have much of His company; if you be married to Christ, you shall have many tokens of His love, which are indeed better than wine; and, if you be married to Christ, He shall take on all your debt. What do you owe? Is there a person here that is not a debtor to the justice of God? Will you come and marry Christ, that He shall take on your debt? Since it is the law of nations that the husband takes on the debt of the wife, I say, come and take spotless Christ as your Husband, and He shall take on your debt. I am sure you have nothing to give Christ, and He desires nothing of you, but that you come and be content to take Him.

Now speak your minds; and what will you say? I would have you, O fighters against this blessed gospel, thinking upon this word, "What then shall I do when God riseth up? And when he visiteth, what shall I answer him?" (Job 31:14). I would pose your consciences today, what will you answer Christ when He rises up and asks that question of you, "What ailed you about Me that you would not take Me?" And have you anything to say as to why you would not take Him? Have you anything to object against Him?

Now I shall leave it all with this: would you make Christ to rejoice? Then, I say, be betrothed unto Him "in the day of his espousals, and in the day of the gladness of his heart" (Song 3:11). Would you have eternal fellowship with Him? Then I entreat you to be married unto Him. Young women, do you not desire to marry? I desire you, then, marry this precious Husband. I leave it with you; it is He who must persuade you once to enter into this blessed contract of marriage; it is He who must stand within, and move you to consent to take Him. Is it not a blessed bargain? Is your heart moving and leaping within you after it? Now, to Him who can persuade you once to enter into this blessed married estate, we desire to give praise.

SERMON 4

Believers are the Friends of God

And [Abraham] was called the Friend of God.
                                        —James 2:23

Preached before the administration of the Lord's Supper.

"What shall be done unto the man whom the king delighteth to honor?" (Esth. 6:6). He shall be admitted to this precious bond of relation, to be a friend of God. "There is an evil which I have seen under the sun, and it is common among men" (Eccl. 6:1), that they talk much of their pedigree, of their descent and alliance—which are but poor boastings indeed—and a disputing about "endless genealogies" (1 Tim. 1:4), as the apostle speaks. But, if they would allow themselves to consider, they would see all men sprung from one common root, and that ere long death, the king of terrors, will cut off all these distinctions of high and low, of great and small, of rich and poor. But the person who indeed has relation to God and may call himself the friend of the Most High, he is truly a person that may boast of this relation, and say that he has descended from a royal Prince.

It was the blessedness of man, in his primitive estate, to have a blessed knot of friendship made up between him and God; but he, by reason of his pride, broke that knot. And we are bound to precious Christ, whose name is "Prudence," and who has found out the knowledge of many witty inventions, and who has found out the precious way of making the blessed and more durable knot of friendship between God and us. There is nothing men do that advances them so much as this: to be a friend of God. Yet I know there is nothing in the world less esteemed than to be a friend of God. I would only say this unto you who are professors: Does not your conversation, does not your communicating, does not your praying speak that you are not friends of God? What if Christ should come unto you today, and say, "Behold the wounds that I have received in the house of my friends" (see Zech. 13:6)? If Christ should present that challenge unto us which Absalom presented to Hushai—"Is this your kindness you show to your friend?"—what would we answer when we were so reproved? Should we not stand speechless before Him, having nothing to answer?

Now, to come to the words we have read. In James 2:14–26, the apostle disputes much against a painted, a counterfeit, and a dead faith, a faith that has not the handmaid of works waiting on it; and, after he has spoken about this, he sums up in verse 23 two great advantages that attend the Christian whose faith is attended with works. The first advantage is that such a Christian has the righteousness of Christ imputed to him. That Christian is the wonder spoken of in Revelation 12:1—he is "clothed with the sun," has "the moon under [his] feet," and is bedecked with "a crown of twelve stars." Yes, that Christian that is in the exercise of his working faith is the Christian that is clothed with these excellent robes, the righteousness of Christ. He has not forgotten his ornaments nor forsaken his apparel.

The second advantage that results unto the Christian who is in the exercise of a working faith is that he becomes the friend of God: "he was called the Friend of God" (James 2:23). Being "called" in Scripture indicates the real being of a thing.

There is only one thing we will speak to from this precious sentence, and it is this: *saints and believers in Christ are advanced to the matchless and inconceivable pitch of dignity, even to this step of dignity, to become friends of God.* This title, friend of God, is given to Abraham three times in Scripture: (1) In 2 Chronicles 20:7, "The seed of Abraham thy friend for ever." (2) In Isaiah 41:8, referring to Jacob, Abraham's effigy: "The seed of Abraham my friend." (3) And here, in James 2:23.

Now, in speaking to this, I will touch a little on three things. First, I will speak a little on the fact that *such a dignity as to be a friend of God is attainable*. First, does not Christ's coming into the world and taking upon Him our nature speak that there is such a thing attainable as to be a friend of God? Would you know what was the great design of love that Christ had before His eyes in coming into the world? It was even this: to renew the broken friendship between God and man, the eternal plot of love that was laid in heaven from all eternity. This was the great upshot of it, that man, who was afar off, might be brought near through the blood of the cross. Would you know what did cast the knot of friendship between Christ and us? It was even His blood (see Eph. 2:13–15). Yes, if Christ had not condescended to die, we should have remained eternally in the state of estrangement from Him. Hence He is called "the counsel of peace… between them both" (Zech. 6:13), to be the blessed "daysman…that might lay his hand upon us both" (Job 9:33). But, second, this may speak that it is attainable, namely, that it is the great design and scope of this everlasting gospel, that you should become friends unto God. Would you have the substance of the gospel in one word, it is this: be reconciled to God. And is there any that will deny such a precious privilege? Third, this speaks that it is attainable, to wit, that it is the end of the sacraments, that this friendship might be made up and confirmed. Would you know what is the great end of the sacrament of the Lord's Supper? It is even to seal up that blessed contract of friendship between Christ and a soul. I tell you this today, Christ has given us the contract to bring down to you, and we are to desire you to put in your names — there is a blank left in the body of it for you to put in your names. And, if you would consent to it, Christ would put in His seal. There is this, fourth, that speaks of the attainableness of it, namely, that Christ has prescribed the means by which a Christian may win this noble dignity of being a friend of God. This is clear in Isaiah 27:5: "Let him take hold of my strength, that he may make peace with me; and he shall make peace with me." Would you know the best and most compendious way to be friends of God? It is even this: to take hold of His strength to make up this blessed friendship. That which, fifth, speaks of the attainableness of it, is this: that all the desires of a Christian, when he is in a right and spiritual frame, run in this divine channel, that he may be friends with God. Would you know what is the great center where all the sober and spiritual desires of a Christian meet? It is even here, that they may be friends to God. Lastly, this speaks of the attainableness of it, that it is the thing the devil does most often contradict; and does not this speak that there is such a dignity attainable, as to be a friend of God? I conceive indeed, there is as much in the very words as may make us to stand still and wonder that the dust of His feet should become a friend of His. I would only say this by the way: blessed is the soul eternally, of whom that word may be said, "[He] was the principal officer, and the king's friend" (1 Kings 4:5). I say, blessed is he who is the King's friend today, for he shall receive these soul-comforting tokens of friendship.

Second, we would propose unto you *these precious advantages that result unto a Christian by being a friend of God*. And the first advantage that results unto a Christian is this: you are the persons invited to the feast today. Know this: except you be friends to God, you shall incur condemnation if you approach the feast today. The Scripture says, "Eat, O friends; drink, yea, drink abundantly, O beloved" (Song 5:1). They are the friends who are invited to eat and drink, "Rise up, my love [or, as the word may be rendered, 'my friend'], my fair one, and come away" (Song 2:10). I do suppose there shall be many here today to whom Christ shall speak these three most sad and most terrible words: first, there are some that here today to whom He shall speak that word, "Friend, how camest thou hither?" (Matt. 22:12). And, if I may so speak, I never love it when Christ begins to compliment, to call you "friends," when indeed you are enemies. There is that second word which we fear Christ shall speak to many today, namely, "Betrayest thou the Son of man with a kiss?" (Luke 22:48). And there are some, third, to whom He shall speak that word today, "Mine own familiar friend, in whom I trusted, which did eat of my bread, hath lifted up his heel against me" (Ps. 41:9). Oh, but it is a dreadful sin to betray and persecute Christ when you are feasting with Him, and at His table to lift up your heel against Him!

In speaking to this precious advantage, that friends only are invited to come, I shall only speak a little to these two things. First, I shall speak to these precious considerations, to provoke friends to come to this feast.

The first consideration is this: Christ, who is the great Master of the feast, invites you. We may say that word to you who are friends, "Be of good comfort, rise; he calleth thee" (Mark 10:49). If you would multiply objections throughout eternity, they may be all answered in this: Christ invites you.

A second consideration to move you who are friends to come is this: that all things are ready, therefore, come. This is Christ's own word, "All things are ready: come unto the marriage [feast]" (Matt. 22:4). Preparation is ready, faith is ready, mortification is ready, repentance is ready, tenderness is ready, Christ is ready, the feast is ready; therefore, come. What objection have you against the feast that is not answered in this, "All things are ready"? What do you lack that is not to be found in Christ? And what do you lack that Christ is not willing to give? What do you lack that Christ does not regret your not employing Him for the having of it?

A third consideration to provoke you who are friends to come to the feast of love is this: that Christ is exceedingly offended with these that stay away. When the invitees in Matthew 22:7 would not come, it is said of the King, "He was wroth." When those that were bidden to the feast would not come, it is said of the King, He was "angry" (Luke 14:21). If you would not offend precious Christ today, then, friends, do not stay away. Yea, Christ vents His wrath further in Matthew 22:7: "He sent forth his armies, and destroyed those murderers." You may ask, what is the reason that persons who will not come to the feast are called murderers? I conceive this to be the ground of it: because a Christian that is a friend may be guilty of the body and blood of Christ by staying away, as well as he may be guilty of the body and blood of Christ by coming; yea, he may be almost as guilty by staying away, if not altogether, as by coming. You may crucify Christ by staying away, as well as by coming.

A fourth consideration that may provoke you who are friends of God to come is this: there is a royal feast prepared for you. I confess, there is not much here for you who lack discerning eyes of faith. But a person that is in the precious exercise of faith will be constrained to cry out, "This is a 'feast of fat things, a feast of wines on the lees, of fat things full of marrow' (Isa. 25:6); it is a glorious feast, it is a purchased feast, it is a dear feast." I would have you, Christians, judging of this feast by the price that was paid for it; and

I would have you judging of this feast by Him that is the Master of the feast (as the Master is, so will the feast be), and I would have you judging of the feast by these noble and spiritual advantages that result to one that eats this feast in faith. I may say concerning the wine you are to drink today, "He that drinks of that wine indeed shall thirst no more, and he that eats of that bread shall hunger no more." Christ is endeavoring to persuade us to come upon this account, that there is a royal feast prepared for you (see Prov. 9:2; Matt 22:3–4).

A fifth consideration to provoke you who are friends to come is this: Christ is so willing and pleased that you should come that He will not take the first refusal off our hand, "He sent forth his servants to call them that were bidden to the wedding: and they would not come. Again, He sent forth other servants, saying, Tell them which are bidden, Behold, I have prepared my dinner" (Matt. 22:3–4). This is an evidence of Christ's willingness that you should come to the feast, that He will not take the first refusal off your hand.

The last consideration to provoke you who are friends to come up to keep the feast of tabernacles, and to sit down at His precious table, is this: that there is not much that Christ does require of you to come with. There are some who think there is so much required of them that they dare not approach. I would only ask these three questions of you. First: Have you a desire to meet with Christ? Then come. "Ho, every one that thirsteth, come ye" (Isa. 55:1)—that is the royal proclamation of grace. The second question: Have you no money in your purse? Then come. It is moneyless folk who are invited to this precious market of grace. As long as you have any money, you are not fit to come; but, when you lack money, you may come with boldness. The third question: Will you come with a price? A Christian has a price in his hand to buy wisdom, and yet He has no price. All that is required of you is to come without a price. Do not think to buy Christ with your preparation, nor with your repentance, nor with your tears; you must come and take Christ freely, as He is offered unto you.

Now, there is that second point which we would speak to from this, that friends only are invited to come to this precious feast. I shall give you *four grounds why only friends are invited to come.*

The first ground, why only friends are invited to come, is that there is none that will be welcome but friends. There are some of us who have a friend's name, but we shall have a foe's welcome. Yea, whoever is a stranger to Christ, we do in the name of the Master of the feast, and in the name of this Bridegroom, desire him to stay away that is not a friend to Christ. Let the person that is a stranger and an enemy to Christ, be *anathema maranatha*; a terrible curse shall be to him if he approaches.

The second ground, why only friends are invited to come, is this: only they who are friends can entertain Christ in the banquet of love. There is nobody that knows how to entertain a condescending, a feasting Christ, except friends; they know how to entertain Him and keep Him in the chambers.

The third ground, why only friends are invited to come, is because there is none that can exercise these graces which are suitable to one who would feast with Christ except one who is a friend. Can an enemy exercise the grace of love? And that is a necessary qualification for one who would come to the table. An enemy cannot exercise the grace of sorrow for offending Christ, and yet that is a qualification of one who would approach the table of the Lord.

Lastly, there is this ground why only friends are invited to come, namely, there is none that is able to discern the Lord's body except friends. As for strangers to Christ, they know Him not; if He were standing by them, they would suppose He were another thing. It is only friends that can discern the body and blood of Christ, therefore they alone are invited to come.

I shall say no more to this except, O friends, rejoice and comfort yourselves in this, that Christ has a mind to entertain you today. This table may be to you a door of hope, this table may be to you the valley of Achor, in which you may sing and rejoice as in the days of youth.

Now, there is this second advantage that comes to the Christian that is a friend of God, and it is this: *that person shall have many of the secrets of God*. That person, who is a friend to the Most High, is a person who shall be taken in to know these deep secrets of the Lord. This is clear from John 15:15: "Henceforth I call you not servants; for the servant knoweth not what his lord doeth; but I have called you friends; for all things that I have heard of my Father I have made known unto you." And that is indeed the very bond of friendship, the communication of secrets, unlike those in Job 19:19: "My inward friends abhorred me"; or, as the word is in the original, "The men of my secrets did abhor me." O Christians, and friends to the Most High, comfort yourselves in this privilege: that you are admitted to hear His secrets, and what is indeed His mind. I will tell you six excellent secrets that Christ communicates to His friends.

The first is this: Christ will communicate unto you the secrets of your own state; He will let you know whether you be in the state of nature or in the state of grace. There is that excellent secret of your eternal election, there is the excellent secret of your having your names written in the Book of Life, that Christ will make known to you: "The secret of the LORD is with them that fear him; and he will shew them his covenant" (Ps. 25:14). As it were, He will bring forth the eternal decree of love that was passed in their favors from all eternity and bid them read: "[The Lord's] secret is with the righteous" (Prov. 3:32).

A second secret that He will communicate to His friends is the secret of light in unknown truths. So He speaks to His disciples, "It is given unto you to know the mysteries of the kingdom of heaven" (Matt. 13:11). Paul says of himself, "We have the mind of Christ" (1 Cor. 2:16). There are many dark and mysterious truths that are hid from those who are strangers to God, yet that Christ will reveal to His friends; yes, there are many dark riddles in religion, many mysteries in godliness, that Christ will unfold to those who are His friends.

Third, there are excellent secrets of duty that Christ will unfold to His friends; He will tell His friends what is the duty of such a time, which others will not know. This is clear in 1 Chronicles 12:32: "And of the children of Issachar, which were men that had understanding of the times, to know what Israel ought to do." A Christian that is a friend of God, when another beside him will not know what his duty is in such a case, he being a friend to the Most High, will know what is His mind and where he ought to walk. There are many secret duties that are made known unto the friends of God that are not made known to others who are strangers to Him.

There is that fourth great secret that Christ does communicate to His friends, even the secrets of providence; He will make these known unto His friends. Sometimes we meet with crosses, and they are barbarians unto us, speaking in an unknown tongue; but Christ does oft-times condescend to give to His friends to hear the voice of the rod, and who it is that hath appointed it. There are some times wherein there is not a providence, there is not a dispensation that a Christian that walks near God meets with, but he can know the language of it, and what God does call for from him in it.

Fifth, Christ will communicate the secret of a Christian's condition to him; yes, He will make known to you what shall be your condition in the world, and how you shall go out of it. And sometimes Christ will make known these things that are dark to you in your condition, and give you clearness about them: "In thy light shall we see light" (Ps. 36:9).

There is that sixth secret that Christ will communicate to His friends, and that is that sometimes Christ will reveal to them secrets concerning the revolutions of kingdoms, and persons, and states; yes, sometimes He will communicate these to His own. When He was to destroy Sodom, "Oh," said God, "Shall I hide from Abraham the thing which I do?" (Gen. 18:17). That strange and remarkable word in Amos 3:7 shows another example: "GOD will do nothing, but he revealeth his secret unto his servants the prophets." As it were, He is under obligation to make known these secrets unto them.

Now Christians, who are friends to God, you may comfort yourselves with this: there are many deep and mysterious things that are made known unto you, that are deep secrets to the rest of the world. Yes, a Christian is living in Goshen, when the rest of the world are under Egyptian darkness that may be felt.

The third advantage that redounds to a soul by being a friend of God is this: they may come with boldness to God, to seek anything from Him. Is God your Friend? Then you may say, "God is my friend; I may be bold with Him." Yes, when you approach to God in prayer, if you could introduce it with this, "O my Friend," you might pray with much confidence and boldness of faith. And when you go to the table, if you could be admitted to say that word to Christ, "O my Friend, come along," this might make you to come with boldness and confidence of faith.

A fourth advantage that redounds to the Christian that is a friend of God is this: he may come to God with confidence of coming speed. If Christ be your Friend, you may go to Him with much soul-persuasion of this, that He will deny you nothing. Christ speaks that word to His friends which Jonathan spoke to David, "Whatsoever thy soul desireth, I will even do it for thee" (2 Sam. 20:4). Does not Christ say that word to His friends which King Zedekiah spoke to his subjects, "The king is not he that can do any thing against you" (Jer. 38:5)? O what can you ask from your precious friend that He will not give you? Did you ever put your precious Friend to do anything which He was not willing to condescend unto? We may say this of Christ: "There is a friend that sticketh closer than a brother" (Prov. 18:24). O had you ever such a precious Friend as this? I may say this to you: you may even prophesy good things unto His part; you may entrust[1] much to His hand.

A fifth advantage that results unto a Christian from this, that he is a friend of God, is this: this precious Friend, this matchless Friend, He sharpens and quickens you to duty. O but a sight of our precious friend, Christ, would make us exceeding swift in the exercise of duty! This is clear in Proverbs 27:17: "Iron sharpeneth iron; so a man sharpeneth the countenance of his friend." Would you know what would make you to go with a divine clarity and speediness in the doing of duty? It is even this, a sight of your precious Friend Christ.

A sixth advantage that results to a Christian from this, that he is a friend of God, is this: he has much communion with God. Would you know the person that dwells much with God? It is he that is a friend of God. Would you know the person that walks much with God? It is the person who can have this engraved upon his forehead, that he is a friend of God. This is clearly imported in the Word, "Can two walk together, except they be agreed?" (Amos 3:3). Which speaks this, that two who are agreed will surely walk much together. David vented his friendship to Barzillai in 2 Samuel 19:33 when he desired him to come over with him to Jerusalem, that he might feed at his table. O if Christ were a Friend to you, and you were a friend to Christ, you would walk much together, you would dwell much together. I would only say this: if you would be friends to Christ, you should have much of His heart, you should have much of His hand, you should have much of His mind. If you would be friends to Christ, you should have much of His heart;

---

1. Original, "lippen."

how should His soul breathe after you! And you should have much of His hand; He would help you in all your straits. And you should have much of His mind; He would communicate to you these precious and excellent secrets that are hid from the rest of the world.

There is this last advantage that redounds to a Christian from his being a friend of God, to wit, that God will give him counsel under all his dark and difficult straits. Is there a difficulty that you are put to? If you be a friend of God, He will give you counsel how to carry yourself under it: "Ointments and perfume rejoice the heart: so doth the sweetness of a man's friend by hearty counsel" (Prov. 27:9). If you were a friend to God, you would sometimes be constrained to sing that song, "I will bless the LORD, who hath given me counsel" (Ps. 16:7). If once you were a friend of God, you might take this up as a ground of your hope: "Thou shalt guide me with thy counsel, and afterward receive me to glory" (Ps. 73:24).

I shall add this advantage also that redounds unto a Christian from his being a friend of God, namely, if he be a friend of God, He will sympathize with you in all the straits and anxieties that you come under. Proverbs 18:24 abundantly states it: "A man that hath friends must shew himself friendly." And is not this the part of a friend, to sympathize with his friend when he is under very anxious and afflicting dispensations? Know, O friends, that Christ is more afflicted with our courses than we are afflicted with them ourselves. "He that toucheth you toucheth the apple of his eye" (Zech. 2:8). Let them but touch the most tender part of your body, and they touch the tenderest part of His body.

Now that which, third, I would speak to from this idea that there is such a precious privilege and royal dignity conferred upon believers as to be friends of God, is this: *to propose unto you some evidences by which you may know whether or not you be friends to God, and God a Friend unto you.* And I would obtest you and charge you in the name of the Master of the feast that, as you would not in this your estate of estrangement venture upon this feast of love, you would search yourselves by these.

The first evidence of a friend of God is this: a friend's love to Christ is constant, according to that remarkable word, "A friend loveth at all times" (Prov. 17:17). If you be a friend to Christ, you will love at all times. There are some whose love to Christ is like the love that Amnon had to Tamar; it lasted but for a very little, and then it was converted into hatred. If you take your love by fits, it is a sad and speaking evidence you are not a friend of God. "A friend loveth at all times." I confess, if Christ should come and search and try our love to Him, He would prove us not to love at all times. Christ will try the reality of your love to Him by crosses, by duties, and by mercies. (1) He will try the reality of your love to Him by crosses. As for some, when Christ begins to speak that word, "Take up [your] cross, and follow me" (Matt. 16:24), they part at that word, and they never meet again. (2) There are others that Christ tries the reality of their love in duties. Sometimes Christ will say to some, "Take now thy son, thy only son...whom thou lovest...and offer him... for a burnt offering" (Gen. 22:2). And, when they meet with such a command, Christ and they part. (3) Now, no doubt, obedience to all the commands of God is an evidence of real love, but there are some who have their obedience to their friend Christ. And He will try the reality of your love by mercies and sweet dispensations, as it were. He will give abundance of things unto you, that you may be tried whether you love Christ or them best. Now I would ask you today, is there any of you who has this mark of a friend, who loves at all times? Are you loving Christ at this time? O if you be not loving Christ, it is bad for you to adventure to approach to Him.

The second evidence of a friend of God is this, that he is the person that has a matchless and high esteem of his Friend: "He is altogether lovely. This is my beloved, and this is my friend, O daughters of Jerusalem" (Song 5:16). If Christ be your Friend, He will be altogether lovely. And as the woman sings, if Christ be your beloved friend, you will sing also, "[He] is white and ruddy, the chiefest among ten thousand" (v. 10). Is Christ matchless unto you? Is He matchless? If not, it is a token He is not your Friend. I would ask this: Who had your thoughts first today? Was it Christ that had your thoughts in the morning first today? I think it is an evidence that person is a friend to Christ, that can cry out that word, "When I awake, I am still with thee" (Ps. 139:18).

The third evidence of one that is a friend of God is this, that everything that is in Christ will be exceedingly lovely to the soul. Is Christ your Friend? There is nothing that is in Christ but it will be lovely: "He is altogether lovely." Christ's rebukes will be lovely, His challenges will be lovely, His sad dispensations will be lovely, His visits will be lovely. There is nothing that Christ can do but you will cry forth, "This is lovely." There is not a commandment that Christ can give but it will be lovely. If you be a friend to Him, you will cry forth, "I have a respect to all the commandments of God." Try yourselves by this: if the rebukes of Christ be lovely, if the sad dispensations of Christ be lovely to you, if the commandments of Christ be lovely unto you, that is an evidence Christ is your Friend.

The fourth evidence of one that is a friend is this: he is a person that will obey all the commandments of God. "Ye are my friends, if ye do whatsoever I command you" (John 15:14). A Christian must be universal in his obedience; that is a friend to Christ. There must not be a duty that a Christian meets with but he must take it in his arms, and cry out, "O good is the word of the Lord." If he will not love the duty for itself, yet will he love it because it comes from Christ.

A fifth evidence of one that is a friend to the Most High is this: if Christ be your Friend, you will be much in telling Him your secrets. There are some things that a Christian will tell Christ, which he will not tell to any in the world; nay, I think it were unlawful for us to tell things to our dearest friends, that we will not tell to Christ. He can put the best construction upon our confessions, and everything we can make known to Him. Yes, believe it—it offends your precious friend when you tell Him not all your secrets.

A sixth evidence of one that is a friend of God is this: absence from Christ will be your exceeding burden. When Jonathan and David were to part one from another, they fell upon one another's necks and wept, till David exceeded (1 Sam. 20:41). And when you and your precious friend depart one from another, should you not weep, and exceed in it? Believe it: it is a token Christ was never the friend to whom absence with Christ was never a burden. Yes, is not that the kindness of a friend, to long to see one's absent friend?

The last evidence of one that is a friend of Christ, and is entered into this sweet and precious bond of relation, is this: you will take delight to walk and converse with Christ. It is said of David and Jonathan, "The soul of Jonathan was knit with the soul of David" (1 Sam. 18:1). If Christ were your Friend, and you were a friend to

Him, there would be nothing so pleasant unto you as to walk all along with Christ. If Christ were your Friend, you would cry out, "Let him kiss me with the kisses of his mouth: for his love is better than wine" (Song 1:2).

The fourth thing that we would speak to upon this is to point out to you *these three remarkable times in which it is of much soul-concern to have Christ as our friend.*

The first time when it is of much concern to have Christ as our friend is when a Christian is put under most sad, anxious, and afflicting crosses. It is much of a Christian's concern to have Christ as his friend when he is put to propose his complaint: "Lover and friend hast thou put far from me" (Ps. 88:18). Yet that soul may comfort itself with this: "Christ is my Friend." A Christian could sit down and say, "I am reproached, yet I comfort myself with this, that Christ is my Friend; I am in poverty and straits, yet I comfort myself with this, that Christ is my Friend; I possess nothing, yet I comfort myself with this, that Christ is my Friend; I am put to wander 'in dens and caves of the earth' (Heb. 11:38), yet I comfort myself with this, that Christ is my Friend; I am put to endure the trial of cruel mockings, yet I comfort myself with this, that Christ is my Friend."

The second time when it is of much soul-concern to have Christ as our friend is on a communion day. It is much of your soul-concern to have Christ as your Friend at this time. O woe be to him that shall feast with an angry Christ! And woe be to him that shall feast with a Christ that has a controversy with him! Yea, know it: there is death if you be not friends to Christ.

The third time when it is of much soul-concern to have Christ as your Friend is at the day of death, when you shall stand upon the utmost line between time and eternity, when you shall look death in the face, and your sins shall stare you in the face, and all your convictions shall be called "a solemn assembly" round about you (Joel 2:15). It is much of your concernment to be friends with Christ at that day, that when you shall have one foot in eternity, and another in time, you may comfort yourselves with this, "My precious friend will guide me through the 'valley of the shadow of death'" (Ps. 23:4).

That which, fifth, I would speak to from this, that Abraham was called the friend of God, shall be this: *to point out to you these ways by which you may win to partake of this royal dignity of being a friend of God.*

And the first is this: be much in the exercise of faith; that is the way to win to this royal dignity, as is clear, in that by faith Abraham attained to this, to be a friend of God. Faith is the grace that does cast the knot of union between Christ and the soul; faith is the grace that makes up complete friendship between Christ and the soul. Without faith you are enemies and strangers unto Him.

The second way how you may win to this, to be friends of God, is this: be much in studying these endless virtues and precious excellencies that are in Him. "Acquaint now thyself with him, and be at peace" (Job 22:21). Would you know (says he) the compendious way to be friends with God, and at peace with Him? It is even this: "Acquaint yourself with him."

Third, would you have that blessed friendship made up between God and you? Then go to Jesus Christ, who is the blessed Days-man, that must lay His hand upon us both. He is indeed the Person that can take up all the quarrels, that can remove every ground of mistake that is between God and us. It is impossible for you to be friends with Him, except you take Christ along with you.

There is this, fourth, that I would prescribe unto you, to wit, that you would be much in the study of what spiritual advantage, what unspeakable liberty lies hid in this, to be a friend of God. Necessity cries out, "O be friends with God." Advantage cries out, "O be friends with God." There is nothing that you meet but it speaks this: "O be a friend of God."

Now I shall shut up our discourse at this time; only I shall propose these considerations to you who mind to sit down and feast with your Friend.

The first consideration that I would propose is this: Will you consider the dreadful disadvantage that comes to Christians who eat and drink unworthily? I would say this to you: if ever there was a sin that was the mother of hardness, if ever there was a sin that was the mother of security, if ever there was a sin that was the mother of atheism, it is the sin of eating and drinking unworthily. Therefore, take heed to the disadvantage that attends eating and drinking unworthily at the table of the Lord. I think there were some that, at the last communion they attended, did contract something that they will not shake off upon this side of eternity. Yea, know it: a Christian may contract as much estrangement and distance from Christ at a feast of love as he will make up while he is on this side of time. You shall never win so near Christ again till you win up to the higher house if, at this feast of love, you contract estrangement with Christ. Therefore "ponder the path of thy feet" (Prov. 4:26) when you go to sit down with Christ.

A second consideration that I would propose unto you who are to sit down to feast with your Friend is this: O have high thoughts of Christ in the day of love, and in the day of His feasting with us; have high thoughts of Him. Is it not most unsuitable to have low thoughts of Christ on the day of His coronation? Is it not unsuitable to have low thoughts of Him on the day when He brings us "to the banqueting house, and his banner over [us is] love" (Song 2:4)? Know it: the person that would sell Christ for thirty pieces of silver is not a person that should approach to the feast of love. Therefore, study to bring your hearts swelling with high, stately, and majestic apprehensions of the Master of the feast. In a manner, when you sit down, you may begin to wonder at the condescending love of Christ, and speak that word which Mephibosheth, feeling unworthy, spoke to David when he was set down at table with the king, "What is thy servant, that thou shouldest look upon such a dead dog as I am" (2 Sam. 9:8). I think, if we saw Him, we would be afraid to approach to Him.

The third consideration that I would propose to you who would approach to feast with your Friend is this: by all means endeavor to have clearness concerning your interest in this friend. Know that it is much of your concern to know that Christ indeed is your Friend. You will win it by the testimony of the Spirit, or you will win it by faith, or you will win it by holy reason, or you will win it by sense, or you will win it by evidences; but, however, be much in requesting the King for this, that you may see a sight of your name written in the book of life before you come to this precious feast of love.

A fourth consideration that I would propose to you who are to feast with your Friend is this, that you would study not only to have your state cleared, but to be in a good and spiritual frame of spirit. If you would feast with your Friend Christ today, study to have a spiritual and excellent frame of spirit. I would only say this: there are eight sorts of frames of spirit, which if you come with, Christ will not regard you, and I would desire you would examine yourselves whether you be under any of these frames.

There is, first, a legal frame of spirit, that is unfit for eating and drinking with Christ. I call that a legal frame, a frame not withdrawn from the covenant of works. Some will not trust upon their works, but they will trust upon their duties, and upon their graces. I say to that person, be who you will: if you have a legal frame of spirit, approach not to Christ's table today.

A second frame of spirit which Christ will not regard is a presumptuous frame. A Christian who will go about this ordinance upon his own strength, who will sit down and eat and drink with Christ upon his own strength, that is a frame that Christ will reject, and say to that person, "Friend, how camest thou in hither?" (Matt. 22:12).

Third, there is the frame of spirit that wants an errand — that is a frame that Christ will reject. Christ will ask that question at you, "What is your errand?" And, if you be under such a frame of spirit that you have not an errand, I would say unto you, do not venture to come.

There is, fourth, a confused frame of spirit, and that is not for the Lord's table. Hence it is, that in 1 Corinthians 11:28, it is required of us before we come to the feast of love that we should search and examine ourselves. We should have clear discoveries of our own condition before we come.

There is that fifth frame of spirit that is not fit for the table of the Lord, and that is an untender and hardened frame. Is it not the work of the day to mourn over Him whom we have pierced? And, if you have an untender and hardened frame of spirit, it is a speaking evidence this will not be to you "a feast of fat things...full of marrow" (Isa. 25:6).

There is that sixth frame of spirit that is not fit for such a precious ordinance, and it is an unmortified frame of spirit. The person that has his idols lying between his breasts, whose whoredoms make him to depart from God, that person is not fit for such a solemn ordinance.

There is that seventh unfit frame of spirit, and it is the frame that has not love in it; that is, the frame that is not loving Christ, that is an unsuitable frame. O but Christ may speak that word unto you which Isaac spoke to Abimelech, "Wherefore come ye to me, seeing ye hate me, and have sent me away from you?" (Gen. 26:27). O what if Christ shall speak unto you, "How can you come unto me, since you hate me, and have put me away?"

The last sort of frame of spirit that is unfit for this ordinance is the heart that is not at all prepared for this precious ordinance. There are some of us here (we may speak without breach of charity) who suppose we doubt much if we took a quarter of an hour's more pains to prepare our hearts to this precious ordinance than we do at other times. There is not any that slight preparation, but it is a speaking evidence of their undervaluing of Christ. We shall only name the rest of the considerations, and close.

There is this fifth consideration that I would propose unto you, and it is this: there are many persons who think they are in suitable frame to partake of this ordinance, and yet no doubt they are in a desperate frame. There are some who examine their condition by the letter of the law, and cry out, "I am blessed." This was Paul's way also, crying out that he was, concerning "the law, blameless" (Phil. 3:6), and he was "alive with the law" (Rom. 7:9). They examine their condition by the letter of the law. Others examine their condition by the peace of conscience that they have. Some, if they have peace of conscience, think all is well. Some judge their condition by the bulk of outward duties, as that who said, "God, I thank thee, that I am not as other men are.... I fast twice a week, I give tithes of all that I possess" (Luke 18:11–12). Some examine their condition by the walk of others; if they see themselves in outward things above them, they sit down, and bless themselves. I would say to you, you who are embracing such a delusion, take heed lest you meet with a snare.

There is that consideration likewise that we would propose, and it is this: that a Christian may be in an exceeding good frame for feasting with Christ, and yet he may suppose himself to be in a very bad frame. Christians mistake their condition and frame, by judging it according to the rule of dispensations. If dispensations speak bitter things to us, we sit down and conclude sad things against ourselves, and cry out, "To which of the saints shall I go?" and, "If I call, there is none that would answer me."

The last consideration that I would propose unto you is this: you are now invited to come to this solemn feast of love; know it, that it may be a day of sad remembrance to many. Yes, give me permission to say it: we look not like feasters with Christ. I think, if a stranger who knows not what we are meeting for today would come in and look to us all round about, he might cry out, "There is no communion here today." Does not "the shew of [our] countenance witness against [us]" (Isa. 3:9)? O are there any who have seen the Master of the feast today? Are there any who have beheld the "goings of my God, my King, in the sanctuary" (Ps. 68:24)?

An Exhortation to Perseverance

Keep yourselves in the love of God.
—Jude 21

Preached after a fast before a Communion.

If precious Christ should propose that question to some of us which once He asked Peter, "Lovest thou me?" (John 21:15), I suppose there are few within these doors who could upon solid and spiritual grounds return Peter's answer to the question, "Thou knowest that I love thee." The grace of love is a royal and tender plant that cannot well grow in our untender hearts. The love of many that are within these doors is like Jonah's gourd—it springs up in a night and perishes in a night. Our love is like the early cloud, and the morning dew, that quickly vanishes. If so we may speak, in a manner of love, we love Christ today, and we hate Him tomorrow. I would only say this to you: O that the divine and precious excellencies of the grace of love were known, that you might be provoked not only to pursue after it, but also to keep it, when you have attained it!

The grace of love has three great questions which it does propose. First, "What wilt thou have me to do?" (Acts 9:6). Love desires no more but to have its orders from Christ, and it will not despise His commandments. A second question of the grace of love in a Christian is this: "What shall I render to the LORD for all his benefits toward me?" (Ps. 116:12). Love is a grace that is ofttimes put to a nonplus; it cannot tell what it should render unto God for all His gifts and precious donations of favor which He has given.

A third precious question of love is this: "Saw ye him whom my soul loveth?" (Song 3:3). Such a question is not very common in these days, which shows that love is dying within us, and drawing towards its grave. Now, though love has three questions, yet it has but one desire, which you will find in Psalm 27:4: "One thing have I desired of the LORD, that will I seek after; that I may dwell in the house of the LORD all the days of my life, to behold the beauty of the LORD, and to enquire in his temple."

I shall, before I come to the words, only desire you to take notice of two things. First, that there are many mistakes in sundry Christians concerning this noble and excellent grace of love. There is nothing we have so much in profession as love, and yet there is nothing we have less in practice and reality than love. In a manner, hatred to Christ may be engraved with great letters upon the walk and conversation of many of us. There is that, second, that I would say: he who has gotten the precious grace of love is eternally made up. O Christians, love will be your eternal companion. Faith will leave you, hope will leave you, repentance will leave you, mortification will leave you, and patience will leave you when you enter in within the gates of that city. But that noble and excellent grace of love will walk in through the gates to the city with you. The day is coming when you shall speak that word which a holy man spoke being near death: "Now farewell faith, farewell hope, and welcome O love."[1]

Now, to come to the words, the great scope of the apostle in this epistle is to guard those to whom he wrote against apostasy and defection, only against a doctrinal apostasy from Christ, that they should hold fast the profession of their faith without wavering, and contend earnestly for the truth. But he desires to guard them against practical apostasy from Christ, that what they had once won, they should study to keep. There is no less Christian policy required in keeping than in attaining; there is as much Christian diligence to be used to keep as to attain our graces. Among the rest of the precious means that God has prescribed by which we might win to a divine steadfastness is this one: keep yourselves in the love of God. By "the love of God" here, we do not so much understand

---

1. John Jackson, *The True Euangelical Temper* (London, 1641), 15.

these sweet emanations of love and the manifestations of it, that are upon God's part, as we understand the love that a Christian has to God, that they should earnestly and vigorously desire to keep. For you would know, love may be either taken in a passive sense, as it points out these sweet outflowings and emanations of love from the heart of Christ, which terminate upon the Christian, or it may be taken in an active sense, as it points out these sweet and excellent actings of love that are in the soul of a Christian that terminate and are fixed upon precious Christ. And by keeping themselves in the love of God, their endeavoring to persevere and hold fast the love they have attained, and withal that they should pursue and earnestly contend for more, is pointed out. We may say (as it were) He desires them to keep within this excellent palace of the love of God; it is one of the most excellent mansions and places of abode that we can have.

Now you may take notice of these four things from the words, which we shall shortly speak to. The first is this: *that the grace of love in a Christian is incident*[2] *and liable to apostasy and decay.* A Christian is prone to nothing so much as this, to make defection and apostasy in the precious grace of love. Love is a tender thing; it must either be well kept, or else it will be lost. We must keep the grace of love as the apple of our eye.

The second doctrine you may take notice of from the words is this: *that it is a duty most incumbent upon a Christian to study to hold fast and keep God's love.* The word that is here rendered "keep" imports, according to its force in the original, for one to keep a thing diligently as with watch and ward, to which they should have a diligent inspection and care lest they lose the precious jewel, love.

The third doctrine you may take notice of from the words is this: *that there is much everlasting and unspeakable soul-advantage that lies hidden in the practice of this duty of keeping yourselves in the love of God.* This we take notice of from the scope, in which the apostle prescribes this as an excellent remedy to guard against apostasy. O Christians, would you go to heaven without a fall? Go all along your way to heaven traveling in the chariot of love. Yea, when love is at a decay, it will make your garment contract many unseemly spots.

---

2. A medicine that "cuts" the phlegm.

Would you know what a loving Christian is? He is a Christian who has two heavens: he has a heaven upon earth, and a heaven when he has done with earth. Would you know where the loving Christian's heart is? It is in heaven. Would you know where the loving Christian's conversation is? It is in heaven. Would you know where the loving Christian's treasure is? It is in heaven. Would you know where the loving Christian's hope is? It is in heaven. Would you know where the loving Christian's eyes are? They are in heaven. I know not what of a loving Christian is out of heaven, but this lumpish tabernacle of clay that cannot inherit incorruption till it be made incorruptible. But a soul that is burning in love is a soul in heaven, according to that expression, "The soul is more where it loves, than where it lives."[3]

The last doctrine I take notice of from the words is this: *that there are many temptations and assaults that a Christian meets with, the great design and intent of which is to rob and deprive him of this excellent jewel, love.* This we conceive is pointed out in that word "keep," not only in the exhortation, "Keep yourselves in the love of God"—which does presuppose there are many enemies—but also the force of the word in the original signifies as much as supposes a diligent keeping of that which is in hazard to be taken away and lost, as if to say, "Keep as with watch and ward, for there are ten thousand temptations at your right hand, and ten thousand temptations at your left hand, that are ready to take away the precious jewel, love, from you." And, if once Satan rob you of this, there is little hope of any subsequent victory over him. Would you know what love is? It is a Christian's strength and his delight.

As to the first thing in the words, to wit: *the grace of love is subject to decay.* I need not stand long to prove this. It is clear from Jeremiah 2:2: "I remember thee, the kindness of thy youth, the love of thine espousals, when thou wentest after me in the wilderness, in a land that was not sown." Which words speak, that love was now gone; the

---

3. Albertus Magnus (1193–1280), *On Cleaving to God* (London, 1971), chap. 12: "For the soul is more where it loves than where it lives, since it is in what it loves in accordance with its very nature, understanding and will, while it is in where it lives only with regard to form, which is even true for animals as well."

love of espousals, and the kindness of youth, was now away; the wilderness-love was now gone and decayed in them; the love they had when they were led through a land that was not sown, was now decayed and gone. And it is clear also from Revelation 2:4: "Thou hast left thy first love." I would only ask this: Is there a Christian within these doors whose heart may not be a proof of this truth, that love is liable to decay? Are there any of you who are here but this may be ingraven upon your foreheads, "Love is decaying, love is waxing old every day"?

In speaking to this truth, I would touch a little to these things. First, I would be clear on what the apostasies of the grace of love are, what it is for love to be in a decay and spiritual consumption. And we conceive it imports these three things.

First, for a Christian to lose these eminent degrees of love that formerly he had. Love in a Christian is sometimes like the coals of juniper, or like the coals of fire, that have, at times, a most vehement flame, yet at other times that love is cold and remiss. So, when you have lost something of the degrees of love, it says, love is in a consumption and decay, drawing towards its grave. Sometimes your love will be like a burning fire, and ere the morrow come it will be like a smoking flax.

Second, the apostasy and defections of love stand in this: for a Christian to lose these strong and vigorous actings of love that formerly he had. It is a known principle in nature, *"Lesa principia habent, lesas tantum operationis"* — when the principle is weakened, it can no longer act. So likewise love, when it is under a decay, has not such strong actings, and is not so vigorous as it was before. Sometimes love in a Christian will act strongly within him; there will be no impediment in the way but love will overcome it. As it were, love is an undaunted grace; love scorns and laughs at difficulties, and mocks at impediments.

Third, the defections and apostasy of love appear in this, when Christians lose these easy and facile actings of love that formerly they had. Is not this known, that sometimes you will win to a greater easiness and facility in acting the grace of love, more than at other times? Sometimes you will get your heart brought to an excellent frame most easily; at other times you will toil yourselves all night before you can get your heart in a holy frame. O but there is a great decay of love as to this in many of us! Will you not subscribe to these two? Will you not subscribe to this, that, if you could get heaven for one good thought, you could never buy it, you could never give a good thought for it? And will you not all subscribe to this, that, if you could get Christ eternally for one act of love, and for one desire, you could not spin it out of your cold, dead, and lifeless heart? O whither is the grace of love now gone! And, believe it, the remarkable decays of the love of God are the very rise of all these other decays that now are with us. The decay of love is that which makes our house to drop through, and our building decay; the decay of love is that which makes us to meet with empty ordinances, with empty prayers, and to have an empty walk and conversation.

That which, second, I would speak to upon this is to point out to *you what are the rises and fountain-causes of the apostasies and decays of the grace of love*. Is not love dying? Alas! The grace of love is lying upon its deathbed; it may cry out to Christ, "Master, save me, for I am ready to die."

First, one rise of it is this: the hearty soul-embracing of our idols. Would you know why you love God so little? It is this: you love your idols too much. Alas! We lodge Christ but in our sight, but we lodge our idols in our hearts. As long as our idols and we are familiar, it is impossible for the grace of love to thrive. "They are all estranged from me through their idols" (Ezek. 14:5). It is as if he has said, "There is an uncouthness contracted between them and me by reason of their idols." "They forgat me," God said, when they "went after [their] lovers" (Hos. 2:13). O cursed be that forgetfulness that makes us forget Christ and to remember our idols! "They forgat me." There is an emphasis in that word "me"—they forgat beautiful me, they forgat transcendent me, they forgat kind me, they forgat dying and glorified me, and followed after their lovers. If you would keep the love of God, you would subscribe a bill of divorce to your idols, which you would have ratified in such a way as that it should never be repealed. O cursed be the person that prefers his idols to Christ! And let all the congregation say, Amen.

Second, another rise of the decays of love is this: the abounding of iniquity within us. There are some who may say they have five predominant idols; yea, in a manner, they know not an evil in them, but they may call predominant. This is the great mother of the apostasies of love. "And because iniquity shall abound, the love of many shall wax cold" (Matt. 24:12). O Christians, your hearts are so full of strangers that Christ cannot get a room to lodge in. What is your name, O Christian? We may call our name Legion, for we are many. O to have a fight against these multitudes of guests that dwell within our hearts! Our hearts are like the house of Bethlehem. It was so full of strangers that Christ with His mother could not get a room to lodge in, but had to go to the stable. We keep Christ at the door through the multitudes of strangers who are within us. Is not that our cursed divinity, "I have loved strangers, and after them will I go" (Jer. 2:25)?

A third rise of the decays of love is much formality in going about the duties of godliness. O but a communion celebrated and gone about formally, a prayer gone about formally, a fast gone about formally, and a reading of Scripture gone about formally are the very mother of the apostasy of love. Would you know what is the reason love is now at a decay? It is even this: formality is sitting upon the throne. This is somewhat pointed out in Scripture: "This people draw near me with their mouth"—that is, formally—and, "their heart [goes] far from me" (Isa. 29:13). As it were, approaching Christ with the tongue, where there is no approaching Christ with the heart, makes an estrangement of our hearts from Christ. There is not a formal prayer you pray, O Christians, but it is (as it were) a step of your departing from Christ. There is not a formal prayer you pray, O Christians, but it is a drop of water upon the fire of love. Therefore, if you would keep your love in life, wrestle much with God like princes in prayer. It was a noble saying of one, "He never came away from God without God, he never left Him till he got Him."[4] Alas! We content ourselves when we go to seek Him, though we find Him not. O put on that divine impudence (for so the word "importunate" may be rendered) that we will take no denial from Him.

A fourth rise of the decay of love is this: much self-seeking in all our devotions, which has great influence upon the decays of love. "Israel...bringeth forth fruit unto himself"—there is self-seeking—

---

4. Source unknown.

and "their heart is divided"—there is a decay of love (Hos. 10:1–2). His heart (as it were) is divided between two objects. It is impossible for a Christian who is much in self-seeking to be much in love; there is nothing so inconsistent together as love and self-seeking. As long as self is your god, the love of God will die within you.

Fifth, this also has influence upon the decays of love: the sin of hypocrisy. This does exceedingly quench the precious actings of the grace of love. If one of you turns to be a hypocrite, if hypocrisy looks out from your eyes, and appears in your walk, then farewell the grace of love. There is nobody who is taken up in the exercise but these who are upright and sincere: "The upright love thee" (Song 1:4).

A sixth rise of the apostasies from the grace of love is this: a Christian's little observation of the precious experience of the love and favor of God that He meets us with. How many favors from God have you received, which you have buried in forgetfulness, and have remembered no more? This may be pointed out in comparing Romans 5:4 with Romans 5:5. Patience brings forth experience. And would you know (says the apostle) what advantage attends the Christian who is much in marking his experience? "The love of God is shed abroad in our hearts" (v. 5). O Christians, shall God have a book of remembrance of your words, and will you not have a book of remembrance written of His actions? How many stones of remembrance have you set up, O Christians? The day is coming when the waters of Jordan shall divide themselves, and the ransomed of the Lord shall pass through, and you shall put up twelve stones of everlasting remembrance to God, who has redeemed your soul from death, your eyes from tears, your feet from falling. I would only say this, that a Christian would observe the experience of restraining love, a Christian would observe the experience of preventing love, a Christian would observe the experience of conquering love, and a Christian would observe the experience of pardoning love. Know this: Christ can forget nothing but your wrongs done to Him, and there should not be anything that you should forget so little as His love.

Now that which third I would speak to upon this shall be to pro-pose unto you *some helps by which you may be afflicted in guarding against the apostasies and decays of this excellent grace of love.*

First, be much in the exercise of faith if you would keep love in life. It is impossible for love to live if faith be at its death. Love and faith are two sister-graces and twins; they grow together and decay together: "That Christ may dwell in your hearts by faith; that ye, being rooted and grounded in love" (Eph. 3:17). These two graces are sweetly conjoined together: "Charity out of a pure heart, and of a good conscience, and of faith unfeigned" (1 Tim. 1:5). I would only clear this unto you a little, that faith has an excellent influence upon the keeping of love in life. (1) Faith is a grace that takes up the tran-scendent comeliness, the passing beauty, that is in the face of Christ. Faith (as it were) draws aside the veil, and says unto love, "Come and see." Faith removes these clouds and brings in love to delight itself in a discovered and seen Christ. (2) Faith has influence upon keeping love in life in this respect; faith is the grace that makes up an interest between Christ and the soul, and the soul has a pro-priety in Him by faith. Now, you know, interest and propriety are the foundation of love. Nothing commends things so much as these two, the excellency of the thing, and, "It is mine, it is mine." That is faith's divinity, "Christ is mine, Christ is mine"; and this makes love to come in and cry out, "Christ is mine, and shall be so eter-nally." So, faith takes a grip of Christ, without wavering; but love takes Christ, clasps its arms about the object, and cries out, "I will never let Him go." Love cannot admit of a separation; love abhors nothing so much as this absence from Christ. (3) Faith is the grace that lets the Christian see the endlessness, the eternity, the breadth, the depth of love that is in the heart of Christ. Faith, as it were, goes over the borders of time into eternity, and takes a view of the eter-nal love that was in the heart of Christ before the cornerstone of the world was laid, and before the morning stars did shout and sing for joy. And when love gets a sight of the eternity of the love of Christ, then it cries out, "O who would not love Him who is the King of saints? Who would not delight themselves in Him who loves me from eternity, and shall love me to all eternity?" "We love him, because he first loved us" (1 John 4:19). (4) This makes it out that faith has an exceeding great influence upon the life of love, even this: faith is the grace that reveals to a Christian the emptiness of his idols; faith is the grace that makes the Christian put to his hand and subscribe amen to the words of Scripture, "Vanity of vanities, saith the Preacher, vanity of vanities; all is vanity" (Eccl. 1:2). O but when a Christian gets a broad sight of the loveliness that is in the face of Christ, and gets a broad sight of the emptiness of his idols, then he cries out, "What have I to do with idols? He is become to me as a green fir tree, from whence my fruit shall be found." Would you know what love is? It is even the silver cord by which the soul of a Christian is immediately knit to the soul of Christ.

There is this, second, that would help to guard against the decays of love: be much in studying the knowledge of Christ. What makes you love so little? It is because you know so little of Him. Do you know Him? If you knew Him, you would be forced to cry out, "O for ten thousand hearts to wear upon him!" "Acquaint now thyself with him" (Job 22:21), that is, grow up in the knowledge of Him, "for then shalt thou have thy delight in the Almighty, and shalt lift up thy face unto God" (v. 26). And what is delight but an intense measure of love which points out the eminent actings of it? Scripture provides the means to attain this: "Grow in grace, and in the knowledge of our Lord and Saviour Jesus Christ" (2 Pet. 3:18). You must bring Christ to your sight before you can bring Him to your heart. O but ignorance of Christ is the reason we love Him so little! Can we love an unknown Christ and can we love a Christ whom we do not believe? O but to have such a sight of Christ as the saints who are around the throne have! To have some immediate views and glimpses of the passing, of the transcendent comeliness and soul-conquering beauty that is in Christ, would make us sick of love, yea, so sick of love as to be content to die of that sickness, even to die in the sickness of love.

Third, we would prescribe this as a help to guard against the decays of love: be much in meditating upon Christ. "I meditate on all thy works," and "my soul thirsteth after thee, as a thirsty land" (Ps. 143:5–6). And what is thirsting? It is the eager, the unsatisfied actings of love. Would you know what love's prayer is? Love in a manner has only one prayer, and that is: give, give, give, give. It is an unsatisfied grace that cannot have enough; it is like the daughter of the horseleech that never says, "It is enough." Give love enjoyments of Christ tomorrow, and it will never say, "It is enough." O meditate upon Him; that is the way to keep love in life. Believe it; I know not a duty that would keep love so much in vigor as meditation. David was in a loving frame when he was meditating; "O how love I thy law! It is my meditation all the day" (Ps. 119:97). Give Christ more of your light, and He shall have more of your heart.

Fourth, we would prescribe this as a help to guard against the apostasies and decays of love, to wit, study to entertain frequent correspondence and communion with Christ, and this would keep love in life. This is clear, "The King hath brought me into his chambers." And what of that? "We will remember thy love more than wine: the upright love thee" (Song 1:4). "He brought me to the banqueting house, and his banner over me was love" (Song 2:4). And what of that? "Stay me with flagons, comfort me with apples: for I am sick of love" (v. 5). Yes, love makes a Christian sick, and it must make a Christian whole again. O but little conversing with Him is that which is the cause that our hearts are dying like a stone within us.

Fifth, there is this which would be a help to guard against the apostasies of love, namely, let a Christian be much in observing the returns of prayers, and that would keep love in life. "I love the LORD, because he hath heard my voice and my supplications" (Ps. 116:1). Know you what a return of prayer is? It is even a sweet declaration of the love and condescending grace that is in Christ. Believe it: there is more love in a return of prayer than eternity will be able to make language of. O study the returns of prayer; there is much bosom-love, much transcendent and heart-love in such a dispensation.

Lastly, we would prescribe this as a help to guard against apostasy and decays of love, to wit, let a Christian endeavor to guard against every temptation that comes to seek his love. Christians, after you have given your love to Christ, answer all the temptations that come to seek your love thus: "O temptation, I am not my own, I am bought with a price; therefore I must glorify God in my soul and in my body." And answer your temptations with this: "You are too late in coming." And certain I am, temptations come too late to the soul that is prepossessed with the love of Christ; if once Christ be within, temptations will not have so easy access. O what a life it is to hold Him all night! I would even prescribe these two things to you:

when you go unto the throne of grace to pray, that Christ go before you in your arms to the throne of grace, and, if it be possible for you to win to it, study even to die with Christ in your arms, that heaven may be to you a going up from the lower to the higher room, that death may be to you a change of place and not of company.

Fourth, I would speak to this: *I would point out to you some evidences that love is in a decay, that love is gone in a great measure and degree.*

First, the little delight we have to correspond with Christ says that love is decaying and under a consumption. O but did we love Him, we ought not keep so much out of His blessed company. Every day's absence from Christ, to the soul that is burning in love, would be a little eternity. Does not this speak that love is in a decay, that you are so little groaning after fellowship with Christ? It was an evidence that love was upon the growing hand in David when he said, "As the hart panteth after the water brooks, so panteth my soul after thee, O God" (Ps. 42:1; see also Ps. 63:1).

A second evidence that love is in a decay is the little delight we have in commanded duties. In a manner, when love is within, when it lodges in the heart, there is not a command that comes from precious Christ, but love will kiss it; there is not a command that will come to a Christian that is in a vigorous exercise of love, but he will cry forth, "God has spoken in His holiness; I will rejoice!" There is not a command that comes from Christ, but love will say, "Good is the word of the Lord." And does not your much disputing of His commandments, and your much neglecting obedience unto them, speak that love is in a decay? "If ye love me, keep my commandments" (John 14:15; see also vv. 21, 23, 24). There cannot be a greater demonstration of love than obedience. O are there not many commandments that come from Christ unto you of which you say, "This is a hard saying; who can bear it?"

Third, this speaks that love is in a decay: even our little weeping and groaning under absence with Christ. Is absence with Christ your burden? Or is it not so much as it was before? That is an evidence love is at a decay. Would you know love's language under absence with Christ? "All ye that pass by...see if there be any sorrow like unto my sorrow" (Lam. 1:12). To a Christian that is in the burning exercise of love, absence with Christ is his greatest cross, and that which does most afflict him.

Fourth, this speaks love is in a decay, and is waxing old within us: even the small esteem we have of Christ. Did you love Him, you would cry out, "Whom have I in heaven but Christ?" And, "There is none in the earth whom I desire besides Him." That is love's motto: none but Christ, none but Christ. Do not these low and undervaluing thoughts of Christ speak that this love is at a decay? In a manner, we are taking up stones to stone Him. And will we stone precious Christ? We will stone Him?

Fifth, our little mourning for offending Christ says that love is at a decay and waxing old within us. Sometimes, when love was in its vigorous exercise, the smallest of sins that the soul could commit against Christ would make it to water its couch with tears. But now the greatest offence we do to Christ will not draw a tear from our eyes—and is not that a decay of love? I would even say that word to you which Absalom spoke to Hashai, "Is this thy kindness to thy friend?" (2 Sam. 16:17). Is this your kindness to your precious friend Christ? There are many wrongs you have done to Him that you never had one sad thought for.

Lastly, this points out the decay of love in our hearts to Christ, even this: our entertaining so much the things which He hates. O will we lodge His enemies within our hearts? Alas! Our hearts are as a sanctuary for many idols. If once you did win to the precious exercise of love, no doubt you would put all things out the door that might interrupt or mar the blest correspondence with God, or that might keep you at distance with Him.

Now that which, fifth, we would speak to upon this first thing in the words is this: *how a Christian may be helped to recover and repair the decays and breaches of the grace of love.* And, first, I would say this: if you would repair these breaches, be much in the exercise of repentance. "Nevertheless I have somewhat against thee, because thou hast left thy first love.... Repent, and do the first works" (Rev. 2:4–5). There is nothing that will recover love so much, when it is almost lost, as repentance. The repenting Christian is the loving Christian; the Christian who goes deepest in the exercise of repentance oft-times ascends highest in the exercise of love. Second, I would have a Christian to be much in looking upon his debt—that is the way to recover love. O Christians, take a look of the debt you owe to Christ. "She loved much: but to whom little is forgiven, the same loveth little" (Luke 7:47). O what if you saw the book of the debt you owe to Christ? It would be an endless work to tell over all the blessed acts of love that Christ has dispensed to you. Third, we would propose this as a means to repair the decays of love, to wit, that you would study to repair first the breaches of the grace of faith. Never think that love can ascend in its growth, if faith does not ascend with it.

Now we shall only speak a word to the second doctrine we proposed, and we shall close up our discourse at this time. The second doctrine was this: that it is a duty incumbent upon a Christian to keep himself, to persevere, and to hold fast the love which he has attained. We shall not stand long to clear this truth. "Hold that fast which thou hast" (Rev. 3:11). The general no doubt takes place in this of love. "I will put upon you none other burden. But that which ye have already hold fast till I come" (Rev. 2:24–25). And it is most remarkably clear in that word, "Look to yourselves, that we lose not those things which we have wrought" (2 John 8). The word that is there rendered "look" imports (according to its force in the original) that a Christian should take heed with both his eyes, diligently to consider, lest he lose what he has gained already. Keep your ground, O Christians; keep your ground. And withal, this may be pointed out, "Continue ye in my love" (John 15:9). Dwell and abide in it. Now, to press this a little more, that a Christian should keep himself in the love of God, I would propose these seven considerations.

The first consideration to press it is this: the soul that is much in the exercise of the grace of love, he is the soul that meets with much enjoyment of God. Would you know the soul that meets with the most manifestations of God? It is the soul that is burning with love. "He that loveth me...I will love him, and will manifest myself to him" (John 14:21). "If a man love me...[my Father and I] will come unto him, and make our abode with him" (v. 23). I would have you to look to the wonderful, deep, and profound mysteries that are in this word: "He that dwelleth in love dwelleth in God, and God in him" (1 John 4:16). Would you know what builds a house to God? Even love. Love builds the house; he that dwells in love, God dwells in him, and the soul dwells in God. O what a mutual dwelling in the soul! Is not this a sweet cohabitation? Is not this a sweet and transcendent mystery? O what love is here, that He who dwells in the light that is inaccessible, that He who inhabits eternity, that He should dwell in our hearts — such a poor cottage! Were there ever any worthy that He should come under their roof?

The second consideration is this: the soul that is much in the actings of love, he is the soul that lives within sight of his interest in God. Would you know what is the cause of so much disputing, of so much unbelief? It is the lack of love. "I love them that love me" (Prov. 8:17). The love that is there spoken of, it is not the love that is first in the heart of God unknown, but the meaning is this: "He that loves me, I will manifest this to him, that I love him." "He that loveth me shall be loved of my Father, and I will love him, and will manifest myself to him" (John 14:21). O Christians, would you go in every day, and look to the ancient records of heaven, and see your name written in great letters in the book of life? Then be much in the exercise of love. Who is the Christian who has the secrets of Christ? It is the loving Christian. Who is the Christian who lives nearest heaven? It is the loving Christian.

The third consideration to press it is this: if you keep not love in vigorous exercise, there are five things that will remarkably decay and wax old within you. First, delight in duty will decay. If once love begins to wax old, then farewell to delight in duty when love is away. Would you know what it is that makes our chariot wheels to move swiftly? It is love. Would you know what makes us to run in the ways of His commandments? It is love. Would you know what makes us to embrace every command? It is love. Second, if love begin to decay, then farewell the grace of tenderness; tenderness will then wax old. What is it that makes a Christian to eschew all appearance of evil? It is love. What makes a Christian to hate the garment spotted with the flesh? It is love. What makes a Christian not so much as take up the name of an idol in his mouth? It is love, and hence is that word, "Ye that love the LORD, hate evil" (Ps. 97:10). No doubt it speaks this, that tenderness is securely conjoined with love. Third, if love be in a decay, then farewell to the work of repentance and mortification. Nothing makes a soul repent so much as love; nothing makes a soul mortify so much as love; nothing makes the soul water its couch with tears so much as love; nothing makes the soul to sit down in secret places, and weep over itself, so much as love. That is the great voice of love unto all its idols. Fourth, if love decay, then bid farewell to patience under sufferings; we shall never bear a cross long patiently without love. What is the mother of patience? It is love; love brings forth patience. "Love is not easily provoked, thinketh no evil" (1 Cor. 13:5). Love (as it were) does not entertain a suspicious thought of Christ; that is love's divinity. It makes us say, "Let Him kill me, yet will I love Him." Fifth, if once love begins to decay, the grace of hope does also remarkably decay; that is gone when love is gone. And the things that are the objects of hope, they will grow tasteless unto you when love is gone. You know the object of hope is the thing promised, and the object of faith is the truth of the promise; and if once love be gone, then farewell the grace of hope. Hope will no more look to heaven, and comfort itself; hope will no more look to the crown, and comfort itself. It is love that will keep hope and faith in life: "Faith which worketh by love" (Gal. 5:6). Yea, love is even that which puts faith to work.

The fourth consideration to press the keeping yourselves in the love of God is this: that the Scripture has put many notes of excellency upon the precious and excellent grace of love; it has put many notes of excellency upon it. I would only let you see these five or six precious notes of excellency that the Scripture has put upon love. First, the grace of love is called "the first and great commandment" (Matt. 22:38). Would you know the first commandment of the gospel? It is love. A second note of excellency in love is that it is worth thousands, yea, tens of thousands of prayers; the grace of love is worth all prayers. There is more excellency in one real acting of love than in a thousand prayers. "To love [God] with all the heart...and with all the soul...is worth all whole burnt offerings and sacrifices" (Mark 12:33), even all of them. O Christians, if you could pray forty years, and fast and weep another forty years; if you want the grace of love, you shall die a stranger to Christ. Would you go to a mountain and weep out your eyes, and waste away your body praying forty years, and weeping another forty; if you want the grace of love, you should be but as a sounding brass and a tinkling cymbal. A third note of excellency that is put upon love in Scripture is this: it is more in the sight of Christ than if you would give your body to be burnt for him. Would you give your body to be burnt for Christ? One act of love is more in Christ's account than that: "Though I give my body to be burned, and have not charity, it profiteth me nothing" (1 Cor. 13:3). This does eminently speak forth that love is of more worth than all sufferings. A fourth note of excellency put upon love in Scripture is this: Would you fulfill the law in one word? Then be much in the exercises of love: "Therefore love is the fulfilling of the law" (Rom. 13:10). You shall even fulfill the law in one word by love. A fifth note of excellency that is put upon love is this: that love is the bond of perfection, according to that excellent word, "And above all these things put on charity, which is the bond of perfectness" (Col. 3:14). Above all things! "Oh," says the Christian, "shall I put it on above faith, and above mortification?" Yea, says the apostle. And I shall add this: among all the fruits of the Spirit that are made mention of, love is put in the first place (Gal. 5:22–24). Love first fills the field of all the graces of the Spirit. The love of Christ knows no beginning of days; let your love to Him know no end of life.

A fifth consideration to enforce this exhortation is this: a Christian should keep himself in the love of God, because it is indeed that which will make a Christian's life pleasant. Would you know the best way to walk to heaven through a valley of roses? Would you know the best way to travel to heaven in a chariot of delight? Be much in the exercise of love. O love will sweeten your way; love will make you to think time both long and short. You will account your seven years' servitude for the love of Christ but short, as Jacob did of the seven years which he served for Rachel. Love will make your time seem long; love never comes out, but it casts its eyes up to heaven, and sings the last words of the Song of Solomon, "Make haste, my beloved, and be thou like to a roe or to a young hart upon the mountains of spices" (Song 8:14). Love longs for the day that these clouds might part, and Christ might appear coming over the mountains.

A sixth consideration to press you to keep yourselves in the love of God is this: it is the grace that will exceedingly help a Christian to the right understanding of all the dispensations of God.

Keep yourselves in love, if you would not create jealousies unto yourselves. Know that as long as there is one jealousy or suspicion within your bosom, your love is in a decay. "There is no fear in love; but perfect love casteth out fear" (1 John 4:18).

The last consideration we would propose is this: keep yourselves in the love of God, for this is the way to attain steadfastness. This is the very scope of the apostle. It will be an excellent pillar for a Christian to stand steadfast by. What do your waverings speak, O Christian, in these days? They speak the decay of love. A Christian in the exercise of love is a Christian who will not be overcome; he is a Christian whose motto may be this: *semper idem*, "always the same."

Now, may we not, from what we have spoken, urge upon you a pursuit after love? I may say that word, and make use of it in a spiritual way, which the poet has said: *omnia vincet amor*, "love overcomes all things." Love will overcome all difficulties and help you to travel to heaven with easiness; love will make you to skip over mountains. Would you know what makes you to think every difficulty insuperable? It is the lack of love. Love will resolve upon impossibilities, and upon things that will never do. Love's desires may be in heaven, when love's practice may be traveling upon the ground. O how far will love be in its designs, and how short in its performances! Now, that you may try whether or not you have gotten this noble jewel love, I would propose these eight properties of a Christian's love, all which may be evidences by which you may know whether or not you love Him.

The first property of a Christian's love is this: the love that he has unto Christ is a matchless and incomparable love; there is nothing that he loves so much as Christ. The soul that is in the exercise of love will cry out that word, "My beloved is white and ruddy, the chiefest among ten thousand" (Song 5:10). Now, I say unto you, is there any here who loves anything more than Christ? That is a token you have not the love of Christ, for this is a property of the love that a Christian has to Christ: it is a matchless love.

A second evidence or property of this love is that it is an obedient and submissive love—it is a love that will give obedience to every commandment that Christ does present to it. Know this: love has a respect to all Christ's commandments. Love is constant in obedience. Love is obedient at all times, according to these two verses: "I have inclined mine heart to perform thy statutes alway, even unto the end" (Ps. 119:112), and, "I have respect unto all thy commandments" (v. 6). I will be constant; I will be uniform in my obedience. I will not obey today and disobey tomorrow. There are some of you who are like the man's eldest in the parable of the two sons (Matt. 21:28–30). You promise fair to Christ, but you perform little. When you are commanded to your duty, you say, "I will go, sir," but you go not. If your love be not obedient, question the reality of it. I love not that love which is separate from duty; I love not that love that disputes His commandments.

A third property of a Christian's love is that it is a sincere love. Alas! There is much hypocrisy in our love. Some show love to Christ with their tongues but show not love to Christ with their hearts. "Grace be with all them that love our Lord Jesus Christ in sincerity" (Eph. 6:24). That infers there is a love that wants sincerity. And so, John says, "Let us not love in word, neither in tongue; but in deed and in truth" (1 John 3:18). Though you could vent never so much love to Christ in tongue or in word, if you vent not love to Christ with your heart, you are nothing.

A fourth property of a Christian's love is this: it is a constant, a permanent, an incorruptible love; is it like the oil in the widow's cruse, and the meal in her barrel, that does not fail. "Grace be with all them that love our Lord Jesus Christ in sincerity" (Eph. 6:24). Or, as the word may be rendered according to the original, "Blessed be all they that love our Lord Jesus in incorruption, these whose love to Christ admits of no end nor period."

A fifth property of a Christian's love is this: it is a love that is never satisfied. "Love is strong as death" (Song 8:6). Love is as the grave; you know the grave never says, "It is enough." So love never cries out, "It is enough." Let love have never so much enjoyment of Christ, this will be its desire: O for more! O for more!

A sixth property of a Christian's love is this: it is an unconquerable love, a love that cannot be overcome. You know, men overcome the world, and death overcomes them; but love in a manner overcomes death. What is so strong as death? Even love. Love is the grace that never knew what it was to yield; love is the grace that will cry forth, *"Nulli cedo nisi Christo,"* ("I yield to none but Christ").

A seventh property of love is this: it is the grace that makes the soul breathe most after complete and full enjoyment of Christ. Have you love, and are you not longing to be in the land of love, to be within the gates of the city? If so I may speak, that is love's great prayer. Christ says, "Behold, I come quickly" (Rev. 22:12). What is love's prayer then? Amen, blessed Lord Jesus, so be it. And it adds that word after it hath said "Amen," "Even so, come, Lord Jesus" (v. 20). Christ will no sooner say, "Behold, I come quickly" (vv. 7, 12), but love will cry out, "Come quickly, Lord Jesus, come quickly!"

The last property I shall now mention of the grace of love is this: it is a growing grace. Grace must be growing up from one degree of perfection to another. This was Paul's prayer, "And this I pray, that your love may abound yet more and more" (Phil. 1:9). Love must be an abounding love.

Now, are these properties of the grace of love with you? I suppose that if Christ were to come to search this house with candles, there would be few of us sound lovers of Him. O soul that is burning with love to Christ, let the grace of love burn within you, till grace take fire of glory. What a day it will be, O expectants of heaven, when perfect love shall perfectly act upon that noble and perfect object! And what a sight it shall be to see the Christian embracing Christ immediately within his arms, and Christ embracing him. Will there not be much joy in heaven, when the report shall be brought to the Father that Joseph's brethren are come, even that the brethren of our blessed Lord Jesus are come to heaven? Will there not be joy in heaven at that day? There is joy in heaven at our conversion; how much more at our glorification! There was joy in heaven when first we came out of the land of Egypt; how much more joy shall there be in heaven when we shall pass into the promised land, and shall eat and drink abundantly, and shall be satisfied with His pleasures! O have you love? Cursed be the person who loves not Christ. Let the person who loves not our blessed Lord Jesus be a *maranatha*, a cursed thing. *Anathema maranatha*, let him be execrable, and cursed of God. Whom can you love, if you love not precious Christ? There is even a refreshing promise which I would have you to take along with you, "He will famish all the gods of the earth" (Zeph. 2:11). There shall not be an idol that you have but God will famish it; and the end of it is this, that you may be brought to bow down to God alone. Therefore He will famish all the gods of the earth. In a manner, Christ puts a necessity upon us to love Him. Did you ever see Him? What were your thoughts of Him when you saw Him? Were you not constrained to cry out, "O what a fool was I, ever to spend so much of my love upon any other thing but Christ"?

Now I shall say but these two words unto you. First, as you would keep yourselves in the love of God, O Christians, expectants of heaven, beware of mortifying your enjoyments of Him. Second, beware to stir up Christ or awake Him before He please. Know it: it will be the foundation of a standing quarrel if you quench the motions of the Spirit, and put Christ to the door, when He desires not to go away. The best way to entertain Christ, and the best way to keep yourselves in the love of Him, is even this: maintain your enjoyments.

I would only say these three things upon this unto you. First, that a Christian, in that part of his prayer in which he meets with enjoyments, should insist most in that with God. To clear this a little more fully to you: some Christians meet with most enlargements in their confessions, and there are some Christians who meet with most enlargement in their desires, when they seek from God by prayer. Some Christians meet with most enlargement in their praises. Now, I say this, whatever be the part of prayer you find most enlargement in, insist much upon that with God. Some Christians get all their enlargements in confessions. I say to that Christian, be much in confessions. Some Christians get most of their enlargements in their praises. I say to that Christian, be much in praising God. Some Christians in their confessions are straitened, and in their praises they are straitened, and in their desires they have enlargement. I say to that Christian, be much in desiring from God. Ordinarily a Christian meets with more enjoyment and enlargement of heart in confession than he meets either in desires or in praises. It is impossible for a Christian to meet with enjoyments in praises, except he be in the lively actings of faith; but the Christian without the lively actings of faith meets with enjoyments in confession. And the reason is confession falls within the reach of sense, but praises fall within the object of faith. Nothing that is the object of praise, but it is also the object of faith. Second, I would say unto you that a

Christian may desire enjoyment of Christ and, when he comes to meet with it, he may undervalue it. A Christian may be sick of love when He is away, and he may loathe Christ when He is come. In Song of Solomon 4:16, she earnestly pursues after, and desires, Christ to come; yet when in chapter 5 He is come, she puts Him to the door (v. 6). Lastly, I would say this, O loving Christians who dwell in this house of love, comfort yourselves with this: there is an eternal, a soul-comforting, uninterrupted feast of love above that is prepared for you. O what a day it will be! What a day it shall be when love shall be in its highest degree! What a day it shall be when love shall go in and take Christ in its arms! Weep much, weep much under the decays of love; and this were an excellent help to win to the repairing of all your other decays. Believe it, believe it—there are many who go down to the pit with this delusion, that they love God; and yet God shall eternally hate them, and they shall eternally hate God. There are some who think their hearts are burning within them all along their way with love to God, and yet they may be burnt eternally in the fire of the displeasure of God. I shall not speak of that which I intended by saying that a hypocrite, a stranger from Christ, may seem to exercise many different acts of love, and yet lack this saving, this precious and real grace of love. Only I would leave this upon you, that you would strive to give your hearts to Christ, and to love Him, and keep yourselves in love when you have attained to it. O Christians, long for your hope. Let even that word in Micah 2:10 be heard in your minds every day, "Arise ye, and depart; for this is not your rest." Where is my rest then? Your rest is above, O Christians; your rest is above. Look up to heaven, and comfort yourselves with this: behold, He comes; behold, He comes. I would never wish a more delightful exercise than for a Christian to be shining in light, and burning in love. Let light and love go along with you.

Now, what more shall we say? Time will fail us—yea, eternity would fail us—to commend Christ and love to Him. But, "Sight, sight, sight" shall be the blessed commentary that shall be given of Christ. Sight will resolve all the dark questions concerning Christ, and all the riddles that are in the precious name of Christ. Sight will answer that question, "What is His name, and His Son's name, if you can tell?" Sight will resolve all the deep secrets that are in the love and heart of Christ. We but now believe on Him, but then we shall see Him. Faith and hope are a Christian's companions here, but sight and love are a Christian's companions above. Faith will give place to sight, and hope will yield its place to love. Faith will fight the war, and sight and love will sit at home and divide the spoil. Hope and faith will guide you to heaven, but sight and love must go in and reap the fruits of that excellent victory eternally. Faith, in a manner, will even say this to love, "Now I yield my place to you," and hope will say this, "Now, O sight, I leave my place to you." And O what a blessed change of predominant graces that will be! Let us wait for Him.

A Call to Behold One Greater than Solomon

Go forth, O ye daughters of Zion, and behold king Solomon with the crown wherewith his mother crowned him in the day of his espousals, and in the day of the gladness of his heart.
—Song of Solomon 3:11

Preached before a Communion.

I have glad tidings from a far country, and precious news to declare unto you today. There is a royal proclamation that is gone out from the Most High unto you, the substance whereof is this: go forth, O daughters of Zion, and behold King Solomon. And I would ask this question of you: Are you willing to embrace such a royal offer, and to give obedience to such an excellent command? Is there any person here today who shall in the day of Christ's coronation cry forth that word, "Shall this man save us" (1 Sam. 10:27)? Is there any person here today, is there any such son or daughter of Belial here, as will despise Christ in his or her heart, and bring Him no presents? Would you know what is the most excellent present you can bring to Christ? It is your heart. If you bring not this, you have not reached the extent of Herod's religion, who was desirous to see Christ. I would only speak these three words to you: first, I suppose the most of you, at the last day of your feast, did feast with a veiled Christ. Did you get a sign of King Solomon in his royal apparel, and in his transcendent comeliness? Second, little mourning under absence from Christ, in secret and in the public ordinances, I suppose, is the great cause why Christ does desert us in these extraordinary ordinances. And there is this, third, that I would say unto you: it is not long that this royal proclamation shall continue. What do you know but this may be the last invitation from heaven unto you, "Go forth, and behold King Solomon"? Yes, before twelve of the clock tomorrow, we may be put beyond the reach of such an invitation.

Now, Solomon having in the former part of this chapter discoursed most divinely of these noble privileges and advantages that result unto a believer through Christ, he does in the last verse of this chapter draw a precious exhortation from that which he had been speaking of before. And in the words we have read we have these four things to be considered.

First, the excellent exhortation and proclamation of love that is here given, which is this: "Go forth."

Second, the persons to whom this exhortation is given, and these are the daughters of Zion. By the daughters of Zion, we either understand these within the visible church who are yet in the state of nature and are strangers unto Christ, or we may understand these who are united to Christ by faith. And, as the exhortation is directed unto the first, we may take the meaning of it to be this: "Go forth," that is, "Desert and forsake your cursed condition; come out from the land of your captivity and from the house of your bondage, and behold Jesus Christ." And, as the exhortation is directed to them who are really united unto Jesus Christ, the meaning of it is this: "Stir up the grace of God that is within you; go forth from your secure estate, and go forth from your lazy estate, and go forth from your unmortified estate, and behold King Solomon."

The third thing in the words are the arguments by which he presses this exhortation, and they are two. The first is that, if they would go forth from their condition, they should get a sight of Christ, who is here pointed forth under the name of Solomon, who was indeed a type of Christ. Would you have sight of Christ? Then go forth. The second argument is, if they would go forth, they should have a sight of Christ in a stately, majestic, and royal way; they should see King Solomon with a crown upon his head. There is indeed in Christ a sweet conjunction of stately majesty, and majestic stateliness; there is in Christ a sweet conjunction of humble highness, and of high lowliness.

The last thing in the words is the description of the crown that is upon Christ's head. And it is described from these three: (1) From the persons who put this crown upon His head. It is the crown wherewith His mother crowned Him. By "his mother" here, we understand the invisible church, and particular believers, who do (as it were) put the crown upon Christ's head. And believers in Scripture are called Christ's mother. Matthew 12:50 speaks of these who do His will: "The same is my brother, and sister, and mother." And in some sense believers may be said to bring forth Christ: "My little children, of whom I travail in birth again until Christ be formed in you" (Gal. 4:19). Now, for the clearer understanding of this crown that believers put upon the head of Christ, we would know Christ is crowned with a threefold crown. First, He has a crown upon His head, as He is God, essentially equal with the Father. Second, He has a crown upon His head, as He is Mediator, "For thou hast made him a little lower than the angels, and hast crowned him with glory and honour" (Ps. 8:5). "For the suffering of death, [he was] crowned with glory and honour" (Heb. 2:9). Christ has this third crown upon His head, to wit, the crown that is put upon Him when He does overcome and vanquish believers unto His obedience. Not that it is to be supposed that believers, subjecting themselves unto Jesus Christ, do add anything to His glory, but only this: believers, by subjecting themselves to Christ and giving up their names unto Him, do give a manifestation of the glory, majesty, and stateliness that is in Christ. So, if you would make Christ's glory to shine, and the beams thereof to appear, give up your hearts unto Christ. If so we may speak, there is not one consent that is given by any to Christ, but Christ looks upon it as if it were an addition to His glory. (2) The second thing by which this crown is described is from the time when He was crowned with this crown: it was in the day of His espousals. In the day that souls are married to Christ, they put, as it were, a crown upon their Husband's head. (3) This crown is described from the noble effects that it had upon Christ. What was Christ's exercise in the day that a believer did put the crown upon His head? It was the day of the gladness of His heart. And I would say this by the way: O sinners, would you make the Father, the first person of the blessed Trinity, to rejoice? Would you make the Son, the second person of the blessed Trinity, to rejoice? And would you make the Holy Ghost, the third person of the blessed Trinity, to rejoice? Would you make all the angels in heaven to rejoice? And would you make all the saints who are round about the throne to rejoice? Then, I say, go forth and behold King Solomon. You cannot do Christ such a kindness, nor can you do anything that will afford yourself such infinite advantage, as this. In a manner (if so we may speak) your unwillingness to give Christ your heart, and to go forth to see Him, interrupts His joy.

Now, to come to the exhortation, which is this: "*Go forth.*" We shall speak of it first as it is directed unto strangers to Christ, and unto aliens from the covenants of promise. And we conceive there are these four things included in this royal proclamation. Christ, as it were, points out to us here, first, our inability and unwillingness we have to come out from our sinful estate. Therefore, it is that Christ is put to hold forth this royal command: "Come forth." Second, it speaks this: that the condition in which we live by nature is a most desperate and miserable condition; hence it is that Christ, who is the great Counsellor of heaven, and the eternal Wisdom of God, does say unto you, "Go forth." Christ, as it were, says unto you, "Even this night go forth from your ignorant estate; go forth from your estate of darkness, that you may behold a wonderful sight." Christ, as it were, says unto you, "Go forth from your estate of estrangement, and be made near unto me this night." Christ, as it were, says unto you, "Go forth from your estate of enmity, and be friends with me." Christ, as it were, says unto you, "Go forth from your estate of cursed subjection to sin and Satan, and subject your-selves unto me." There is this, third, that is in the exhortation, and it is the estate into which we are called; it is a most excellent, most choice, and most precious estate. Must it not be an excellent estate and condition into which the Prince of heaven does invite you? The condition must be excellent, because the Caller unto it is so. Lastly, this is imported in the exhortation: there are many temptations that meet us in the way, that hinder us from going forth and deserting our sinful condition; therefore, He will command and will convey strength in the command, by which you may give obedience unto it.

Now, in speaking to this exhortation, I shall touch a little at these three things.

First, I shall propose unto you from the words these six excellent considerations, *to provoke you to go forth*.

The first consideration is this, *O atheists and strangers: go forth, and you shall get a sight of Christ*. As long as you stay in the house of your bondage, in the land of your captivity, you can never get a sight of Christ. And it is not a small sight. When you go out to see Him, you shall not go out to see a reed shaken to and fro with the wind; when you go out to see Him, you shall not go out to see one clothed in soft raiment; when you go forth to see Him, you shall behold a Prophet, yea, one that is greater than a prophet. And I know not if all the rhetoric that can be used will persuade you, if this do not persuade you. The queen of Sheba shall rise in judgment against the people of this city who came from a far country to behold king Solomon. And behold, One greater than Solomon is here. O come and see this pleasant sight! Him who is the first-born among many brethren; Him who is the Ancient of days, the exalted Plant of renown, the Flower of the tribe of Judah, the precious Root that sprang of the root and stem of Jesse. Come and behold this bright and morning star. O come and behold this precious Son of righteousness; look to Him till you love, love Him till you rejoice, rejoice till you wonder, and wonder till you be put to silence. Between these let your exercise be taken up. If once you saw Him, you would almost never desire to see another sight. I would even give that counsel unto you which Philip gave to Nathanael, "Come and see" (John 1:46). It is even Christ's commandment unto you this night, "Come and see." O shall ever these cursed eyes of yours behold such a pleasant sight?

A second consideration from the words that may provoke you to go forth is this: *that Christ is exceeding willing unto this, that you should go forth*. I shall point out these eight things that speak forth Christ's willingness that you should go forth and see Him, that you should give Him one visit before you go hence and be no more.

First, does not the long journey that Christ took, travelling between heaven and earth, speak that He is willing that you should go forth? Christ came from the Father's bosom, as it were, to draw you from the state of sinfulness and estrangement from Him. Nay, further, there is not a wound in Christ's hand, nor in His side, nor in His feet, but it says He is willing you should go forth. There is not a reproach Christ commands me here upon earth but this is the language of it: Christ is willing you should go forth.

The second thing that speaks Christ's willingness that you should go forth is this: that He has made the offer of this gospel so large. You may see the largeness of it: "And let him that is athirst come" (Rev. 22:17). The door, as it were, not being enough opened, He calls open the gate of the gospel a little wider, and says, "Whosoever will, let him take the water of life freely." There is not a gate between you and Christ but your own unwillingness; and, if once you were past this gate, it would be a closed bargain. Christ does not seclude any from coming to Him but these who seclude themselves.

Third, what speaks Christ's willingness are these many blessed means that He has taken to gain us to Himself, and to persuade us to go forth. I would only have you look to these two places to hold this forth. First, Hosea 11:4, where there are four precious means that Christ makes use of to persuade you to go forth. The first noticed there is that He draws us with "the cords of a man." He begins to convince our sight, and to use many pressing arguments with us, why we should go forth and behold Him. And the second is this: He draws us with the "bands of love." When the cords of a man will not do it, He will not give over His project; He will then begin to draw with the cords of love, these sweet, invincible, constraining, and overcoming cords of love. And, if that will not do it, He will use a third means: He will take the yoke off our jaws, and ease us of our burdens; He will give unto us many precious dispensations of love. And, if this will not do it, Christ has yet a last arrow to shoot: He will lay meat before you; as it were, He will bring all the excellent dainties of heaven before you, and say that word, "Arise, eat and drink abundantly." The second place is Song of Solomon 5:2, 4. Christ will speak to the bride, that she would open. And, if that will not do the turn, He will fall to a second means, and it is this: He will knock at the door of our hearts. And, if that will not do it, He will speak kindly unto us, and cry out, "Open to me, my sister, my love, my dove, my undefiled." And, if that will not do it, He will use this: He will propose arguments unto her to gain her consent to His desire—"for my head is filled with dew, and my locks with the drops of the night." And, if this will not do it, Christ is not put to a nonplus; He will take a more sweet way: "My beloved put in his hand by the hole of the door, and my bowels were moved for him." Yes, Christ will pursue till He overtakes and wins you over to His love. And does not all this speak that Christ is willing that you should go forth and behold Him?

Fourth, the many desires that Christ has that you should go forth, and that you should come to Him, speak His willingness. Is not this word a most sweet sentence of love: "My beloved spake, and said unto me, Rise up, my love, my fair one, and come away. For, lo, the winter is past, the rain is over and gone" (Song 2:10–11)? That is, as it were, Christ's word to us in preaching, "Come away, come away." There is not one hour's delay of obedience to this precious command, but it is as it were a sword piercing His precious bones, and does exceedingly affect His heart. And does not that speak His willingness? "I said, Behold me, behold me, unto a nation that was not called by my name" (Isa. 65:1). When you are little minding Christ, He is minding you. And what would you have more? You shall get Christ; and, once you see Him, there is no more requisite for your getting of Christ. O give Christ but one look, and you shall have Him; give Him but one look, and you shall have the eternal possession of Him. There are indeed some of you who shall sing Balaam's song, "I shall see him, but not now: I shall behold him, but not nigh" (Num. 24:17). You shall get one sight of Him, O atheist, you shall get one sight of Christ, when He shall come in the clouds, and you shall wish you were blind in the day.

Fifth, this speaks Christ's willingness that you should go forth and see Him: even these many regrets that He has why you will not go forth. "And ye will not come to me, that ye might have life" (John 5:40). And that word, "O Jerusalem, Jerusalem…how often would I have gathered [thee]?" (Matt. 23:37). And in Luke 29:41 Christ wept over Jerusalem, because they would not go forth. O Glasgow, Glasgow, what do you know but Christ is groaning thus in heaven, "O Glasgow, how oft would I have gathered thee under my wings, as a hen does her chickens, and you would not!" And what know you but this decree is past in heaven against you, your house is left unto you desolate, until you cry forth, "Blessed is he that comes in the name of the Lord"? Yea, know it: Christ weeps more for us than we weep for ourselves. And I would say to Christians, "O blessed,

blessed, blessed are you, that ever you made choice of Christ!" Oft-times Christ is praying for us in heaven, when we are asleep.

Sixth, the blessed oath of the everlasting covenant speaks Christ's willingness that you should go forth and behold Him. Is not this the oath of the everlasting covenant? "As I live, saith the Lord God, I have no pleasure in the death of the wicked…turn ye, turn ye from your evil ways; for why will ye die, O house of Israel?" (Ezek. 33:11). He hath confirmed His willingness by an oath, that by these two immutable things we might have strong consolation and hope.

The seventh thing that speaks Christ's willingness for a soul to go forth is this: that Christ takes so many repulses off our hands, yet does not desist to cry out, "Go forth, go forth!" What if Christ had taken us at our first word? Where would we be? O how often have we said that word to Christ, "We will not go forth"? How often have we cried that word to Christ, "It is our strength to sit still, and to delight ourselves with our idols"? O patient Christ! O condescending Christ, who can take so many affronts off our hands! Is not this a mystery, that He who is white and ruddy, in whose face there is no spot, should come to these who are black as the tents of Kedar, whom the very daughters of Jerusalem would despise, and yet, when He is wooing, take many refusals off their hands? O what if Christ should say that word unto you when you refuse Him, "Be it unto you according to your desire!"

There is this, lastly, that speaks Christ's willingness that you should go forth and behold Him, even this: that He is content to take you whenever you come unto Him. Will you come to Christ at the sixth hour, or will you come to Christ at the eleventh hour when you have but one hour to run? In either case, He will accept you. Only I would say this: do not delay the time; oh, do not delay the time. Christ's accepting of souls whenever they come says that He is willing we go forth. Does not Christ's accepting of many in their old age say He is willing we should go forth? I will only in the last place add this to all the rest: when you will not willingly go forth, Christ will compel you; He will constrain you to go forth, according to that word, "Go out into the highways and hedges, and compel them to come in" (Luke 14:23). And I would not, even if I had great happiness outside of heaven, be without the sweet compelling force and overcoming power of Christ.

A third consideration from the words to provoke you to go forth is that *there will be an intimate relation made up between you and Christ; you shall become indeed unto Christ a mother* (Luke 8:19–21). This is clear from the words wherein all believers are signed with this note of excellency, that they are mother unto Jesus Christ. We conceive indeed, there is a mystery in this which none can unfold: there is a divine mixture, a spotless orderly confusion of relations between Christ and a soul. O what a mystery in nature and among men were this, that one should be a mother, and yet a son! That one be a son, and yet a brother unto Him to whom he is a son! That one should be spouse, and yet a mother! But here we are at a loss, and are like blind men groping for the wall.

A fourth consideration from the words to provoke you to go forth is this: *that hereby you shall indeed put a crown upon Christ's head.* You know, it is a noble prerogative, and esteemed a great privilege among men, to have access to put the crown upon the king's head. O that you were covetous and ambitious of such a noble dignity, especially to put the crown upon the head of Him who is the King of kings, and upon whose head are many crowns (Rev. 19:12)!

A fifth consideration from the words to provoke you to go forth is this: *there shall be a marriage relation between you and Christ; it shall indeed be the time of espousals.* And what greater blessedness imaginable than this, to have that golden, everlasting, and precious knot of union between Christ and your souls made up!

The last consideration from the words to provoke you to go out is this: *that you should indeed rejoice the heart of Christ; He desires nothing so much as the prosperity of the saints.* Would you make the heart of Christ to be glad, which was once filled with sorrow because of our sins? Would you make His heart to leap within Him? Then go forth, for that should be to Him the time of the gladness of His heart.

Now that which, second, I would speak to from this exhortation, "Go forth," shall be this: *to propose unto you some impediments that hinder you to go forth, and to embrace this royal offer and proclamation of heaven.*

The first impediment that hinders you to go forth is this: there are many temptations within you that cry out, "Sit still, sit still." The world cries out, "Sit still." Carnal ease cries out, "Sit still." Your house, your land, your pleasures cry out, "Sit still." Yea, there is not a bosom enemy that is here but there is a proctor for the devil within it, that is strongly pleading his cause. When they were invited to come, some cried out this, "Suffer me first to go and bury my father," and then, they said, they would follow Him (Luke 9:59). There are some of you who must bury your idols in your grave before you can come to Christ. Our idols will leave us before we leave them. O will you take Christ and lay Him in the balance with your idols?

A second impediment that hinders you to go forth is your ignorance of King Solomon. "He that cometh to God must believe that he is" (Heb. 11:6). Are there not some of you who know not if there be such a person in heaven as Christ? And, if you know that He is, you are desperately ignorant of what He is. And, know it: you must receive Christ in your sight before you can receive Him in your heart. O but, once you knew Him, you would cry forth, "It is good for us to be here." You would say that word which the four lepers spoke, "This day is a day of good tidings, and we hold our peace" (2 Kings 7:9). Will you speak nothing to Christ? Have you not this to say to Christ, "I will go forth" (1 Kings 22:22)? And have you not this word to speak to Christ, "Thy people shall be willing in the day of thy power" (Ps. 110:3)? And have you not this to say to Christ, "Draw [us], we will run after thee" (Song 1:4)?

A third impediment is this: your not having the faith of these things that are spoken unto you. "The word preached did not profit them (Heb. 4:2), and why? Because it was not "mixed with faith." You think all these excellent declarations of love to be but notions and fancies.

A fourth impediment is this: the lack of right taking up and conceptions of Christ. "Who hath believed our report?" (Isa. 53:1). And the ground of it is in the following words, in which he points forth the low and abject conditions which Christ was to be in among them; yea, in verse 2 they cry forth, "There is no beauty that we should desire him."

A fifth impediment that hinders you to go forth is your slothfulness. Sometimes you will begin to set about going forth, and before you can even say, "What is this?", even presently, slothfulness kills your resolutions. And you may go home this night with this resolution, "I will go forth from this desperate estate"; and, before you are aware, this resolution may be gone.

A sixth impediment that hinders you to go forth is that you are not convinced of your desperate estate and miserable condition. This is your divinity, "I thank God I am not like other men." I think we may say the last part of it unto you: you are not like other men. I think, if once you were brought this length, to cry out, "Alas! I am undone," you were in a more fitting capacity to go forth, and you would necessarily go forth. I would say this to hypocrites and atheists: there are many of you who live in a fool's paradise. You dream that you eat, but behold, when you awake, you shall be empty; you dream that you drink, but when you awake, you shall be thirsty. It shall be a dreadful wakening unto many, when in hell they shall wake up from their deluded condition; it will be a dreadful day to many, when their hope shall vanish as a dream, and their expectations fly away as a vision of the night. There are some here of whom this word shall be verified, "Thou shalt go forth from him, and thine hands upon thine head: for the LORD hath rejected thy confidences" (Jer. 2:37).

The last impediment I shall mention as hindering you to go forth is this: you trust too much in your own righteousness, and will not trust yourselves to the righteousness of Christ. "For they being ignorant of God's righteousness, and going about to establish their own righteousness, have not submitted themselves unto the righteousness of God" (Rom. 10:3). That is the cursed frame of our hearts—we desire to be as little obliged to Christ as we can. We would love well to travel to heaven by a covenant of works; but, if ever we win there, we shall be constrained to cry out, "O blessed be He who has guided me all along the way! To Him be the glory of my salvation!" There is not a song of merit in heaven; all the songs that are there are songs of free and eternal grace.

There is this, third, that I would speak to from this, namely, I would propose *some evidences by which the most part of you may know that you have not as yet gone forth and obeyed this excellent exhortation and royal proclamation of heaven.* And I would charge all of you, as in the sight of King Solomon that does desire you to go forth, that you would search and examine your own hearts, whether or not indeed you have gone forth.

The first evidence that you have not gone forth is the low esteem you have of King Solomon. Does not that say that you are not gone forth? I think it is impossible for a soul to go forth and see Christ and not to have at one time or another a matchless esteem of Christ. I think it is impossible for a person to go forth, and not to cry out this word, "Whom have I in heaven but [Christ]?" (Ps. 73:25). And there is none in the earth whom I desire besides Him. I think, if once you did go forth, this would be your word sometimes in the morning, and in the silent watches of the night, "My beloved is white and ruddy, the chiefest among ten thousand" (Song 5:10). I charge your consciences with this: Are there not many things you prefer unto Christ? Is not that your cursed divinity, which says, "Loose Barabbas, and crucify Christ; Give me my idol, and let Christ go"?

A second evidence that you are not gone forth is this: the commandments of Christ are your burden. Is not prayer your burden? Is not believing your burden? Is not mortification your burden? But, if once you had gone forth and seen King Solomon, you would cry forth, "Where the word of this precious King is, there should be obedience." If once you had gone forth, you would sing Psalm 119:16, "I will delight myself in thy statutes." You would love His commandments, because they come from Him, and if there were no more but because these commandments come from Him. Love will cry out, when it meets with such a command, "Good is the word of the Lord." You would know this: a Christian, when first he engages with Christ, loves Christ for all His dispensations; but, after he engages with Christ, he loves His dispensations because they come from Christ. I would ask you this. Is there a command in Scripture that you love and delight yourselves in? I tell you what you say when you meet with a command, even that word which Ahab spoke to Elijah, "Hast thou found me, O mine enemy?" (1 Kings 21:20). There is not a commandment that comes to you but you think it a thing not very pleasant to behold; and that is an evidence you have not gone forth.

A third evidence that you have not gone forth is this: the offending of King Solomon is not your burden. Did you ever sit down in secret and groan under this thought, "O wretched me, O ungrateful me, that I should have offended Him! And what iniquity, O my heart, have you found in Christ, that you take such pleasure in your idols, and to offend Him?" Did you ever water your couch with your tears because of your offences? Were ever your eyes fountains because of your whoredoms and departings from Christ?

A fourth evidence of your not having gone forth is this: that, since the first day you heard of Christ, absence with King Solomon was never your burden. And is not that a speaking evidence that you are not gone forth? If once you saw the uncreated red and white that is in His face, there would not be an hour's absence with King Solomon but you would cry forth, "O when will He return?" And you would cast up your eyes to the mountains of Bether, and cry out, "Turn, my beloved, and be thou like a roe or a young hart upon the mountains of Bether" (Song 2:17). And I would tell you this: the person that never groaned under absence with Christ, he shall never see King Solomon.

A fifth evidence that you have never gone forth is this: you never knew what this meant, to be under the pangs and shocks of the new birth. Did you ever know what it was to have Moses crying out, "Touch not the mountain, lest ye be thrust through" (see Heb. 12:20)? Did you ever stand at the foot of mount Sinai trembling, and crying out, "I am undone, because I have not obeyed all that is written in this law"? Some of you come to Christ before ever you go to Moses; and, if ever you come to Christ, He will send you back to Moses again. Should not this be a mystery, for one to be brought forth before birth, or without pain? So it is a mystery in religion, for one to be brought forth before he knows the pangs and throes of the new birth.

A sixth evidence that you have not yet gone forth is this: some of you never knew what it was to distinguish between hardness and tenderness, between faith and misbelief, between absence and presence. Have you ever known what it is to cry out, "Mine heart is turned within me" (Hos. 11:8) and at another time, "My heart is dying a stone within me" (see Ezek. 11:19)? At one time you will cry forth, "My beloved is mine, and I am his" (Song 2:16); at another time you will cry forth, "What is my strength, that I should hope? And what is mine end, that I should prolong my life?" (Job 6:11). At one time you will be constrained to cry out, "He brought me to the banqueting house, and his banner over me was love" (Song 2:4); at another time you will cry forth that word, "I sought him whom my soul loveth: I sought him, but I found him not" (Song 3:1). Do you know such things as these? Some of you have an unchangeable frame of spirit, yet you are always one.

I shall mention this last evidence of your not having gone forth, to wit, the little desire you have to pursue after fellowship with Christ. Had you once seen Him, you would cry forth sometimes in the morning, "My soul thirsteth for thee, my flesh longeth for thee in a dry and thirsty land, where no water is" (Ps. 63:1). Yes, you would shut out your tongues for painful thirst, and would long to see these clouds above gathering, which would be the forerunner of rain. Now, are there not many of these evidences with you that you have not gone forth?

We shall shut up our discourse at this time in speaking a little to these two things further from the words "go forth." First, I shall propose these five considerations that may *provoke you immediately and presently to endeavor and set about the duty of going forth.*

The first is this: What do you know but this is the last proclamation of Christ, "Go forth"? What know you but, before twelve o'clock tomorrow, Christ shall say that word, "Go forth eternally, and see my face no more"? And if you obey not this "go forth," you shall surely obey that second one. Your life hangs by a thread. We know not but the strongest who are here are walking upon the borders of eternity. What know you but this is the eleventh hour of your day, and there remains only one hour for you to walk in? Therefore, go forth.

A second consideration to provoke you immediately to go forth is this: Christ is expecting your answer. What shall I report to our Master concerning you this night? For I must return Him an answer. What answer shall I return concerning you? Shall I carry back this report to Christ, "They will not go forth"? Yes, Christ is waiting for your answer. Think of it. How we shall answer, "Will you go forth? Will you go forth?" For we must have an answer. O sweet, patient Christ waits upon you. Should He not rather be wooed than be a wooer? Yet He is condescending, and does take the pains. I may allude to that word, "It was so, that all that saw it said,

There was no such deed done nor seen from the day that the children of Israel came out of the land of Egypt unto this day: consider of it, take advice, and speak your minds" (Judg. 19:30). Now, what is your mind concerning? Are you content to take King Solomon? And know it: you cannot take Christ with better will than He is willing to give you Himself. Could you enlarge your desires as the sand of the seashore to take Him, He is willing to take you.

A third consideration to provoke you immediately to go forth, and to think of this so great, everlasting, and so weighty a thing: that you would consider the party who invites you to go forth. O is it not Christ? Is it not Christ who calls you to go forth? Shall there be such a thing heard as this, a refusal given to Christ? Tell it not at Gath, publish it not at Askelon, let not the daughters of the Philistines rejoice. O shall such a report of Glasgow be heard in heaven this night, "Yon people would not submit themselves to Christ"? Shall Christ speak of this to the Father? O think of it, consider, advise, and deliver your minds.

A fourth consideration to provoke you immediately to go forth is this: there is not one hour's delay that you make but it incapacitates and disenables you to go forth. Stay but one hour longer, and you shall be more unable to go forth than even now; you are therefore to go forth immediately and behold King Solomon. I know there are some here who will say, "Yet a little sleep, a little slumber, and a little folding of the hands to sleep" (Prov. 24:33). I would only say of that person tonight, "Boast not thyself of tomorrow; for thou knowest not what a day may bring forth" (Prov. 27:1).

The last consideration I would mention is this: the sooner you go forth, you shall be the more welcome to King Solomon. As we have sometimes told you, Christ loves young religion. Well, therefore, immediately go forth. Now, to seal up this upon your conscience, I would speak this by the way. I take heaven to witness, and all the angels in heaven, and all the saints who are round about the throne, and the stones of the walls of this house, and all who are here, I take you to witness—this has been declared to you from heaven, "Go forth, and behold King Solomon." And if there shall be any who shall be found disobedient to this royal command of love, let them appear before Christ at the great day, and answer for it. And here there are persons who shall stand witnesses against you that you have been desired to go forth. Consider, therefore, if you go not forth, the vengeance of the Most High will overtake you; the sword of the everlasting indignation of God is bathed in heaven, and will come down and make a sacrifice of these who go not forth. The day is coming when some persons who are here will cry forth, "O that I had been born in Sodom, when I was born in Glasgow!" Therefore, consider it, and go forth.

There are these six things that I would have you take home with you, which shall be the *six thoughts which one day you shall have if you go not forth.*

First, you shall have this thought, when you are eternally scorching in the fire, "O what a fool was I, that would not go forth!" You shall cry out that word, "O call time again, call time again! O for one preaching of the gospel! O for one 'go forth'!" But that shall be denied you.

There is this, second, that shall be your thought in that day, to wit, the remembrance of the many exhortations and proclamations of love that you have met with, and the many "go forths" that have been spoken unto you. They will be an aggravation of the charges against you, and an increase of your pain. Believe it—the day is coming when there shall not be an exhortation to go forth nor to believe, but you shall remember. You shall then say, "I remember at such a lecture I was bidden to go forth, and at such a sermon I was bidden to come and behold King Solomon."

Third, I would say this unto you: in the day that the smoke of your torment shall ascend up to heaven, you shall be thinking, "What a foolish exchange have I made! I embraced a present world, and rejected a beautiful Christ."

There is this fourth thing that you will think in that day: "Not only was I commanded to go forth, but sometimes I had desires to go forth, and these I quenched and put out." That shall be a great aggravation of your pain and misery. You will then cry out, "Cursed me, cursed me, that ever I quenched these desires that were within my breast to go forth!"

There is this, fifth, that I would say unto you, to wit, in the day that you shall be under the lashes of the everlasting indignation of God, you will think this, "The time was when I might have gone about duty, and was commanded to do known duties, and to follow after Christ, and I would not." How often do you go to your most unnecessary work, and neglect prayer? There are some had rather be bound to a tow than to sit down in their houses and pray. Know it, you who never prayed — you shall once both pray and sit on your knees. The promise that is given to Christ, "Every knee shall bow to [Him]" (Rom. 14:11), is not accomplished till that day when the stoutest atheist and strangers to Christ shall sit down upon their knees and cry forth, "Alas that ever I was born!" Will you think upon this day? He comes! Behold, He comes! He has a crown in His right hand and a sword in His left hand.

Lastly, I would say this unto you: when you shall stand upon Christ's left hand, and shall see others who are here standing upon Christ's right hand, you shall then say, "What ailed me, that I did not consent as well as these?" Ere long there shall be an eternal and dreadful separation.

Now I shall ask these three questions of you. First, what think you of King Solomon? And is your heart burning within you while you hear the report that is given of Him? Second, are you thinking of Him? Alas, alas! He is not in all your thoughts. And may we say, O precious Christ, come Thyself and woo! It is not for lack of respect that He sends ambassadors in His name, but this is the reason that He sends ambassadors, and why He does not come Himself: you could not abide a sight of Him. I tell you the reason why ambassadors are sent: I think if He would come Himself, it would be the occasion of much misbelief. If you saw Him, you would cry out, "Will He ever take me?"

A second question that I would ask you is this: will you not from this night forward give up yourselves to King Solomon? I have this to report in our Master's name: He is stretching forth His hands, and desiring you to come forth. Shall He say to any of you this night, "Welcome, O stranger?" He will not much tell you your faults when you come home—He will bury them in eternal forgetfulness.

A third question that I would ask you is, dare you upon your peril give a positive dissent to this request? Or dare you delay, and say, "Tomorrow I will think of it?" Know that God may strike you dead, so that you shall never again hear an exhortation to go forth. I would have you to make this night a joyful night in heaven.

Would you make it a night of gladness of heart in heaven? Then go forth and embrace Him. Shall He see of the travail of His soul, and be satisfied?

I have one word to say, which was the saying of a pious man when he was going from a sermon, who, being asked by one if the preaching was done, he answered, "Alas! It is said, but it is not done." I suppose there are some of you, when you go home, may say, "The sermon is said, but it is not done." May we hope we shall all meet in heaven? Will you think of it? Will you not have one serious thought of this desire that is given you, "Go forth and behold King Solomon"? Your cursed feet never went to such a blessed gate before, your cursed eyes never saw such a pleasant sight before, as Christ. O go forth, go forth!

I will leave this with you: the blessing of Him who is King of kings, who is the Prince of peace, who is King of righteousness, who waits for your answer, who has the keys of the house of David, which He alone opens and no man shuts, which He alone shuts and no man opens. The blessing of Him who is the beautiful rose of Sharon, who makes both heaven and earth heartsome, who is the joy, the desire, and the love of all who are round about the throne. The blessing of Him on whom are all the blessings of these precious many thousands, of Him who was dead and is alive, and who lives forevermore. The blessing of Him who is the Prince of righteousness, who can make this a night of going forth—may this blessing be upon the head of the person who will go forth, and has gone forth, to behold King Solomon.

The Saint's Resolution to Pay His Vows

I will pay my vows unto the LORD *now in the presence of all his people.*
—Psalm 116:14

Preached after a Communion.

It would be an endless work for some of us to declare all the bonds and covenants we have broken, the conviction of which makes some of us to be resolved in nothing so much as to resolve no more. I confess, indeed, it is our precious advantage that changeable creatures have to do with an unchangeable God; that, when we lose our grips on Him, He does not lose His grips on us; that, when we break our promises and vows, He does not break His promises and vows unto us.

I would say these two things unto you. First, a Christian is tied to God by a fourfold chain and cord that is not easily broken. He is tied to God by the invisible cord of faith that makes up the union between Christ and the soul. He is tied to God by the sweet and precious cord of love, which indeed we may call Leah; for, when a Christian is in the exercise of it, he may cry out, "Now…shall my husband be joined unto me," and there is that precious cord of heavenly desires. For a Christian, while he is here, is both in Christ and out of Christ; he is in Christ in regard to union, yet he is out of Christ in regard to the complete enjoyment of Him, and he is going to Christ in regard to the complete union that he shall have with Him when time to him shall be no more. And, lastly, there is the bond of resolutions and vows by which a Christian is tied to God.

Has not this resolution been ofttimes with you, "I will never leave [him], nor forsake [him]" (Heb. 13:5), "until I [have] brought him into my mother's house, and into the chamber of her that conceived me" (Song 3:4)? There is that second thing that I would say, and it is this: I think our resolutions for the most part are like Jonah's gourd—they spring up in a night, and they perish in a night. We resolve and bow tonight, and we have broken it tomorrow. All our resolutions are like the morning cloud, and all our vows like the early dew that quickly passes away. This is the cursed divinity of our hearts, "Let us break His bands and cast His cords from us." Cursed be the hands that break these blessed bands. Should not these bands be as a chain of gold round about your neck, and as an ornament of grace to your head?

But, to come to the words that we have read—in them we have these seven things to be considered.

First, that sometimes Christ does take bonds, vows, and resolutions upon Himself. He, as it were, would knit His duty to His heart by the bond of resolutions. This is clearly presupposed in the words which David says, "I will pay my vows unto the LORD" (Ps. 116:14).

The second thing we would take notice of from the words is this: that it is a duty incumbent upon Christ to pay His vows, and to perform His resolutions and promises unto God. "I will," says He, "pay my vows; I shall have this debt over my head; I shall have a discharge, shewing that I paid this vow unto God."

Third, you may take notice of this from the words: that a Christian, in paying his vows, and in performing his promises and resolutions that he has made, should admit of no delay. This was David's practice here. He said, "I will pay my vows unto the LORD," as if he would have said, "I will not take one moment's delay, but immediately pay them; I will not defer them till I be in a more suitable frame of the work. I will pay them now."

Fourth, you may take notice of this from the words: that a Christian's resolutions are ofttimes much above his performances. It is said of David here, "I will pay my vows unto the LORD"; but we do not see where he did it. If you will read, you will find that word three hundred times in the psalms, "I will," I will do such a thing. I shall only cite two places that may show the abundance of "I wills" that are in the psalms. Psalm 9:1–2 uses "I will" four times in two verses: "I will praise thee, O LORD, with my whole heart; I will shew forth all thy marvellous works. I will be glad and rejoice in thee: I will sing praise to thy name, O thou most High"; this is an excellent resolution, as is also, Psalm 145:1–2 "I will extol thee, my God, O king; and I will bless thy name for ever and ever. Every day will I bless thee; and I will praise thy name for ever and ever." And so it is in the words we have read, "I will pay my vows unto the LORD." But we never heard tell that David did pay his vows. Not that we think all David's resolutions fell to the ground; God forbid! But we think that resolutions may drive and move as the chariots of Ammi-nadib, when practice will be moving very slowly like the chariots of Pharaoh. And, as we have sometimes said, resolutions may be walking upon the borders of heaven, when practice is walking upon the borders of hell. Promises and resolutions are as the forerunners of an army that run swiftly before, when practice is as the body of an army that marches more slowly. O when shall it be that practice and resolutions shall be commensurable, and of equal extent? That if you say in the morning, "I will," you may say at night, "I have done it!" That would be most excellent.

Fifth, you may take notice of this from the words: that the vows a Christian takes on are indeed debt. This is imported in the statement, "I will pay my vows unto the LORD." As it were, David has that much honesty, that he desires to not owe debt. I would say this: there is a threefold debt that a Christian is under. There is the debt of sin, and that Christ has paid for us, which we will never be able to pay. There is the debt of duty that lies upon us, which we would strive to pay today and from henceforth. And there is the debt of divine resolutions that lies upon us, which a Christian should endeavor to pay.

I would only ask you this by the way: Think you ever, O Christians, that you will pay all your debt to Christ? No, I think you shall never pay it. And I give you these three grounds, by the way now, why a Christian will never get the debt paid that he owes to Christ. First, he desires not to pay the debt of love; yes, believe it—I think he desires not to pay the debt of love. I may say, blessed be the man who is under the debt of love. The more we are under the debt of love, we are the richer; our riches, Christians, consist in debt. Again, second, the debt of love is an infinite debt. The saints in heaven, as it were, will tell this to Christ, even that they never came up to the half of the thousandth part of what they owe. The third reason why a Christian cannot pay his debt is this: a Christian, in paying the debt of love, is constantly contracting more debt. Would you know what is the exercise of the saints in heaven? They are paying and contracting debt. What are their praises? Are they not the paying of the debt? And yet there is not a song they sing to the Lamb but it is a new addition of debt to what they owed before.

Sixth, you may take notice of this from the words: that the paying of resolutions and vows to God that we have taken on is an honorable and excellent work. Says a Christian, "I will pay my vows in the presence of all God's people," as if he would have said, "I will never be ashamed of this precious work. I shall tell heaven, 'I am now come to pay my debt to God'; I will even pay it in the presence of all who are in heaven."

Lastly, take notice of this from the words: that it is a great mystery in religion for a Christian to have a divine end in paying his debt of vows and resolutions. Therefore, this is put in among the rest, "I will pay my vows unto the LORD." There are some of us, as it were, when we pay a vow, or perform a resolution, it is to ourselves; but here says David, "I will pay my vows unto the LORD," as if he had said, "God is the noble center and period unto whom I will march in paying all my vows and resolutions."

Now, before we shall speak to any of these things we have proposed, we would have you take notice of these things, by comparing our text, verse 14, with verse 18, where the same words are repeated. And we conceive the repeating of this resolution holds forth these things. First, it holds forth the certainty that was to be of the performance of this resolution; he would certainly conclude this thing. Second, it holds forth this: that there is a great difficulty for a Christian to adhere to divine resolutions and precious designs. Therefore David, having vowed and resolved in verse 14, before he comes to verse 18, meets with something that had almost put him from his design; therefore, and over the belly of opposition, he cries out again, "I will pay my vows unto the LORD in the presence of all his people." And it points forth the great delight that David had in this blessed exercise. As it were, he was paying in verse 14 and, before he comes to verse 18, he finds occasion to engage to pay again. This points out the easiness and delight that David found in paying his debt and in performing his resolutions. There is this, lastly, to take notice from it, namely, that the repetition of the resolution points out what spiritual advantage and gain David found in this duty of paying his debt to God. He, as it were, says, "When I pay my debt, I grow rich." This is a mystery that is not known, that the saints grow richer by paying their debts, as if a saint would say, "I grow ever richer when I pay that which I owe to God; my riches do then increase upon my hand."

Now, I come to speak a little to the first things in the words, which was this: *that sometimes Christians do find themselves obliged to take vows, resolutions, and purposes upon themselves.* There are frequently such practices in Scripture. For clearing it, I shall propose these seven times when especially a Christian does take on the vows of God, and has most divine, excellent, and precious resolutions.

The first time is immediately after a Christian's conversion to Christ, and union with Him—that is a vowing time; that is resolving time. When first a Christian sees the beautiful face of Christ, he cries out, "I shall never leave Him, I shall never forsake Him." A Christian, when first he is united to Christ, cries out, "His will shall be my law, His people shall be my delight, and His righteousness shall be my refuge."

A second time when especially a Christian does resolve and take vows is when he is seeking some great thing from God; then does he pass promises and resolutions that, if God would give him such a great thing, he would then do such a thing after that. This is clear: "If God will be with me, and will keep me in this way that I go, and will give me bread to eat, and raiment to put on, so that I come again to my father's house in peace; then shall the LORD be my God" (Gen. 28:20–21). There was Jacob's resolutions that, if God would give him that precious suit, he would engage himself to be more united to God than he was before. This is also clear in 1 Samuel 1:11, where Hannah, seeking a son from the Lord, entered vows and made promises. There Hannah said, "If thou wilt give unto thine handmaid a man child, then I will give him unto the LORD all the days of his life." I would only say this by the way: cursed be the Christian who engages such a thing to God, when he is

seeking something from God, if he does not perform his engagements. And, indeed, we do not perform our engagements; we let
God perform His promises, but we never perform our engagements.
What now if God should from heaven read out, "O Christian, woe
for all thy resolutions, covenants, and vows that you have broken
against Me? Might not you cry out against yourself, 'O perfidious
wretch that I am'?"

A third time when Christians take on vows and resolutions is
when they are under much affliction; that is a time when a Christian enters into bonds and resolutions. This is clearly presupposed
in Psalm 66:13, 14, "I will pay thee my vows, which my lips have
uttered, and my mouth hath spoken, when I was in trouble." An
afflicted time is a vowing time. "Oh," says the Christian, "if I could
win out from under this cross and sad dispensation, Christ would
find me a different man than ever I was before." And, alas, when
we come from under crosses, we become ten times worse than we
were while under them. I would only say this concerning vows
made under affliction: never rely[1] too much upon your own heart.
What deathbed vows have you not broken? And what vows when
God has been calling as in a solemn assembly all your terrors round
about you? What vows then made have you not broken? It shall be
an uncomfortable cross which you shall have, when you shall come
forth of one cross, and go into another cross with this conviction: "I
have not performed the last vows that I made to God in affliction."
And that conviction will be as wormwood and gall to you, when
you meet with the next cross.

A fourth time when a Christian does engage himself under
solemn bonds and resolutions is when he is under much divine
enjoyment of God. When a Christian is near God and is admitted
to see Him who is white and ruddy, that is a resolving, and a vowing time. When the spouse gets a grip of Christ, then she resolves,
"I held him, and would not let him go, until I had brought him
into my mother's house, and into the chamber of her that conceived
me" (Song 3:4). The time of much enjoyment is a vowing time. This
is clear also when Jacob took on his resolution and vow in Gen-
esis 28:20, 21. Was it not when he was brought to sing that word,

---

1. Original, "lippen."

"The LORD is in this place; and I knew it not" (v. 16)? I would only say this by the way: O Christians, beware to resolve under a communion time too far. I confess I love not big resolutions, especially from atheism and presumption.

A fifth time when a Christian does engage himself under bonds and vows to God is upon the receipt of some excellent deliverance once sought earnestly of God. This is not much different from the former. "For thou hast delivered my soul from death, mine eyes from tears, and my feet from falling. I will walk before the LORD in the land of the living" (Ps. 116:8–9). "Thy vows are upon me, O God: I will render praises unto thee. For thou hast delivered my soul from death" (Ps. 56:12–13).

A sixth time when Christians enter under vows, resolutions, and purposes is when God begins to recover them out of their apostasy and declining. When first a Christian begins to recover his steps after much apostasy from God, that is a resolving time, a vowing time. Israel is upon the returning hand, and the first word she speaks when she is come home is, "Asshur shall not save us; we will not ride upon horses" (Hos. 14:3). And the first sentence that is in the mouth of the recovering church is this: "I will go and return to my first husband" (Hos. 2:7)—that is a brave resolution. I would only say this: if a Christian afterward breaks the vows that he made when he began to recover from apostasy, it is one to a hundred if he go not down to his grave with much halting. Therefore, O Christians, study to keep vows taken on after apostasy; for, if the devil overcome you then, you may go down to your grave with the justice of God piercing both your sides.

A seventh time when a Christian engages in solemn vows and promises to God is on a communion day; that is a vowing day. These are resolving days, covenanting days. I shall tell you six ordinary resolutions that Christians take on at such a time. Some Christians take on such a resolution at a communion day as this: "I shall never have a hard thought of Christ anymore; there is never a dispensation I shall meet with but I shall give Christ a good construction; I shall ever entertain a favorable opinion of His doings after this"; and that is a good resolution. A second resolution some Christians take on at a communion day is this: "I shall never delight myself with my idols so much as I have done in times past." Yes, sometimes we speak thus when we sit down at communion tables, "What have I to do any more with idols?" (Hos. 14:8), and yet, ere three days go by, we change our song and say, "Yet a little solace with my idol." A third ordinary resolution is this: "I shall never be so negligent of prayer and other duties as I have been; the Lord keep me from being so neglectful as I have been." That is our language then—we will now be His servants, and we will be content to nail our ears to the posts of His door, and we will say, "I desire to have a nail bored through my ear to the post of the door, that I may be declared to be His servant forevermore." A fourth resolution some Christians take on at that time is this: "I shall never be so formal in duty as I was before; I am now convinced what a dreadful sin it is to pray formally, and what a dreadful sin it is to communicate formally; now I take on this resolution to stir up myself to take hold of God, to wrestle as a prince with Him in every duty till I prevail." A fifth ordinary resolution that a Christian does take on at times is this: that he will be obliged to Christ in every step of his way to heaven—"I shall never trust the guiding of myself to myself; I will make Christ the guide of my youth and old age." And, if ever you go to heaven, you must be under the tuition of Christ. Christ has been guiding souls to heaven now almost six thousand years, and He never misguided any of them. There is not a grave between you and heaven upon which this may be written, "Here lies one that Christ did misguide." And, lastly, there is that resolution of a Christian at such a time, namely, "I shall never quench the motions of the Spirit so much as I have done before times." O how often have we quenched His motions in preaching! How often have we quenched His motions of love! How often have we quenched His motions of life! How often have we quenched His motions of desires! We no sooner get them, but we kill them. O many a precious resolution have we killed, since first Christ and we did meet; how many a precious conviction have we killed since first Christ and we did meet! How many a precious motion of the Spirit have we killed since first Christ and we did meet!

We shall now, from this, take notice of these five conclusions. First, since there are so many times when Christians take on vows and resolutions upon themselves, then know that it is a duty lying upon you to take on the vows of God, and to sing before you go out of these doors, "Thy vows are upon me, O God: I will render praises unto thee" (Ps. 56:12). To vow and resolve is a duty that is commanded: "Vow, and pay unto the LORD your God" (Ps. 76:11). Second, you Christians who have taken on vows, beware to make enquiry after them. There are some whom Solomon makes mention of who make enquiry after vows; that is (says he) to devour that which is holy (Prov. 20:25). I tell you what it is to make enquiry after vows: it is to have a sad heart that ever you vowed such a thing; it is even to study to get a way to set yourselves from under such a resolution. Make not enquiry after vows. Third, I would say this: O Christians, in making vows, resolutions, and promises, be most deliberate. We may more than allude to Solomon's words, "Be not rash with thy mouth, and let not thine heart be hasty to utter any thing before God" (Eccl. 5:2). As we used to say, there is no disadvantage after good advisement. *Ubi nulla eft elctio, ibi nulla eft deliberation*—where there is no choice, there should be no advisement, said one, when he desired to forsake Christ. Fourth, I would say this unto you: when a Christian does resolve, he should do it with much fear. That is a remarkable word; after Solomon has been pressing this point upon folks in the fifth chapter of Ecclesiastes, he says, "But fear thou God." This would no doubt make us to perform more than we do. O Christians, when you speak the word to God, even have a holy jealousy over yourselves; say, "I will, I fear, never get this performed." Lastly, I would say this: comfort yourselves in this, O Christians, that if the breach of vows and resolutions be thy cross and burden, the day is coming when you shall break resolutions no more, and you shall break vows no more. Yes, the day is coming when you shall be made a glorious pillar in the house of Christ's God, and shall go no more out, and these unsteadfast hearts shall be set upon Him who is the precious Rock of ages.

Now we shall come to speak a little to the second thing in the word, which is this: the duty of a Christian to pay these vows, resolutions, and promises that he makes unto God: "I will pay my vows." And is not that commanded ofttimes in Scripture? It is clearly commanded, "If a man vow a vow unto the LORD, or swear an oath to bind his soul with a bond; he shall not break his word, he shall do according to all that proceedeth out of his mouth" (Num. 30:2). And it is clear also, "Pay thy vows unto the most High" (Ps. 50:14). Also, "Thy vows are upon me, O God: I will render praises unto thee" (Ps. 56:12). I conceive there is none that question but this is a duty that lies upon all, to pay their vows to God, and covenants made with Him.

In handling this, I shall speak a little to this question: *What is the reason that Christians break their resolutions, purposes, and vows to God so often?* What can be the reason of that?

The first reason, we conceive, is this: we do not resolve and vow in His strength. In whose name do you resolve? "In my own name," you say. If a Christian resolve in the strength of Christ, and vow in His name, then he would win more certainly to the accomplishment of his vows than ever he did before, when he did resolve upon his own strength. If we could sing that song, "Surely…in the LORD have I righteousness and strength" (Isa. 45:24), we would keep our vows and promises to God more often. Would you know why Peter broke his vow? He resolved much upon his own strength. And, know it: a Christian is never nearer a fall than when he is upon the highest pin and presumption of self-pride.

A second reason of it is that, if we vow in Christ's strength, we do not put Christ much to it to give us strength to perform our vows; we are not often in a needy dependence upon Christ. What should a Christian's life be? It should be misery looking up to infinite mercy; it should be emptiness looking up to infinite fulness; it should be a Christian, as having nothing, looking up to Christ who possesses all things; it should be a Christian's sitting in the dust, acknowledging himself to be less than the least of all mercies, and acknowledging himself to be the greatest of all sinners, yet taking hold of the strength of a Mediator. A Christian may be both ascending and descending at one time. A Christian, when he is nearest Christ, will be nearest the ground. O Christians, put Christ to it. Seek strength from Christ—that will be the way to perform your resolutions.

A third reason of it is this: you resolve more with light than with the heart or love. What is it that leads you to resolve? It is light. I persuade you of this: there are not many of us here whom love leads to resolve and vow, but it is light that does it. A Christian knows this is his duty to resolve, and therefore he resolves; but it is not love that puts him to resolve or come under vows. There is, as it were, a contradiction between his heart and his light.

A fourth reason why a Christian breaks his resolutions so often is this: there is much hypocrisy in our resolutions. "Nevertheless they did flatter him with their mouth, and they lied unto him with their tongues. For their heart was not right with him, neither were they stedfast in his covenant" (Ps. 78:36–37). A hypocrite will never make out his word long; a hypocrite is changeable as the moon, but a Christian is more steadfast.

A fifth ground of it is the instability of our hearts. I cannot give a description of the unsteadfastness of our hearts. I think it would be impossible to write a chronicle of the motions of our hearts. O but our hearts are wanderers! Where are your eyes? Are they not at the ends of the earth? Your heart is likely there also. O if you would seek a settled heart from God! Then you might sing that song, "My heart is fixed, O God, my heart is fixed" (Ps. 57:7), and say, "I will pay my vows."

A sixth ground and reason why a Christian breaks his vows and resolutions so often is self-indulgence and self-ease. I am sure that the damnable idol of ease and self-indulgence treads upon the necks of very many. What convictions has it slain? What resolutions has it broken? What motions of the Holy Ghost has it quenched? That is the divinity of our heart—O pity yourselves. Believe it: if we took more pains, we would see more noble effects of our resolutions, which we shall never see while we are under this idol's power. When will you be set free from this idol of self-ease? Is not this certain, O Christians, that sometimes you have gone from a sermon with your heart full of convictions? And what did you do with them? Self-ease did kill them. And sometimes you went with many noble designs in your heart from a communion, but self-ease killed them much before night. We may say this: pride has slain his thousands, but laziness has slain his ten thousands.

Now I would say this: Were you ever convinced of the sinfulness of the sin of breaking vows and covenants with God? I would ask you, are there not many here who never shed a tear for the breach of covenants with God? I would have you in a holy jealousy that God and you never entered a covenant together, if you mourn not for the breach of vows. Know that if you were united to Jesus Christ in the everlasting covenant, it would be impossible for you but to mourn for the breach of covenants with God. God will avenge the quarrel of a broken covenant made between Him and us; God will be avenged for broken resolutions and broken communion vows. Sometimes when Christ comes to us and bids us take on resolutions and vows, what do our hearts answer? Do not our hearts answer, "O Jesus of Nazareth, why art thou come to torment me before the time?" (see Matt. 8:29). Cursed be the tongue that speaks that word to Christ.

That which, second, we would speak to shall be to point out *some considerations to press you to pay and perform your vows unto God.*

The first consideration is that a Christian, by not paying his vows to God, does contract a deal of guilt. Scripture makes this clear, "Suffer not thy mouth to cause thy flesh to sin" (Eccl. 5:6; see also Num. 30:2–3; Deut. 23:21–23). Then there is much guilt in breaking resolutions and vows unto God. It speaks this: that you are persons who care not for God, and you are persons who do not walk perfectly with God.

A second consideration to move you to pay your vows unto God is this: the not paying of vows has many sad disadvantages and consequences with it. I shall name these to you. The first disadvantage that waits upon the breach of vows is this: it will mar your confidence when you go to God with a new strait. Some Christians who have dealt treacherously with God, when they have been put to a new strait, dare not go to God to seek anything from Him, the breach of former vows so staring them in the face. I would only say this: Would you have confidence in your straits to see anything from God? Then, say I, be much in paying of your vows to God. O but a Christian who has this to say may come to the throne with much confidence, "There was never a vow I made to God, but in some measure I set about to perform it." O he were a blessed Christian who could say that.

There is that second disadvantage that waits upon the breach of our resolutions, namely, it will make God angry at many of our prayers: "Suffer not thy mouth to cause thy flesh to sin; neither say thou before the angel, that it was an error. Wherefore should God be angry at thy voice?" (Eccl. 5:6). It is known by experience: some

Christians have remained dumb many days for the breach of vows; the breach of vows has been the reason that we are stricken dumb before God and have had nothing to say.

A third disadvantage that attends the breach of vows is this: if God condescend to give you a mercy upon which you make vows and promises to God, and if you do not perform those vows, that mercy shall prove a notable curse, be whom you will. I never desire a greater curse upon any than the receipt of a precious mercy from God, upon which we engaged to do such things if we should receive it, and yet not setting about the accomplishment of that engaged for duty. Solomon, when he is pressing the paying of vows, continues, "Wherefore should God...destroy the work of thine hands?" (v. 6b), the meaning of which we conceive principally to be this: What is the reason you would put God to destroy the mercy He has given you? I shall only give you these two grounds, that by your not performing of vows, or not setting about the performance of them, the mercy received, which was the occasion that these vows were past to God, proves to be a notable curse. First, that mercy is the mother of much presumption and pride. Let a mercy be received upon vows, and a Christian not set about the performance of these vows, he shall sit down and sacrifice to his own net; from this it proves a remarkable curse. A second ground of it is this: a mercy received upon vows, and when we set not about the accomplishment of them, it makes that mercy the mother of security. I think there is much sad and woeful laziness that has been the fruit of such a mercy.

A fourth disadvantage that attends the breach of vows is this: it does exceedingly interrupt the quiet and peace of conscience that a Christian should have. O but the breach of covenants and vows makes a Christian to have his way to heaven wearisome! O but we might have sweet ways to heaven! In a manner, there is not a step of our way to heaven, but our conscience checks us. Would you have peace of conscience, O Christians? Then study to perform your vows.

A fifth disadvantage that attends the breach of vows is this: it does exceedingly interrupt the exercise of love, the exercise of faith, and the exercise of diligence. O but the breach of vows will make a bad understanding between God and you! The breach of vows will put such a jealousy between Christ and you as will not be taken off for many days.

The last disadvantage that attends the breach of vows is this: it will make your departing sad and dreary, if you be a Christian. I have known that some most tender Christians, when they have been looking eternity in the face, there was nothing that troubled them so much as the breach of vows. O how many precious covenants have we broken! How many precious communion vows have we broken! How many excellent resolutions have we broken! You who have broken many vows, I would say that if at all you shall be saved, it shall be so as by fire (see 1 Cor. 3:15).

Third, we would propose the following considerations, in order to induce Christians to pay their vows.

The first consideration is: Christians, I would have you paying your vows without delay, because this is commanded. "When thou shalt vow a vow unto the LORD thy God, thou shalt not slack to pay it" (Deut. 23:21). And, "Better is it that thou shouldest not vow, than that thou shouldest vow and not pay" (Eccl. 5:5). It was also the practice of David, "I will pay my vows unto the LORD now in the presence of all his people" (Ps. 116:18). I would say this unto you, Christians: after the receipt of your mercies, strive to pay your vows. I will give you these four grounds of it. First, a Christian has biggest thoughts of his mercy immediately after it is received; and so it helps to the performance of your vows, because your heart is filled most with the mercy then. Second, a Christian, immediately after the receipt of mercies, is in the most suitable temper for performing his vows to God. Yes, then, a Christian moves as the chariots of Amminadib. A third ground of it is this: a Christian will think best of the performing of his vows immediately after the receipt of mercies, when the thoughts of the mercy are growing big within him. If we then perform our vows and resolutions, it will not seem much in our eyes; but, if we perform our vows twenty days after the receipt of the mercy—then, it is one to a hundred if we grow not proud. A fourth ground of it is this: if a Christian delay to perform his vows, one to a hundred if ever he perform them. Delays of the performance of vows is a breach of vows. Heard you never that word, "Delays are dangerous"? Indeed, delays of performing the vows of God are most dangerous.

A second consideration is this: Christians, comfort yourselves with the fact that your resolutions, purposes, and vows lie within a promise. You may say, "How will I win to pay my vows unto God?" Your vows, your resolutions, and your purposes lie within a promise, within the bosom of a promise. It is said of Egypt, "They shall vow a vow unto the LORD, and perform it" (Isa. 19:21). And, "Thou shalt pay thy vows. Thou shalt also decree a thing, and it shall be established unto thee" (Job 22:27–28). We think the doubling of the promise speaks the certainty of the thing, and it shall be established. There is not a covenant, not a purpose, nor a resolution that we have but it lies in the bosom of promises. Christ, as it were, *nolens volens*,[2] that is, He leads you to the performance of it.

A third consideration that I would propose is this: a Christian should by all means study to have his resolutions commended to Christ. There is not a resolution you have, O Christians, but this should be the prayer you would pray unto Christ with it: "O precious Christ, breathe upon this resolution." I confess, it is a noble art of Christianity to do all in the strength of Christ. We commit our persons to Christ; this is ordinary, and O that it were more common! But do you know what this is, to commit our graces to Christ, to commit our duties to Christ, to commit our resolutions to Christ, to commit our convictions to Christ? There is nothing that you have but you should commit it to Christ; He is the surest hand to which you can commit them. Yes, commit your gifts to Christ; they will be best kept by Him. Make Him the place of refuge, where all your strength lies.

A fourth consideration that I would propose to you is this: Christians, when you are in a tender frame, beware of resolving according to your extraordinary frame, but resolve according to your ordinary frame. Is it not known that when a Christian is near God, he takes on big resolutions? But I would say this word unto you: "Look unto the rock whence ye are hewn, and to the hole of the pit whence ye are digged" (Isa. 51:1). Christians, resolve by your ordinary frame, and not by the rule of your extraordinary frame. Be very sober in your resolutions; as it were, never resolve without asking Christ, "O Christ, shall I resolve this?"

---

2. "*Nolens volens*," unwilling or willing.

There is this fifth consideration that I would propose to you Christians who are here: I charge you in the name of Christ—who is the Master of the feast unto which you were called—do not delay the accomplishment of your vows. Christ may speak that word unto you at the next communion you go to, "Where is the performance of your vows made at Glasgow's last communion?" I confess, it will make you to feast with much bitterness when you have nothing to say when you are thusly reproved. I would say that word, "Boast not thyself of to morrow; for thou knowest not what a day may bring forth" (Prov. 27:1). May we not all be in our grace before a day passes?

A sixth consideration we would propose unto you is to state some differences between a Christian's resolutions and a hypocrite's resolutions, for a hypocrite may resolve most strongly. There is much difference between a hypocrite's resolutions and bonds that he takes on, and these excellent cords of love that a Christian takes on. The first difference between the resolutions of a hypocrite and the resolutions of a Christian is that a Christian ofttimes (I will not say always) resolves upon the strength of another person than himself; but a hypocrite, I think, resolves always on his own strength. "Yea," says the Christian, "if Christ were not in heaven, I would never have resolved." "But," says the hypocrite, "if Christ were out of heaven, I would have resolved." But know this: without Christ you can do nothing. It would be good to go to communions with this, to prayer with this, to conference with this, to the streets with this, to the smallest duty of religion that is required of you with this: "Without Christ I can do nothing" (see John 15:5). A second difference between the resolutions of a Christian and a hypocrite is this: I think the breach of communion vows and resolutions never affects a hypocrite's conscience. It is never the matter of a hypocrite's washing his bed with his tears. But there is nothing that will affect the heart of a tender Christian so much as the breach of communion vows; these will affect his heart exceedingly. I would say this to you who never groaned under the breach of communion vows and resolutions: you are either an exquisite Christian or an exquisite hypocrite. I tell you three sins that a hypocrite never mourned for: there is original sin, and the sin of unbelief, and the sin of abusing the Lord's table. These are three invisible sins over which we think a hypocrite never mourns. It is impossible for a hypocrite to mourn for original sin; I doubt much if he wins to the conviction of it in seriousness. Did ever any of these three sins affect your heart? I would say to you who were never affected with any of them: you may go back and weep over the foundations, and say, "Alas for the day that I began to pray and profess!" A third difference between the resolutions of a Christian and the resolutions of a hypocrite is this: a hypocrite, in his resolving, never has his heart wholly taken up about the thing that he resolves, but a Christian sometimes in his resolutions has his heart much engaged to the thing. A hypocrite resolves more with his light than with his heart. The heart of a hypocrite is never, in his resolving, engaged to the thing that he resolves. But it is love—the constraining, overpowering, quickening, besieging principle of love—that leads the Christian to many divine resolutions. I know that love travails and is pregnant with[3] eminent resolutions. Sometimes love will make a Christian too resolved upon impossibilities, as in John 20:15: "If thou have borne him hence, tell me where thou hast laid him, and I will take him away." It was impossible for her, a poor weak woman, to carry in her arms a dead man's body; but love made her to say it. Love consults more with its duty than with its own strength. A fourth difference between the resolutions of a hypocrite and one who is godly is this: a hypocrite, in his resolving, is not constant. A hypocrite is a most inconstant creature in his resolutions. He will resolve today and he will break tomorrow. But a Christian will win to some steadfastness sometimes—though not always—in his resolutions. O are there not many here who may lament that word, "My purposes are broken off" (Job 17:11), my love purposes and my affliction purposes are broken off! Sometimes God has bold designs in not giving us strength to perform our resolutions, "that he may withdraw man from his purpose, and hide pride from man" (Job 33:17). Sometimes, if we could win to do the thing which we resolved to do, we would grow proud and conceited. Not everyone can bear the glory of an eminent enjoyment; this is a mystery. Give Christ the burden of your enjoyments to bear. Believe it: public and eminent enjoyments are a burden which your shoulders are not able to bear; therefore, when you meet with emi-

---

3. Original, "big with child of."

nent enjoyments of God, let your song be, "Not unto me, not unto me, but unto Him be the glory of my salvation!" The last difference between them, that I shall now mention, is this: a hypocrite in his resolutions seldom or never has a sweet and precious design; this is almost always wrong. He will resolve to be a diligent Christian, that he may be beautified when he comes abroad. A hypocrite will endeavor to mortify such a lust and his idols as far as he can; but it is that he may have peace with his conscience. For I doubt much if a hypocrite be very desirous of peace with God, but peace with one's conscience, that is the great desire of a hypocrite. But a Christian, in his resolutions, has always some sweet design and precious target at which all his arrows are shot.

I shall close our discourse at this time with this: I know, whatever has been the temper of our spirits, this has been a resolving time. And I would say this: if a Christian would pay his vows, it would be a precious day, a praising day. Hence it is that praise and vows are put together so often in Scripture, they are seldom found separate. In the psalms, thanksgiving and paying of vows are two things that go together. Second, I would say this: if you would pay your vows, be much in the exercise of prayer. There is such a fitness between praying and vowing that the one of them is sometimes pointed out under the notion of the other. "For thou, O God, hast heard my vows" (Ps. 61:5). Now, how many sweet knots have you unloosed? Even cast one knot before you go hence out of these doors; though in a manner you cannot keep them fast, study by all means to cast one knot between you and Christ. I doubt much if we will all meet again; only we shall all meet in one place, and that is in the grave. I doubt much if we shall all meet in heaven. I would say this, and close with it: the breach of vows so constantly, and so little mourned for, is an evidence of the lack of sincerity. I may allude to that word, if not more than allude to it, "Lord, who shall abide in thy tabernacle?... He that sweareth to his own hurt, and changeth not" (Ps. 15:1, 4). Is there such a person here, one who has sworn to God and has not changed? The many unrepented of and unmourned for breaches of our vows are a token that we shall not abide in the tabernacle of God, or that we have not the solid hope and expectation of being once with Him.

Now even take these three resolutions away with you. Take Peter's resolutions away with you today, "Although all shall be offended [by Christ], yet will not I" (Mark 14:29). O to take that resolution away, and to take it away with us in sincerity! If Christ should never have one to back Him but me, I will back Him; I will never loosen my grip on precious Christ; even death shall not separate us. I shall die with Christ in my arms. If you condescend to do so, go away with that resolution today, "Though all men should forsake Thee, I will not forsake Thee." Second, go away with this resolution: "I will walk before the LORD in the land of the living" (Ps. 116:9). I think there is much in those words, "before the LORD." I shall never be out of His sight; I shall walk before Him in the land of the living. Would you know Enoch's walk? As it were, he began at the east end of the world, and took Christ in his hand, and went out of the west end of the world. Enoch walked hand in hand with Christ; as it were, he knew no other thing but even to go along and seek Christ. That is even Christ's way of guiding you to heaven. He has a string of love about your heart; the one end of the string is about our hearts, and the other end is in heaven, and Christ is drawing us by that string. The one end is here, and the other end is in the hand of the Mediator, and He is always drawing us along the way sweetly. A third resolution that I would have you go away with is this: let the world choose whom they will, but "as for me and my house, we will serve the LORD" (Josh. 24:15). Let all the world choose their idols; I will choose precious Christ. Know it: you will sing that song that made the bargain, "I will bless the LORD, who hath given me counsel" (Ps. 16:7). To Him be all the praise.

Self-conceit Proves Self-deceit

For if a man think himself to be something, when he is nothing, he deceiveth himself.
                                                        —Galatians 6:3

Conceitedness and presumption are weeds that grow in every garden. Are there not many who think of themselves above that which they are? That are going down to the pit in a golden dream, and are spending their days living in a fool's paradise? It is certain, delusion and conceit are things that stick most near to many of us, that by appearance we shall go down to our graves with a lie in our right hands, deceived hearts having led us aside. I would only say this: it is the duty of us all to search our own hearts by the candle of the Lord, lest we be deceived in that which is of our soul and everlasting concern. Be persuaded of it: where one goes to hell who thinks he is going there, there are thousands who go to hell who think they are going to heaven. For, if discouragement has slain its thousands, I am persuaded presumption has slain its ten thousands.

The apostle, in the first two verses of Galatians 6, is pressing two most precious and excellent exhortations upon those to whom he writes. The first is that they should in meekness restore such a one who falls away by the power of temptation and an evil heart (v. 1). The second exhortation is that excellent doctrine and duty of Christian sympathy, that we should bear one another's burdens (v. 2). And, in the words that we have read, he brings in a strong and pressing argument to this duty of Christian sympathy. It may seem strange that such an argument should be used to press such an exhortation, but we conceive the strength of the argument lies in this: it is impossible for a man who thinks of himself above what he ought, to be much in the exercise of the duty of Christian sympathy.

In the words we have these things to consider. First, that there are many within the visible church who are under mistake, presumption, and conceit. Scripture makes this clear, "For if a man think himself to be something, when he is nothing, he deceiveth himself" (v. 3). Second, that presumption and conceit is a most groundless and reasonless thing. This is also clear — is there anything more unreasonable than for a man to think himself to be something when he is nothing? Can there be anything more unreasonable than for a man to judge himself to be that which he is not? The third thing is the disadvantages that follow upon presumption and conceit. There are two of them in the words. The first is that the person who is under the power of presumption and conceit deceives himself. The second disadvantage in the words that wait upon presumption and conceit is that it is impossible for that man to be in the exercise of Christian sympathy. It is only the humble Christian who is the sympathizing Christian.

Now, for the first, presumption and conceit are a thing incident to many. I shall, before I prosecute this point, speak a little unto these two: (1) to what presumption and conceit are, and (2) that they are an evil incident to many.

For the first, we conceive that conceit and presumption stand in these three. First, for a man to believe himself to be that which indeed he is not, is a great part of presumption. The second part of presumption is for a man to think he has more than indeed he has. The third part of presumption is for a man to desire not to appear that which really he is, and to desire to appear that which really he is not. That is indeed the woeful root of bitterness that is rooted and springs up in the heart of many.

As for the second, to clear that such is an evil incident to many: First, is it not clear from these commands? "Be not highminded, but fear" (Rom. 11:20). "For I say…to every man that is among you, not to think of himself more highly than he ought to think; but to think soberly" (Rom. 12:3). "Let no man deceive himself. If any man among you seemeth to be wise in this world, let him become a fool, that he may be wise" (1 Cor. 3:18). Second, is it not clear from the woeful experience of many who are under the foot of this evil?

"There is a generation that are pure in their own eyes, and yet is not washed from their filthiness" (Prov. 30:12). It is not one person, or two persons, who are under the foot of presumption and mistake; there is a generation of those folks. And likewise it is clear in Revelation 3:17, where Christ charges that fault upon many, yea, by appearance upon the whole church, that they thought themselves to be rich when they were poor.

The third thing that clears presumption and conceit to be evil incidents to many are those reproofs that Christ gives unto persons because of this evil. "Yea, and why even of yourselves judge ye not what is right?" (Luke 12:57). Christ reproves persons for this, that they have misconstruing conceptions concerning their own state.

Fourth, it is clear that mistake and presumption are evil incidents to many from the many marks and evidences that are given in Scripture by which persons may be helped to examine their state and condition. To what end were all these marks of real grace that are given in Scripture, if there were not too much presumption and conceit?

In prosecuting this somewhat more, I shall speak a little unto four things.

First, I shall speak a little unto *some considerations to press you to guard against presumption and mistake of your own condition*; for this is indeed the lot of many, to go down to the pit, and suppose themselves not to be going thither.

The first consideration that I shall propose to press you to guard against mistake and presumption is this: there are many who are mistaken and have thoughts of themselves above what they ought; therefore, I entreat you, guard against mistake. This is clear from that place we cited, Proverbs 30:12, as well as Matthew 7:22, where it is said, "Many will say to [Christ] in that day, Lord, Lord...." There are many who, when Christ shall come and judge the world, shall be in a delusion and mistake. If there were but one of a hundred who was mistaken, yet we ought to search. But since it is more than probable that where there is one who does not mistake, there are six who do mistake, therefore I entreat you search, lest God be provoked to search and find out your iniquity.

The second consideration is this: if once a person be under mistake concerning his condition, it is an evil he will not be easily driven from. "They hold fast deceit, they refuse to return" (Jer. 8:5). As it were, they keep the presumption with both their hands; and, let any man speak what he will unto them, they will go down to their grave with this, "I am in Christ." It is exceeding hard for one, under the power of mistake, to quit his mistake.

The third consideration to press you to guard against mistake and presumption is this: it is a great mocking of God. "Be not deceived, God is not mocked" (Gal. 6:7). As it were, it is a denying of the justice and omniscience of God for a person to live under a mistake.

The fourth consideration that I would propose to press you to guard against mistake is this: of all the evils that are within a person's heart, this evil of presumption and conceit is one of the greatest. "These six things doth the LORD hate: yea, seven are an abomination unto him" (Prov. 6:16). And what is that which leads a man to these seven things? It is a proud look. And now I say this unto you: as you would not make yourselves hateful in the eyes of the Lord, I beseech you guard against presumption. There are some who say, "Stand by, for I am holier than thou"; these are a smoke in His nostrils, and a fire that burns all the day long.

The fifth consideration that I shall propose is this: the person who is in a presumptuous frame, it is hard (if not exceedingly hard) for him to be converted. There is nothing that hinders the success of the gospel upon many men's and women's hearts so much as this: they think they stand not in need of Christ. "Seest thou a man wise in his own conceit? There is more hope of a fool than of him" (Prov. 26:12). And there are lies in their right hands, so that they cannot deliver their souls (see Isa. 44:20). I tell you two sorts of persons who lie furthest off from their conversion by the gospel: the presumptuous person and the hypocritical person. These two the Scripture has declared to lie furthest off from the stroke of the gospel.

There is a sixth consideration to press you to guard against presumption and mistake, and it is this: a mistake concerning yourself in this is, if you pass the borders of time, a most anxious and endless mistake. I would have you searching yourselves in this. What a dreadful day will some have, those who think they are going to heaven, when they shall go down unto those everlasting flames, and shall see their hope has been but as a spider's web, and as a morning dream? I confess, it is one of the saddest and most lamentable things that can be for any person to be under this evil of presumption and mistake; it is just like an ox going with peace to the slaughter.

Second, I shall speak a little to these things *that are the rise and origin of this conceit, presumption, and mistake that is in these days.*

The first rise and origin of mistake and presumption is this: many persons, in judging themselves, take a wrong or false rule to judge themselves by, and so they draw a wrong conclusion from their search and examination. I shall set before you these eight most false and erring rules by which many persons judge themselves.

First, many judge themselves more by the letter of the law than by the spiritual meaning of the law. This was the rule Paul took before his conversion; "I was alive without the law" (Rom. 7:9), and, "Concerning…the law, [I was] blameless" (Phil. 3:6). Now, I say, there are some who, when they sit down to search themselves, take the letter of the law—without the spiritual meaning of the law — to be their rule. A person may be, concerning the letter of the law, blameless unto his apprehension, to whom Christ shall say, "I never knew you: depart from me" (Matt. 7:23). You would know this: the law does reach not only the outward man, but the inward man also. If you should never commit one act of iniquity, if you think but one evil thought, the law cries forth, "O curse upon thee!" And I am persuaded, if many of us who are here would sit down and judge ourselves by the spiritual meaning of the law, we might be constrained to cry out, "Woe is me! For I am undone."

The second false rule by which some judge themselves is this: they judge themselves more by their duties than by their graces; that is, they judge themselves more by their work than by its quality. Some persons, if they fast twice a week, think heaven is theirs without debate. This was the rule by which that man judged himself, "I fast twice in the week, I give tithes of all that I possess" (Luke 18:12). I say, you may pray twenty times every day and yet be a stranger unto God, and one who shall never see His face. Therefore, I would say this to you: judge yourself more by your graces than by your duties.

The third false rule by which some persons judge themselves is the rule that hypocrites take, and that is, some judge themselves more by their extraordinary frame than by their ordinary walk and conversation. Some persons, if ever they have any thing that looks like enlargement, and the visions of God, they will judge themselves by that; and yet their walk and conversation is most dishonorable to God. I say, whoever would judge themselves aright, they must judge themselves by their ordinary walk and conversation, and not by their extraordinary frame.

The fourth false rule by which some judge themselves is this: they judge themselves more by the testimony of their conscience than by the testimony of the law, and that is an erring and false rule. Some persons, if their consciences speak no evil of them, think all is sure. But I would say this to you: the law has much to say to you when your conscience says nothing against you. Some think peace of conscience or a silent conscience is a foundation upon which they may build their eternal blessedness, while perhaps the devil has taken the tongue out of their consciences, that they will not speak. And I say this: though your conscience should cry out to you, "Peace, peace unto you," yet "sudden destruction cometh upon them" (1 Thess. 5:3). O do not believe your conscience always.

The fifth wrong and false rule by which some judge them-selves is this (and it is a most ordinary rule): some judge themselves more by their intentions than by their practice and endeavor. And so, when we come and admonish their actions, they answer, "O sir, I have a good intention, though I can win no further." I say, if you judge yourself by your intentions, you may be under a very great mistake. An atheist may judge himself more by his endeavors than by his practice and attainments, but I never thought that a good rule for persons to judge themselves more by their resolutions than by their endeavors and practice. I say, if a good meaning and intention could bring a person to heaven, then all the sluggards should be in heaven, for the soul of the sluggard desires and has nothing. And you would know this: the gospel and the law require practice, and not intention only.

The sixth false rule by which some persons judge themselves, and which is more refined than the rest, is this: some persons judge themselves more by their gifts than by their graces and practices.

But if you could speak of God like an angel, and could understand all the mysteries within the Scriptures, and still did not practice in some measure what you know, God would say unto you, "I know you not." For what advantage will you have by the knowledge of all the excellent things of God, if you bring not forth these things in practice? O know it: if knowledge could have brought persons to heaven, then Balaam would be a shining star in heaven today. Therefore, do not judge yourselves by your gifts and knowledge, but by your graces and practices.

There is this seventh false rule by which persons judge themselves, namely, some judge themselves more by human approbation than by divine approbation. There are some who say, "I have approbation of all the saints, and therefore I may conclude I shall go to heaven." I say to you, though the approbation of the saints may sometimes have its own weight, yet I am sure there are some in hell who have had much approbation of the saints and excellent ones of the earth. But let Christ's testimonial and approbation be the rule by which you judge yourself, and do not so much care what men say of you. O what if all ministers should call you saints, if Christ call you a reprobate; what poor advantage does that amount to?

The eighth false and erring rule by which some judge themselves is this: they judge themselves by God's outward dispensations. Are there not many who cry out, "I thank God, for He has been good to me all my days. He never afflicted me before; I always had meat and drink and clothes"? I say, you may have all these things in abundance and yet be a stranger unto God. Do not judge of your state by God's outward dispensations. What do you know but that all your enjoyments in the world are only as a bone cast to a dog? And what know you but that all you have is only the fattening you for the day of slaughter? I would charge you and would earnestly desire that you would not judge of your state by the dispensations of God; for these things may have their own mistake. I confess indeed, there are some dispensations of God that may be a confirmation to a Christian of his peace, but I say this: let never a Christian make the dispensations of God the rules of his judging of himself.

The second ground and rise of presumption and mistake is this: many persons are not much taken up in the exercise of self-examinations; this is the rise of their presumption and mistake, as is clear by comparing our text with the verse which follows it, where the apostle, to help the Galatians guard against presumption, gives them this direction, "Let every man prove his own work" (Gal. 6:4). I say, be much in searching yourself by the Lord's rule, and you shall win to some distinct discoveries of yourself. I confess, there are some who have no will to examine themselves because of their discouragement; and some have no will, neither will they set about the examination of their own state, because they have passed a conclusion already: "O what do I need to search? Am I not certain of this, that Christ is mine?" I would only say this by the way: we can never be too sure of our interest in Him.

The third ground and rise of presumption and mistake is this: many persons are void of the spiritual exercise of the grace of faith. There is nothing will help a Christian so much against presumption and mistake as the spiritual exercise of the noble grace of faith. "By what law," says the apostle, is boasting excluded? Not by the law of works, "but by the law of faith" (Rom. 3:27). Faith will exceedingly help a Christian to a humble walking with God.

A fourth rise of conceit and presumption is persons not believing these two things: first, that all things that they have, they have them of another, and second, that all things they have are freely given. Paul, reproving that fault that was among many (their boasting of those things they had received as though they had not received them), says, "What hast thou that thou didst not receive?" (1 Cor. 4:7). Therefore, I entreat you to walk under the impression of that, and it will keep you humble.

A fifth rise of presumption and conceit is this: many persons are not much in reflecting upon original sin and the body of death. That is indeed the thing that is the mother of pride and presumption. There is a most remarkable instance of this in Romans 11:25 where, speaking of original sin, the apostle says, "I would not... that ye should be ignorant of this," and why so? "Lest," says he, "ye should be wise in your own conceits." The lack of distinct apprehensions—and a spiritual study—of original sin and the body of death is indeed the rise of conceit and presumption.

A sixth rise of presumption is this: men's not reflecting upon what they ought to be. If a person would compare his attainments with what he ought to be, it would help him to crush his presumption. This is clear: if a man thinks he knows anything, he knows nothing as he ought to know. Let all your attainments be laid to the command, and that will help you to cry out, "O how far am I behind!"

A seventh rise of presumption is: we compare ourselves with those who are more gross, and do not study to compare ourselves with those who are more eminent. Some judge themselves by the walk and conversation of others who are more gross, and therefore cry out, "I thank God I am not like this man!" This was the ground of that Pharisee's conceit and presumption, who compared himself (as he thought) to an extortioner and adulterer, and thereupon prayed his thanks to God (Luke 18:11). Now, you would study to compare yourself more by those who are above you than those who are below you. I would have you take notice of this: the discouraged Christian compares himself with those who are above him, and the presumptuous Christian compares himself with those who are below him; now this is a fault in both of these comparisons.

An eighth rise of presumption and mistake is this: persons do not consider and seriously ponder what they will at last be. If once a Christian did seriously ponder that blessed perfection that he is to arrive at, it would make him to have low and undervaluing thoughts of all that he has striven for.

Now that which third I shall speak to is this: I shall propose unto you *some grounds upon which conceit and presumption do build themselves*. And I entreat you search whether or not your conceit and presumption are built upon such a sandy foundation.

The first false ground of it is this, namely, applause and approbation from men. Nothing is more ready to lift up a Christian's spirit than to be much applauded and approved by the excellent ones of the earth. I may allude (if not more than allude) to the practice of Uzziah, when his fame spread abroad through the countries, and he became great—his heart was lifted up, and he became proud to his own destruction (2 Chron. 26:14). I confess, I thought it a notable prayer of one whom I thought knew his own heart better than most of us who are here. He earnestly entreated God thusly: "Lord, keep me from applause." Believe it: it is a hard thing to keep low, being applauded. When the wind of applause is high, man is near a shipwreck. It is a question most difficult in Christianity, whether it be easier for a Christian to bear a cross or to be applauded? I think this: a person will never be able to bear applause till he begins to know that his applause is a burden. There is a strange expression in the Scriptures where, speaking of the building of the temple, Zechariah says, "[Christ] shall bear the glory" (Zech. 6:13). We may take notice of these two things: first, that applause is a burden, and second, that it is best and most suitable for Christ's shoulders to bear it. I think it much for a Christian to steal to heaven, and never have one wit he is going there; Yes, and if it were possible not to let his own heart know he is going there, I think he would be blessed. I confess indeed, a precious name is better than much riches; but I would say to you that pride does ofttimes rise out of the root of approbation and applause. And I would only say this by the way: there are two great and most erroneous mistakes among Christians that are most faulty in their walk. First, there are some who never have peace in their consciences except when they have approbation and applause; as it were, their peace hangs upon applause. Second, this is faulty in their walk—they think their lack of approbation from the saints a matter of exceedingly great discouragement, but I say, if all the Christians you know will not own you, but will call you a hypocrite, you may yet grasp Christ and take hold of Him. Take this strange exercise of faith, "Doubtless thou art our father, though Abraham be ignorant of us" (Isa. 63:16). I think it is one of the great mysterious acts of faith that though Christians should condemn us for hypocrites, yet we put a "doubtless" to our faith and cry out, "Doubtless thou art our father!"

The second bad ground and foundation of presumption is this: the gift of knowledge, which is ordinarily the ground of mistake and presumption—"Knowledge puffeth up" (1 Cor. 8:1).

There is this, third, which is the ground of presumption: a Christian's self-denial and humility. That may seem strange, that humility should be the ground of conceit and pride, and yet it is no more strange than it is true. Some persons, if they can have no other ground of their conceit, will be proud[1] that they are humble. And therefore, I say, it is hard for a Christian to be mortified to his

---

1. Original, "conceity."

mortification, and to be humble to his humility, and to be denied to his self-denial, and to be nothing to his being nothing. If pride can have no other root, it will rise out of the root of precious humility.

A fourth ground of presumption and conceit are our duties, and the concomitants of our duties. Some are conceited about this, that they are diligent in duties; and some of this, that they have liberty in duties; and some of this, that they are successful in duties. Now, there are none of these three things that ought to be the ground of presumption or conceit. You should not be conceited about this, that you are diligent in duty, nor of liberty, nor of success in duty. Though I confess a Christian will win to this, not to be conceited about of his diligence, yet it is hard for him not to be conceited about his liberty.

A fifth rise of presumption and conceit is this: many persons do indeed suppose all is right with them, and this makes them presumptuous. Are there not many who cry forth, "I am, and there is none else besides me," who are utterly mistaken?

That which, fourth, I shall speak to are *six observations concerning conceit and presumption.*

The first observation is this: that it is easier for a Christian to be mortified to his duties than to his gifts. A Christian will be more easily denied to his diligence than to his knowledge. Knowledge is that which makes many to have their hearts lifted up in them.

The second observation concerning presumption is this: that it is easier for a Christian to be mortified to his graces than to his enlargements. A Christian may be mortified to his humility, to his patience, to his faith, and yet not mortified to his enlargements. I say, it is harder for a Christian to be mortified unto his enlargements than it is to be mortified to his graces.

The third observation that I would give you concerning presumption and conceit is this: that it is easier for a Christian to be mortified to his natural qualifications than to his religious qualifications.

Fourth, it is easier for a Christian to be mortified and humble in the time of affliction than in the time of prosperity, for prosperity is the time when pride does blossom.

The fifth observation concerning presumption and conceit is this: that it is easier for a Christian to be mortified to his surprising enlargements than to be mortified to his expected and waited-for enlargements. It is easier for a Christian to be mortified to those enlargements that come to him by way of surprise than it is for him to be mortified to these enlargements to which he can sing that song, "Lo, this is our God; we have waited for him," and He has come unto us (Isa. 25:9).

The sixth observation concerning presumption and conceit is this: it is easier for a Christian to be mortified to his private enlargements than to his public enlargements.

I shall conclude our discourse at this time, only I would wish that I may undeceive many of us, and that we may know how it stands between God and us. I entreat you to search and examine your condition. Are there not many who are here who put it beyond all question, and say, "Now I am going to heaven"? Now, that you go not down to the pit with a conceit of the goodness of your estate, I shall point out nine steps that a person may take and yet not win heaven. Search yourselves whether or not you have gone beyond these steps.

First, a person may go this length, that he lacks but one thing to attain everlasting rest, and yet never comes there. Is not that a strange thing, that you may come that length, that there shall be but one thing wanting, and yet never come to heaven? This is clear from that which is recorded of that young rich man who came to Christ, to whom Christ said, "One thing thou lackest" (Mark 10:21). O is not that to be near heaven, and never to come there? You may be within the gates of that city. I shall ask you, and desire you to search yourselves, are there not many here who, if they were seriously asked, dare not say that ever they stepped one step into heaven? And O then how far are you short of those persons!

There is a second step that one may take and yet never win heaven, and that is: a person may seek and pursue after heaven, and yet never win there: "Strive to enter in at the strait gate: for many, I say unto you, will seek to enter in, and shall not be able" (Luke 13:24). Now, is not that a great step? And yet many shall step that step, and not get into heaven. Are there not some here who never knew what it was to seek with earnestness the kingdom of God? I say, you may be a seeker of it and yet never enter into it. Yea, the word that is rendered "seek" in that verse imports seeking with some sort of diligence and earnestness, and yet that person may still be shut out of the kingdom of God. Are you indeed seekers of it? I say, you may be such, and yet be shut out.

The third step that one may take and yet not go to heaven is this: a person may have strong desires after eternal life and yet never win there. If desires and wishes could have brought persons to heaven, Balaam would be there. "Let me die the death of the righteous, and let my last end be like his!" (Num. 23:10). Now, I would ask you, are there not some of you who not once in a month, yea, not once in a year, will have one serious desire for heaven? I say, you may have strong desires and yet be eternally shut out, and never enter there.

A fourth step that one may take and yet never inherit those everlasting joys is this: a person may be admitted to taste of the sweetness and powers of the world to come. I say, heaven may be made refreshing unto them, and the probable expectation they have that once they shall go there. I say that may be, and you shall go there; I say, that may be, and you shall never go to heaven. For the tasting of the powers of the world to come is but a common work of the Spirit. Now, I would pose you with this question: Are there not some of us who are here who, if they would speak the truth, dare not for a world say that ever heaven was sweet unto them? I say, it may be sweet unto you, and yet you will never possess it.

The fifth step that one may take and yet never go to heaven, and enter into those precious and everlasting mansions, is this: a person may be convinced of the excellency of that state, and of his need of it, and yet be one of those who shall never go to heaven. Are there not some here, who since they ever had knowledge, had an excellent and strong faith, and yet never knew what it was to stand in need of Christ, and to be convinced of the advantage that flows unto them who are close with Him? I say, you may be sensible of your lost state, and yet never go to heaven. This is clear in the instance of Simon Magus; he is brought to this, that he sees he is in the gall of bitterness, and in the bond of iniquity, and yet says,

"Pray ye to the LORD for me, that none of these things which ye have spoken come upon me" (Acts 8:24).

The sixth step that some may take and not enter into that precious and everlasting rest that is purchased for the saints is this: some persons may do many things willingly and gladly when they hear a sermon, and yet those persons never win heaven. If the doing of many things at preaching's command had brought persons to heaven, then Herod would be in heaven. Now I would ask you who have lived forty, fifty, or sixty years under preaching, if for all the commands that ever you heard, on supposition that you speak the truth, do you dare say that you ever obeyed one of them? O what a dreadful account are many of us to make for all that we have heard!

There is this seventh step likewise that a person may take and yet never win heaven, namely, to forsake all for Christ, and to follow Him for a while, and yet not be saved. It was said of all the disciples that they forsook all and followed Christ; and Judas was one who forsook all his possessions, and yet he was damned. I say, you may forsake all your enjoyments in the world for Christ, and yet never win heaven.

An eighth step one may take and yet never win heaven is this: a person may sit down and mourn over some sins that he has been guilty of, and yet that person never wins heaven. For if mourning over some sins had brought persons to heaven, then Esau, who mourned for the sin of selling his birthright, would be in heaven. Such is the mourning that Judas had for selling his Master, when he went and hanged himself. Now I would charge you, as you would not meet with an eternal disappointment, that you do not think yourselves something when indeed you are nothing. I confess indeed, it would be no small thing for any man to preach you and your hope asunder if your confidence were truly built upon Him who is the eternal Rock of ages. But this is certain: there are many of us who are here whose hope shall be swept away as a spider's web, and shall vanish as a dream, and fly away as a vision of the night. I would give this advice unto you: believe not your own heart.

Now, what say you of yourselves? Are you put to this question, "O am I under this mistake and delusion?" I say, the person who is furthest from it will be most ready to ask the question, "Is it I?" Now, will you go home and search yourselves, and see how it stands between God and you? I am sure, if many of us would search ourselves, we would find God is not at peace with us. I will tell you but four errors in the way of many presumptuous persons. First, many persons forgive themselves before God forgives them; they pardon themselves for their iniquities before God does. I say, that pardon shall be rent, because it has been taken from the court of our erring and deceitful consciences. And, second, many persons are friends with themselves before God is friends with them. Third, many persons forget their iniquities before God forgets them. There is that last fault that is among many: they assume peace, peace in their own hearts, when in fact there is nothing to them from God but sudden destruction. Are there not some who sing of joy to their souls whom God shall put to eternal sorrow?

O search! It is a matter of eternal concern; for, if once you pass the borders of time with a lie in your right hand, there is no hope. And when you shall pass through the gates of your eternal prison, will you not be constrained to cry out, "O whither is this self-deceiver now going?" It is one of the most dreadful and most terrible things we can be, a deceiver of our own selves! Now, do you think you are in a mistake? O that many of us could believe that all the faith that ever we had was but presumption! I am persuaded God does account it so. Now I shall say no more. O do not think yourselves to be something, when indeed you are nothing.

The Great Danger of Hypocrisy (Part 1)

But the hypocrites in heart heap up wrath: they cry not when he bindeth them.

—Job 36:13

I am sometimes constrained to think that many of the Christians of this time shall meet with a dreadful disappointment; their hope shall vanish as a dream and fly away as a vision of the night. I suppose there are two things that are almost at their height. First, we suppose hypocrisy was never at a greater height, and second, presumption was never so abundant and universal. I desire not to preach much against hypocrisy, lest these who are strangers to God should take advantage. Oh, is it not sad that so many should think they are going to heaven who by all appearance shall be eternally shut out from the enjoyment of God and the fruition of His face? And are there not many who have the testimony of their consciences that they are going to heaven to whom I fear Christ Jesus shall say, "I never knew you: depart from me" (Matt. 7:23)? I think hypocrisy never looked so like real godliness in any generation as it does in this. I confess, reflecting upon the Scriptures might make the most part of professors to stand astonished that, if there be but ten professors, there are five of them hypocrites. I think it is a duty incumbent upon every one of us who have a name among the living in Jerusalem to ofttimes ask that question to our own hearts, "Am I a foolish virgin?" It is known that many lodge Christ in their tongues who never lodged Him in their hearts, and many do speak much good of Christ here who shall eternally curse God hereafter. I shall say that word to you, "Be not deceived; God is not mocked: for what a man soweth, that shall he also reap" (Gal. 6:7). I may also say this to you, that if the hearts of some of the professors of this time were painted out on a board, and we were admitted to behold and see what is within them, would we not stand astonished and wonder how such a one could take on a profession? Believe it: it is not so easy to be a Christian as the most part of us think it to be. Know it: hell is full of self-deceivers; there are many painted Christians now in hell who are cursing God night and day.

Now, to come more particularly to the words. Elihu, in the former part of Job 36, has been setting forth the carriage and advantages of the truly godly, under the saddest and most afflicting cross that he can meet with. And, in opposition to that, he comes and points out the case and state of a hypocrite. In verse 13 we have three things concerning the hypocrite presented. First, the name and qualification of the hypocrite: he is called the hypocrite in heart, which we conceive points out these three things. First, that one may be a hypocrite and yet his hypocrisy be hidden and dark, not only to himself, but to others also, and so the meaning of the words may be this: a secret and unknown hypocrite. Second, it may take in this, namely, a person taking delight in hypocrisy, and approving himself in it. Therefore, a hypocrite in heart is one who delights and solaces himself in his hypocrisy. Third, a hypocrite in heart points out this: he is even a hypocrite in his thoughts, that is, there is a contradiction between a hypocrite's expressions and his thoughts, between his walk and his mind, between his outward man and his inward man, between his profession and his practice. So that I think, in short, a hypocrite is a compound of contradictions, and his walk and conversation is but a continued lie unto God. The second thing concerning hypocrisy in the word is this: that he is a person who heaps up wrath; that is the very constant exercise of a hypocrite. Let him continue doing what he will; let him go to communions or to fasts, and to secret prayer, and to all the meetings of Christians. This is the very substance of his work—he heaps up wrath, that is, every action he goes about doing is adding to the cup of the wrath of the Almighty, which once he shall drink of. For the word which is here rendered "heap" may also be rendered he "adds up wrath"; that is, for every action he takes, he does (as it were) put a drop into the cup of the eternal wrath that he shall drink. The third thing concerning hypocrisy in the words is the evidence and mark of a hypocrite; and it is in these words, that he cries not when God binds him. By binding is principally understood afflictions; that, under sad and afflicting dispensations, he does not furiously seek unto God, which is held forth in that word "cry," which ordinarily in Scripture imports a serious seeking unto God in affliction, as if Elihu had said, "I know a hypocrite may seem to seek unto God in affliction, but he does not cry unto Him." And by "binding," we conceive, may be understood desertion and bands, that when they are under bands, and distant from God, they do not cry unto God for all this.

Now there are five things we shall speak a little unto from this verse. The first is this: that hypocrisy and dissimulation is a thing incident to many. This is clearly presupposed. The second thing that we shall speak to shall be this: that hypocrisy and dissimulation is a thing which may be hidden, not only from the person himself, but also from all others who look upon the person. This is clearly held forth in that word, "the hypocrite in heart"; that is, the unknown, secret, and dark hypocrite. Third, there is this that we shall take notice of: that hypocrisy is that wherewith the hearts of some are at certain times solaced and delighted. This we cleared to be the force of that word, "the hypocrite in heart." Fourth, you may take notice of this from the words: that the constant and perpetual exercise of a hypocrite is to be a heaper up of wrath. Let him do what he will and say what he will—this is the thing he is taken up with, this is his work: he heaps up wrath. And the last thing we shall take notice of from the words is this: that this is an undeniable evidence of hypocrisy, and of one who is under the power of dissimulation, not to cry when God binds him. That is, under all the straits, anxieties, and difficulties that he can be put to, he does not cry to God.

Now, to come to speak a little unto the first of these, that hypocrisy is a case incident unto many. I conceive I need not stand long to clear it. I suppose Matthew 7:23 does abundantly clear it, that hypocrisy is a thing that is most common. That word in Isaiah 9:17 speaks this abundantly, "The LORD shall have no joy in their young men, neither shall have mercy upon their fatherless and widows: for every one is an hypocrite," in a manner charging a whole visible church with this fault of hypocrisy. "I will send him against an hypocritical nation" (Isa. 10:6). As if the prophet had said, "Hypocrisy is such a rife and predominant evil among them that they may be called a hypocritical nation." And Matthew 25 clears this to be a thing most rife where, among these who are professors, there are five who are foolish, and but five who are wise. Now, in speaking to this, I shall speak a little to those three, which will be the foundation to the rest of our discourse.

First, we shall speak a little unto this: What is hypocrisy? And we conceive, hypocrisy is *that by which a man desires to appear to be that which he really is not, and desires not to appear to be what he really is.* Hypocrisy, in short, is this: for a man to be a Christian in his tongue, and an atheist in his heart. But, that we may be a little clearer on the nature of hypocrisy, I shall point out these ten steps in which hypocrisy does stand, all which may be undoubted marks of one who is a hypocrite.

The first thing wherein hypocrisy stands is this: when a person has this as the end of all his actions, to be seen by men when a person is more covetous; and when he prays, to be seen of men, rather than to be seen of God. "But all their works they do for to be seen of men" (Matt. 23:5). "Do not sound a trumpet before thee, as the hypocrites do in the synagogues and in the streets, that they may have glory of men" (Matt. 6:2). So, I say, look what is your end of doing duty. And I would pose your consciences with this: Is it not the great end of the most of our duties to be seen of men? I would say to that person that word, "Take heed that ye do not your alms before men" (Matt. 6:1). I confess, there are some of us, when we are doing anything that is good, who cry out, "Come with me, and see my zeal for the LORD" (2 Kings 10:16). It is to be suspected that, if some of the professors of this time were sent to live upon the top of a mountain, they would leave their profession behind them. This is our woeful evil—we go about the most part of our duties to satisfy our natural conscience, or else to be seen of men. Now, is there any person here who is not guilty of this step of hypocrisy? Do you not sometimes go to communions to be seen of men? I shall say no more to this step of hypocrisy but only this: you shall have your reward.

There is this, second, in which hypocrisy does stand, namely, when a person is more taken up in the love of public than private duties. Are there not some persons who will pray six times when they are in company, who will not pray once when they are alone? Yes, will we not pray twenty times with delight when we are in company, when we will not pray once with delight being alone? "They love to pray standing in…the corners of the streets" (Matt. 6:5)—it is not said of these persons that they love to pray in secret. I say to that person, be afraid your religion is but a fancy. I never loved public religion, that is, religion altogether in public, and not at all alone. There are some professors in public who are atheists when they are alone. I wonder that some of us, when we go to prayer, do not meet with such a voice from heaven, "Arise, sir; why do you lie unto the Holy Ghost?" I say more: let your religion be more in secret than in company, or you shall never have a reward. I think Ephesians 5:12 is a strange verse, and is applicable to the most part of us who are here: "It is a shame even to speak of those things which are done of them in secret." If the stones of the walls of our secret chambers could speak unto us, they would tell us that we exercise not ourselves unto godliness.

A third step of hypocrisy is this: for a person to be more taken up in the pursuit of outward than inward holiness, to be more taken up with outward conformity to the letter of the law than inward conformity to the spiritual meaning of the law. This is an eminent step of hypocrisy, as Christ especially reproves this fault: "Ye are like unto whited sepulchers, which indeed appear beautiful outward, but are within full of dead men's bones, and of all uncleanness" (Matt. 23:27). And likewise, this is a mark of hypocrisy: "[They] come to you in sheep's clothing, but inwardly they are ravening wolves" (Matt. 7:15). Now, are there not many of us who study much to have our outside without spot who never study to have our inside so? Are there not many of us who have Jacob's voice and Esau's hands? Are there not many of us who concerning the letter of the law are blameless, and concerning the spiritual meaning of the law are gross breakers of it? But oh, since God is one who does behold the secrets of the heart, be not content with external holiness. I think there is as much difference between a hypocrite and a real Christian as is between a painted man and a real man. A painted man has all the parts of a real man, but he lacks the life of a man; so a hypocrite has all the parts of a Christian, but lacks the life of a Christian.

I will tell you five sorts of persons whom Christ will reject.

First, those who keep their tongues with all diligence, and do not keep their hearts with all diligence. Some there are who will not speak iniquity, but they practice iniquity to work hypocrisy. I say, if a man does not keep his heart as well as his tongue, he shall be nothing. Many persons speak of Christ that which they believe not; yea, some have gone to that length of impiety as to speak good of Christ with their tongues and hate Him in their hearts. I shall say no more to that person but this word, "Whose hatred is covered by deceit, his wickedness shall be shewed before the whole congregation" (Prov. 26:26). Is there a person whose hatred of Christ is covered with a profession? I say, that person's iniquity shall be preached before the whole congregation. The day is approaching when the person who is not a real lover of Christ shall meet with this reproach: "Lo, this is the man that made not God his strength" (Ps. 52:7). I think God is yet to sift us in a sieve that is smaller than any we have met with. I entreat you therefore, search yourselves, for the day is approaching when none shall be able to abide the storm but those who are built upon the Rock. I fear the day is coming when Scotland's trial shall cast many fleeces of professors. Therefore, I entreat you to be as much Christians in heart as in tongue.

The second sort of persons whom Christ will reject are those who divide the law. That is, they are first-table Christians but not second-table Christians; they love the works of holiness—at least to appearance—but they hate the works of righteousness, such as those persons who love sacrifice better than mercy, and burnt offerings better than compassion (see Hos. 6:6). There are some who love the first table of the law better than the second. O the religion of such a person who pretends to love God and hates his neighbor, that is a religion which was never approved of by God; and therefore, if you would be persons approved by God, divide not the law.

The third sort of persons whom Christ will reject are Christians who divide the gospel, and there are many such Christians in these days. Some will embrace the promises of the gospel but will reject the commands of the gospel, like those who believed in Christ, and yet cried out, "This is an hard saying; who can hear it?" (John 6:60). You shall never be a Christian approved by God if you embrace not the commands as well as the promises. Some Christians do embrace the promises before they believe the threatnings; that Christian's religion is weak.

The fourth sort of Christians whom Christ will also reject are these who are for dividing Christ; those He will reject. I mean this—some Christians will take Christ for righteousness who will not take Him for sanctification; some Christians will take Christ for wisdom who will not take Him for redemption. But know it: there shall none get Christ but these who will be content to take the whole Christ. I would ask that question of you which Paul spoke, "Is Christ divided?" (1 Cor. 1:13). And will you not take the whole Christ? For what has He which is not necessary for us?

The fifth sort of Christians whom Christ will reject, and who shall not be approved by Him, are visible Christians, that is, those who are Christians abroad and are not Christians at home. These are persons whom Christ will not approve.

A fourth thing in which hypocrisy does stand is this: for a person to be more taken up in pursuit after the approbation and applause of men than after the approbation and applause of God; that is an eminent step of hypocrisy. This is clear from John 12:43, where it is said, "They loved the praise of men more than the praise of God." I would pose your consciences with this: are there not many here who have been a hundred times more affected with the approbation of a minister or Christian than with the approbation of God? Are there not many who love the praise of men more than the praise of God? I know if some of us were searched, we would rather have Christians speaking good of us than Christ speaking good of us.

The fifth step of hypocrisy is this: for a Christian to be exercised in the doing of some duties, and yet slighting some more substantial duties of the gospel; this is an evidence and mark of hypocrisy. Scripture makes this clear, where the hypocrite is charged with paying tithes of mint, anise, and cummin, and leaves the weightier matters of the law, such as judgment and mercy, undone (Matt. 23:23). The same is made mention of, "Ye tithe mint and rue and all manner of herbs, and pass over judgment and the love of God" (Luke 11:42). I tell you four of the duties the hypocrite is most taken up with: there is the duty of prayer, the duty of keeping public ordinances, the duty of reading, and the duty of keeping the conversation without spot. These are the four great duties in which the diligence of hypocrites does vent. But as for the duty of self-examination, and the duty of keeping the heart with all diligence, and exercising themselves unto godliness, those are the duties the hypocrite is not at all taken up with.

The sixth thing in which hypocrisy does stand is for persons to strain at gnats, and to swallow camels. I tell you three things a hypocrite will exceedingly strain at: 1. An oath, he will exceedingly strain at that; 2. He will exceedingly guard against giving offence unto any who are religious, and against the neglect of public duty. And yet there are camels that he will swallow, and not strain at them.

There is this, seventh, in which hypocrisy does stand, namely, for a person to be much taken up in censuring the small faults of others, and neglecting their own that are more gross. "Thou hypocrite, first cast the beam out of thine own eye; and then shalt thou see clearly to cast out the mote of thy brother's eye" (Matt 7:5). There are some persons who can see their neighbor's faults better than their own. It is reported of a certain beast that it can see none within, but it can see excellently without. I think a Christian ought to be like the cherubims: "Their faces were inward" (2 Chron. 3:13); they looked within.[1]

Eighth, hypocrisy stands in this: for a person to be more taken and affected with the lots of approbation from men than with God's approbation. I would ask you, are there not some here who were affected with more sorrow by the loss of approbation from a Christian than the loss of approbation from God?

The ninth step of hypocrisy is for persons to be more studious to enlarge their profession and appearance, than to enlarge their practice and work. There are some persons whose great work it is to enlarge their profession and to make their name conspicuous; but, as to bettering their practice, they are strangers to that. "They make broad their phylacteries, and enlarge the borders of their garments" (Matt. 23:5); that is, they make broad their profession. There are some persons more covetous to be seen as followers of Christ than really to be so.

There is this, lastly, in which hypocrisy does stand, even this: for a person to have a constant contradiction between his light and

---

1. Original, "that way."

his practice. Christ says, "All therefore whatsoever they bid you observe, that observe and do; but do not ye after their works: for they say, and do not" (Matt. 23:3). I confess there is in hypocrisy a six-fold contradiction. First, there is a mighty contradiction between a hypocrite's light and his practice, for he knows many things that he never sets about to do. Second, there is a mighty contradiction between his profession and his practice; he professes one thing, and he practices another. Third, there is a contradiction between his walk when he is alone and his walk when he is in company. Fourth, there is a contradiction between his outward and his inward man. Fifth, there is a contradiction between his desires and his endeavors, for sometimes a hypocrite may have excellent desires, but seldom or never has he excellent endeavors. Last, there is a mighty contradiction in a hypocrite between his tongue and his heart.

Now that which, second, I shall speak to is this: I would clear a little unto you *that it is your duty to guard against hypocrisy.* "Beware ye of the leaven of the Pharisees, which is hypocrisy" (Luke 12:1). The word that is there rendered "beware" imports so much. First of all, "beware" (as it were, this is the *imprimis* of a Christian's duty) to guard against hypocrisy. And I shall say no more to press this to be your duty but this: I think those great and everlasting woes that are pronounced against hypocrisy in Matthew 23 speak that it is your duty to guard against hypocrisy.

Third, I shall point out to you three sorts of hypocrisy. First, there is a hypocrisy which is consistent with real grace. For you would know this: everything that is done in hypocrisy does not make a Christian a hypocrite as to his state. I confess, if we took notice that every act of hypocrisy does not give a Christian sufficient ground to call himself a hypocrite, we might reprove hypocrites with more advantage. This is clear in Galatians 3, where Peter, James, and Barnabas are charged with hypocrisy, that they walked not uprightly. Yet, I think, all are persuaded that these were not hypocrites. Second, there is a dark, unknown hypocrisy, so as neither the person himself nor any that observes his walk knows him to be a hypocrite, whom the Scripture describes as "deceiving, and being deceived" (2 Tim. 3:13). Some persons may be hypocrites and they not know it; yea, all others who know their walk will not be able to call them hypocrites. There is a third sort of hypocrisy that is most gross, to wit, known and presumptuous hypocrisy; that is, for a person to play the hypocrite and yet know that he does it, for a person to be impersonating a Christian and yet know that he is an imposter. Scripture describes this person as "speaking lies in hypocrisy" (1 Tim. 4:2). This is a dreadful sin, when a person can play the hypocrite and know he is doing so.

Now, before I prosecute this truth any further, I would have you guard against anything that may be spoken by them who are profane and gross, who are ready to think all religion but hypocrisy, and all the duties of religion but a form. I would say to that person who hates religion under the veil of hypocrisy, do not think we are speaking against the form of religion. Though I confess there may be a form of religion in which there lacks the power of religion, yet there may be much of the power of religion where there is the form of religion. I would ask this question of these who hate religion under the veil of hypocrisy, of these who say they cannot tolerate that such hypocrites should get leave to do as they do, I would ask this question of them: What is the reason that you hate hypocrisy? "Oh," say you, "I hate hypocrisy, but I hate not religion." But would you know why indeed you hate hypocrisy? It is this: you hate not only the image of Christ, but you hate the very picture of it. Some hate not only real Christians, but they hate the very picture of them. I say this of the person who hates hypocrisy and is profane: he may say what he will; he hates not hypocrisy, but he hates the very shadow and picture of Christ. Second, I would ask this question of you, which will clear this: O you who hate hypocrisy, what is the reason you hate not drunkenness, swearing, and whoredom also? Some person will persecute hypocrisy and yet he will swear, lie, and add drunkenness to his thirst. I tell you why the profane person hates hypocrisy and yet loves drunkenness: he hates hypocrisy because it is a sin that looks like godliness, and he loves drunkenness because it is a sin that looks like the devil. A third question that I would ask of such is this: What will you say on that day when Christ shall ask that question of you which Gideon asked Zebah and Zalmunna, "What manner of men were they whom ye slew?" (Judg. 8:18). And you shall answer, "As Thou art, so were they; each one resembled the similitude of a prince." I confess, I never loved the person who hated hypocrisy and yet loved profanity and gross sins.

At this time, I shall go no further, but shall speak a little to seven steps unto which a hypocrite cannot go. First, a hypocrite cannot go that length as to mourn over original sin. Have you ever sat down in secret and cried forth, "O wretched man that I am! Who shall deliver me from the body of this death?" (Rom. 7:24)? This is a token you have passed from death to life. I would give you two reasons why a hypocrite cannot mourn over original sin. First, because the guilt of original sin is only taken up by faith; nothing can discover the guilt and filthiness of original sin so lively as faith. Faith is that which exposes to a person that woeful root of bitterness that is within him. The second ground why the hypocrite cannot mourn over original sin is this: so long as a person is a stranger from Christ, he looks upon original sin as none of his own. Are there not many who think original sin is none of their own? They will groan under actual sins because they cannot put them by, but they are their own; but O they cannot believe that original sin, which was committed five thousand years ago, should be theirs. Now, till once a person begins to engage with Christ, it is impossible for him to believe original sin to be his own. Are there any here to whom sometimes original sin has been their burden? I say that is a step a hypocrite never took, nor ever shall take. I think he is an excellent Christian who can live under these three: (1) to think original sin as great as any actual transgression, (2) to believe original sin is as much his own as if he had eaten the forbidden fruit (and no doubt it is as much his own as if indeed he had eaten it, though it is hard for a Christian to believe it), and (3) to believe that the root of every iniquity that ever was vented or named in the world is within his cursed heart, and that upon a suitable temptation we would be brought to act and commit such an evil.

There is a second step that a hypocrite cannot take, namely, a hypocrite can never win this length: to have a higher account of Christ than of anything in the world beside. A hypocrite may win to love Christ in some respect, but he can never win to this length: to love Christ above all things. Now I would ask you this: Did you ever bring your hearts to this—that you could take angels to witness—you desired nothing so much as Christ, and Christ had all your desire? That if Christ had been put in one balance, and all your idols into another, in your apprehension Christ would have weighed them down exceedingly? Alas! It is certain: many of us who are here, if we would not lie, we dare not for a world say that Christ is preferred above all things. I confess indeed, Christ should have the preeminence in all things, but, alas! Many of us give Him the preeminence in nothing.

Third, a hypocrite can never go this length: to mourn over his unbelief and contempt of the gospel. Did you ever in secret pour forth your heart to God because of your misbelief? That is a length a hypocrite cannot match. And I give you these reasons why a hypocrite cannot mourn for unbelief. First, because he does not take up the sinfulness of the sin of unbelief. I think it is one of the great arts of a Christian to take up and comprehend the sinfulness of that sin of unbelief. Second, because it is impossible to think unbelief an exceedingly sinful sin, till once the matchless excellency, beauty, and worth of Christ be discovered.

There is a fourth step which a hypocrite cannot take, to wit, a hypocrite cannot come this length, as to mourn over the eating and drinking unworthily the body and blood of the Lord. A hypocrite seldom (or never) wins to a hearty mourning over his eating and drinking unworthily; that is a sin which ofttimes lies outside of the reach of a hypocrite's confession and prayer.

The fifth thing which a hypocrite cannot at all times win to (which if you have done, you may conclude you have passed from death to life) is this: he can never win to a heart renunciation of his own righteousness, to be totally denied unto his own righteousness, and to flee wholly for refuge unto Jesus Christ. It is a great mystery of a Christian practice to be wholly denied to the righteousness of the law, and to flee to the righteousness of the gospel, as having nothing. I say, upon strict search you will find it a most difficult practice for a Christian to deny his own righteousness.

There is a sixth step which a hypocrite cannot take, namely, he cannot mourn secretly and seriously for vain and sinful thoughts. It is a notable evidence of sincerity when a person can win to a real mourning for those sinful thoughts that are within his bosom. Can you take heaven to witness, that vain thoughts and the imaginations of your own heart do trouble and afflict you? There are some indeed who care not for their thoughts; they think their thoughts are free. But know this: God will judge you as much for your thoughts as for your words and practice.

There is this seventh step which a hypocrite cannot take, to wit, he can never win to a stayed and composed walk with God; all a hypocrite's religion is by fits. This is certain, that upon serious search it will be found that many persons do not know what it is to be constant in walking with God. There are some times indeed they will take on many excellent fits of religion; but, as for a constant walk with God, they are utterly strangers unto it. I tell you six times when a hypocrite takes on his fits of religion.

First, a hypocrite takes on his fits of religion under the cross. That is the time when a hypocrite, who is indeed profane, will turn religious. "When he slew them, then they sought him: and they returned and enquired early after God" (Ps. 78:34). Some persons will be profane in prosperity, and when God begins to smite them, they will put on some fit of godliness. A second time when a hypocrite puts on his fits of religion is when he is drawing near unto his grave, when death and he begin to yoke. Some persons never mind religion till once death and they begin to speak together. I say, it is one to a thousand if these fits of religion will bear you through. A third time is when he is under some deep, pressing, and strong convictions. Sometimes, when God awakens a Christian's conscience, he will put on excellent fits of religion, and will cry out when their consciences are pricked, "Men and brethren, what shall we do?" (Acts 2:37). The fourth time when a hypocrite puts on many excellent fits of religion is when he is called to extraordinary duties. Sometimes a hypocrite will put on excellent fits of religion at a communion, and he will lay aside all those fits till the next communion comes about. A fifth time when a hypocrite puts on excellent fits of religion is when there is a crown to be gotten for following Christ; as Jehu cries, "Come...and see my zeal for the LORD" (2 Kings 10:16). It is not much for a person to be religious when Christ is in fashion. But O it is much for a person to be religious when Christ is persecuted. The last time I shall mention when a hypocrite puts on his fits of religion is when he is in religious company, and in a religious family. Some will be religious in a religious family, and profane in a profane family. I say to that man or woman, the everlasting curse of God shall light upon your head if you do not repent. O guard against this, that you be not religious only in religious company. I think if some were searched, they would be found always religious in religious company, and when in profane company, they would turn profane. What is that? To turn into so many shapes, and to deny Christ who bought you! Now, O search whether or not this evil root of bitterness be in you, that you may mourn and lament over it, and desire that He who is the God of truth may give you a heart endued with this precious plant of sincerity, that before you go hence and be no more, you may have that testimony, "Behold an Israelite indeed, in whom is no guile" (John 1:47).

The Great Danger of Hypocrisy (Part 2)

But the hypocrites in heart heap up wrath: they cry not when he bindeth them.

—Job 36:13

Are there not some who, upon a serious and impartial search of their own hearts by the candle of the Lord, may be constrained to suspect all their religion is but hypocrisy, that all their enjoyments are but delusions, and all the duties they have gone about are but formality and lying to God with the tongue? I suppose there are some of us who are here, who have taken our hearts too soon upon trust; there are some of us here who are "famous in the congregation, men of renown" (Num. 16:2), and yet it may also be said of us, "Thou hast a name that thou livest, and art dead" (Rev. 3:1). I have thought it a strange expression in Jude 12, where the apostle, pointing forth the hypocrite, calls him a person who is "twice dead," that is, he is not only dead in respect of his natural state, being a stranger to God, but also he is dead in that the life that once he seemed to have in the ways of God is now gone and departed from him. I wonder that some of us who are here are not made beacons upon the top of a mountain, and monuments of the everlasting displeasure of God. And I think it also a wonder that some of us are not carried dead from our prayers when we go to them, for it is certain many of us can speak our prayers unto God while we cannot heart our prayers unto God. I do not question but a hypocrite wearies of God, and I think God wearies as much of him. I would earnestly entreat you all to be impartial in the search of your own hearts, lest you go down to the grave with a lie in your right hand, a deceived heart having led you aside. I suppose hypocrisy does not only appear in the principle that leads us unto duty, but also in the manner of our going about duty, as likewise in the end which we have before us in going about duty. I wonder God does not present this challenge to us in the multitude of our prayers: "Who hath required this at your hand?" (Isa. 1:12). There is a desperate boldness that has overtaken the spirits of many, so as they can speak lies unto God with as great confidence and as little fear as though God were indeed a mere idol. Are there not many of us who make a fashion of prayer, while our consciences bear us witness that sometimes the half of our prayers are damnable lies? Do we not sometimes desire such a thing from God in prayer, and we care no more for it than for the street under our feet? Is it not certain that we will sometimes seem to confess a sin to God in prayer, and be no more weighed down with it than if indeed it were no sin? And is it not certain that we will in prayer praise God for such a thing as for sending Christ into the world, and for giving us this blessed and everlasting gospel, and yet our hearts will be no more affected with those things than if they were fancies, and not real truth? I confess, there are some of us who are not able to speak much against hypocrisy. I suppose we may go down to our graves with this lamentation: "Our hearts are not right with God, nor steadfast in his covenant" (see Ps. 78:37). O believe it: hypocrisy may be spun with a small thread, and we may (as it were) paint religion and hypocrisy both upon one board. And he would be a very discerning Christian who would be able to discern between religion and hypocrisy. Yea, know it: there are some brought within sight of the city who shall never go there; as it were, they have been brought to the walls and ports of that excellent city, and yet never enter therein. For I am sure there is not a hypocrite in heaven today, but there are many thousand hypocrites in hell. I make the supposition that if there were a hundred professors in this church today, it would be much if fifty of us were sincere, and the root of the matter were with us. O hypocrisy, hypocrisy (though in them but partial, and not in its dominion) is that which has made many of God's own children to go mourning to their graves, bedewing their way with tears all along as they went.

In the forenoon we told you there were five things we intended to speak to from Job 36:13, the first whereof was that there is such a thing incident to many as hypocrisy and dissimulation. This was clearly presupposed in the words. It is not said, "the *hypocrite* in heart," but, "the *hypocrites* in heart." And we have cleared this a little, that there is such a thing incident to many; I could wish that many of us who are here were not a confirmation of this truth. And we have spoken a little to what hypocrisy is, and likewise given ten steps in which hypocrisy does stand, and to several other things concerning this grand predominant and master sin that is among us, and does so much take up our hearts.

Before we leave this first doctrine from the words, we shall speak a little to three things. First, *to propose to you some considerations to press you to guard against hypocrisy.* And this I speak not only to these who are indeed hypocrites, but also to those who are acquainted with God, who may have some tincture of hypocrisy.

The first consideration to press you to guard against hypocrisy is this: *the person who is a hypocrite is never at real peace.* I tell you three things upon which a hypocrite does especially build his peace. First, he does ofttimes found his peace upon the approbation of the saints. As long as a hypocrite has a fair gale of applause, he almost never disputes his interest. The second foundation upon which a hypocrite does build his peace is his diligence, that he fasts twice a week, that he prays twice a day. The third thing whereon a hypocrite founds his peace is his external holiness and conformity to the letter of the law. I confess, sometimes a hypocrite may have exceeding much carnal joy and contentment, but it is when he has the fairest gale of the world's applause. I would have you take along this observation, which I suppose is certain: I think it is impossible for a hypocrite ever to have peace or joy when he wants applause. Let all the things of the world concur to create peace to a hypocrite, but he shall not have it if he lacks applause.

A second consideration to press you to guard against hypocrisy is those names that hypocrisy gets in Scripture, which may enforce and press upon you to guard against hypocrisy. And there are four names that indicate hypocrisy is a very great sin. First, hypocrisy in the Scripture is called "blasphemy," a strange name: "I know the blasphemy of them which say they are Jews, and are not" (Rev. 2:9). Yea, I say this: hypocrisy is a very near step to that unpardonable sin against the Holy Ghost. Now, if there were no more to discommend hypocrisy unto you but this, that Scripture calls it blasphemy, it would be more than sufficient. Yet there is more. Second, in Scripture, hypocrisy is called "wickedness," and eminently is it so called. This is clear by comparing Matthew 22:18 with Mark 12:15. In the one place it is called hypocrisy, and in the other place it is rendered, "But Jesus perceived their wickedness," which indicates that hypocrisy is a sin odious and detestable to God. Third, hypocrisy in Scripture is called a lie unto God, "Nevertheless they did flatter him with their mouth, and they lied unto him with their tongues" (Ps. 78:36), speaking of their hypocritical prayers. "[They] say they are Jews, and are not, but do lie" (Rev. 3:9). Now, there is a fourth name hypocrisy gets in Scripture; it is called a flattering of God, and that is one of the most dreadful names that it has. It is indeed the sin which thinks God a liar, and therefore will be pleased with fair words and compliments. Therefore, it is said, "They did flatter him with their mouth" (Ps. 78:36). There is a fifth name that hypocrisy gets in Scripture, and that is where the hypocrite is called "a double minded man" or, as the word indicates in its own language, a two-hearted man or a man who has a heart within a heart (James 1:8). This shows that the hypocrite is a person who has two hearts and, as it were, two tongues. The same can be found in Psalm 12:2 where David prays to be kept from the deceitful man, the one "with a double heart." If so I may speak, the hypocrite has one heart to God, and another to the devil. Now, I say, all those trusted together do point forth the odious nature of the sin of hypocrisy; may it not be an argument to press you to guard against hypocrisy?

The third consideration to press you to guard against hypocrisy is this: it is the sin which God does especially hate and abhor. Would you know the thing which God does especially hate, and His soul does loathe? It is the evil of hypocrisy. "These six things doth the LORD hate: yea, seven are an abomination unto him" (Prov. 6:16). And would you know what leads the van? There is, first, a "proud look" that looks to conceit; second, there is a "lying tongue," which is hypocrisy (v. 17). It is evil for a man to speak fair to God and yet have abomination in his heart. The same may be gathered from Proverbs 11:20: "But such as are upright in their way are his delight." By the rule of contraries, he who is not straight and upright in his way is abomination unto God. I am afraid the soul of the Lord is disjoined from many of us, and that He hates us; as it were, He does not hear us speak, nor hear us pray. The sacrifice of the hypocrite is abomination unto the Lord. Why? Because he brings it with a wicked mind. There are some who can paint their prayers, who can never make spiritual prayers.

The fourth consideration to press you to guard against hypocrisy is this: that hypocrisy is that which keeps a Christian from a stayed, composed, and constant walk with God. "A double minded man is unstable in all his ways" (James 1:8). You will never find the hypocrite where you left him at another time. I tell you what the hypocrite is: he is that which we call the weather cock that is put in some high place, which turns as ever the wind turns. He is, as it were, in a perpetual circle and motion. It is a searching word which Christ has for us in Matthew 6:16, where Christ makes mention of some who were Christians in their faces, but who were not Christians in their hearts. There are some who lodge Christ in their looks, who never lodge Him in their hearts; these are they who disfigure their faces and appear outwardly to fast, but within are nothing. I say, would you be fixed, trusting in the Lord? Then by all means study to guard against this evil of hypocrisy.

The fifth consideration to move you to guard against hypocrisy is this: that hypocrisy is the mother of pride, and pride the daughter of hypocrisy. In short, hypocrisy and pride will never sunder. I defy a person to be proud, but he is a hypocrite; and to be a hypocrite, but he is proud. "Behold, his soul which is lifted up is not upright in him" (Hab. 2:4), that is, the soul who is presumptuous is not sincere. For clearing of this, I would have you take notice of this: pride does ofttimes consist more in the affections than in the thoughts; pride does stand more in desire than it does in our light. Some persons, when they are thinking of themselves, will say, "O I am but a poor unworthy man," and, "There is none like me," and yet that person will fret if any other body speak anything of him but good; he will desire all men to speak good of him, and to have high thoughts of him, though he has something in him which may seem to say he has no high thoughts of himself. Therefore, observe this: pride consists as much in desires and affections as in thoughts. For though you should have no high thoughts of yourself yet you desire others to have high thoughts of you, and your being affected with sorrow for lack of those high thoughts of you in others, that is pride. I do think the hypocrite has these three steps of pride ordinarily attending him. First, he cannot abide that any should excel him in gifts; that is a thing very anxious to him. Second, he cannot abide that any should exceed him in applause. And, third, he cannot abide that any should excel him in diligence, at least the report of it. The hypocrite's pride vents itself in that; he cannot abide that any should be above him. And O is not this the language of our cursed hearts? "I am, and there is none beside me." Yes, such is the desperate pride of our hearts, that when any will speak good of us, then most ordinarily our hearts will begin to speak good of themselves.

The sixth consideration to press you to guard against hypocrisy is this: it is impossible for the person who is under the foot of hypocrisy to profit by the preaching of the word. What is the reason that you profit not by all that is spoken to you from day to day? It is even this: you are not upright and sincere. "Do not my words do good to him that walketh uprightly?" (Micah 2:7). That is, God's words do good to them who are sincere; and, upon the contrary, it does not profit them who are hypocrites. I suppose much sincerity would make us excellent by hearing sermons. I tell you three great ends the hypocrite has in coming to sermons. First, a hypocrite comes oft to the church rather to edify his light than to better his affections, that is, rather to have his knowledge increased than to have affections in order. That is a cursed design. I know, a person may come to have his light bettered; but O do not make it your only design and end to have your light bettered. There is a second end of a hypocrite's coming to the public ordinances, and that is to satisfy his natural conscience or, third, to be seen of men. Now, none of these are gracious, right principles of obedience. Or, fourth, this is ordinarily our end in coming to the public ordinances: to satisfy our curiosity more than to satisfy our case; hence it is that in preaching we are more taken up in the hearing of gifts than in the application of what is said. Now, what is the reason you profit not by preaching? It is this: your hypocrisy. "As newborn babes, desire the sincere milk of the word" (1 Pet. 2:2), and "[lay] aside all…hypocrisies" (v. 1).

The seventh consideration to help you to guard against hypocrisy is this: the lack of sincerity, and the having of hypocrisy, is an obstruction of communion and fellowship with God. Would you know the reason why some persons are admitted so seldom to converse and correspond with God? It is even this: we are not sincere. "For an hypocrite shall not come before him" (Job 13:16), that is, be whom he will that God does admit before Him, the hypocrite is never the man. "His countenance doth behold the upright" (Ps. 11:7). And, by the rule of contraries, the person who is not sincere shall not behold the countenance of God. I am persuaded of this: if sincerity were our royal attainment, and if we pursued sincerity and truth in the inward parts, we would have six enjoyments of God where we have not one; for the hypocrite can neither seek enjoyments nor improve them when he has them. "The upright shall dwell in [God's] presence" (Ps. 140:13). Would you know the person who is admitted to fellowship and communion with God? It is the sincere and upright Christian. The hypocrite is the person who is not admitted at all to dwell in His presence. And I may say that the hypocrisy even of His sons and daughters is that which does exceedingly impede that noble and precious correspondence which should be between them and heaven.

The eighth consideration to help you to guard against hypocrisy is this: the person who is a hypocrite is a person who is near a fall. Would you know the person who will keep his feet best in a stormy day? It is the sincere Christian. "He that walketh uprightly walketh surely" (Prov. 10:9). A sincere Christian will wrestle through many difficulties and overcome many temptations which would overtake the hypocrite. O you who would overcome temptations, I would press this upon you, to study truth in the inward parts.

Now that which, second, I shall speak to shall be this: *What is the reason that hypocrisy is such an abundant[1] and universal evil among many?* I shall name to you these five reasons why hypocrisy is so common an evil.

The first reason of it is this: most folks love exceedingly well to be spoken of, and therefore it is that hypocrisy is so common. In short, I think pride is the very rise of hypocrisy. Believe it: if there were less pride, there would be less hypocrisy; for there are many

---

1. Original, "rife."

persons who desire to be spoken of, and will take on a profession that they may attain the applause of men. However, I think indeed it is but a poor heaven for a person to have the approbation of men who are liars.

The second thing which is the rise of hypocrisy is that persons are not afraid to take on a profession without fear. Many take up religion at their foot and are not afraid they shall not be answerable to their profession. I think it were suitable for a person, when he takes on a profession, to tremble three days in the bitterness of his soul. Alas! I fear there are many fearless professors in this time, and that will make many apostate professors in the time of trial.

The third reason why hypocrisy is so common is this: many persons live not with trembling before the omniscience of God. Oh! Did you know that He is a searcher of the hearts, and trier of the reins? This knowledge would indeed help you much against hypocrisy. David, rendering a reason of his sincerity and uprightness, says, "I know also, my God, that thou triest the heart" (1 Chron. 29:17). If we did believe that God did behold us better than we do ourselves, we wouldn't dare practice so much counterfeit religion, but, alas, We say, "God does not see."

The fourth reason why hypocrisy does so much abound is this: persons are destitute of the fear of God. This may be gathered from Joshua 24:14 where he presses them to sincerity, from the fear of the Lord. I am sure if we were walking much under the impression of the fear of the Lord, we would not dare practice counterfeit religion so much as we do.

The fifth reason that hypocrisy is so common is this: persons are not convinced of the necessity of sincerity. Many think profession an excellent thing, but they cannot abide to be bound to all the duties of religion. I think it is too ordinary what an atheist spoke, "The profession of religion is pleasant, but the practice of religion is unpleasant." Some love the coat of Christ but love not the real grace of Christ; some would have a form of godliness but care not indeed for the power of godliness.

That which, third, I shall speak to shall be this: I shall propose six marks of the hypocrite whereby you may know whether or not this discourse has been to you.

The first mark of a hypocrite that I shall give shall be from our Scripture: "They cry not when [God] bindeth them" (Job 36:13); that is, under the cross a hypocrite cries not unto God. There are three crosses that will be exceeding great trials to a hypocrite: the cross of desertion, the cross of darkness, and the cross of outward poverty. All these crosses will be great trials to a person's sincerity. Now, are there not some who, let Christ desert them never so often, they cry not when God binds them? Though their spirits be under never so many bonds, they do not cry unto God. I say, it is an undeniable evidence of a hypocrite not to cry when he is under desertion and bonds; and I suppose, if that be a mark of a hypocrite, many of us may cry, "Guilty!" I would ask you this question: Are there not many who have been called Christians who it is thirty days since they saw the King [by faith] and yet never sent a sigh unto God for that? And are you not then the persons who cry not when God binds them? O is there not a man or woman here who will own this, that they cry not when God binds them? Are there not many bonds upon the spirits of many and yet they cry not when God binds them? I tell you who the hypocrite is like: he is like Issachar, couching down between two burdens (Gen. 49:14). O fear and stand in awe, you who cry not when God binds you, lest you be a hypocrite. Now I would press this home upon you: Are there not many who, under the sad and afflicting dispensations they meet with, know not what it is to cry unto God? I tell you the worst cross a hypocrite can bear: it is reproach.

The second mark of a hypocrite (which will be yet searching, and indeed ought to put you to trial) is this: it is an undeniable mark of a hypocrite to be more affected with one spot upon his face than with ten spots upon his heart. Before there was one blemish upon his face, he would rather have a thousand blemishes upon his heart. O but, before we would see anything wrong without, we would rather let all go wrong within! I am sure, be who he will, that is the person of whom the text speaks, and he is the hypocrite in heart. Many are more afraid to be found sinners by men than by God. Some would rather be known by men to be Christians, yet would choose to be damnable atheists unto God, and let none know of it. I would ask you thus: Are there not some, as long as their sin is hidden, and none of the world knows of it, who will never shed a tear for it? But let once the world know of it, and their hearts will be distracted with sorrow. There are some who are guilty of the sin of fornication, of which the world does not know, and in this case, they will never have a sad heart for it. But let once the world know it, and they will weep bitterly. And this is the reason: we choose rather to lose the approbation of God than the approbation of men. Yea, know it: some would rather lose the approbation of heaven than the approbation of ministers.

The third mark of one who is a hypocrite (and I would desire you to search yourselves by it) is this: as for the hypocrite in heart, it is the very scope and end of the most part of his duties to be seen of men. "But all their works they do for to be seen of men" (Matt. 23:5). Are there not many of us who, when we go to pray, wish that all our acquaintances would know we are praying at such a time? Yea, is not this a secret piece of our hypocrisy, that we will be glad when others do surprise us [while we are] praying? Some can never say that ever they prayed from a right principle, nor to a right end. I think when the books shall be opened, many of our prayers, and the ends of our going to communions, shall make us ashamed. I do not discommend the duties but, alas, the most part of our actions are to be seen of men.

The fourth mark of one who is a hypocrite is this: he is a person who never did suspect his hypocrisy. Hypocrites have the confidence that they are always sincere. I say, sincerity is ofttimes joined with some suspicion of hypocrisy.

The fifth evidence of hypocrisy is this: a person who is a hypocrite loves many things more than God, he trusts many things more than God, he obeys many things more than God, he desires many things more than God, and he fears man more than God. So that there are these five great idols of a hypocrite: love, fear, obedience, desire, and faith. I call the idols of faith anything that a person trusts in more than God. I call the idols of love anything a person fears more than God; and I call the idols of desire anything a person desires more than God. Now, I say, a hypocrite has all these five idols dwelling within him.

The sixth evidence of one who is a hypocrite is this: he is more taken up in the pursuit of visible holiness than of invisible holiness, and is more taken up in pursuing after the shadow of religion than after the substance of religion. I would have you know this: there are some who have indeed begotten themselves into a lively hope, whom Christ did never beget (Matt. 23:26–28). It is a strange word in which Job compares the hope of the hypocrite to a spider's web (Job 8:14). Now, what is the reason that the hope of the hypocrite is like the spider's web? This is one ground of it: as the spider's web is spun out of its own bowels, so the hope of a hypocrite is spun out of his own conceit and bowels, without any foundation or ground from God. Alas! The day is coming that fearfulness shall surprise the hypocrites in Zion.

I have these five questions to ask the hypocrite, and then I shall close.

The first question that I would ask the hypocrite is that question that Abijah asked of Jeroboam's wife, "Why feignest thou thyself to be another?" (1 Kings 14:6). O hypocrite, what is the reason you pretend[2] to be a real Christian, since you are not indeed real? What is the reason you pretend to be so?

The second question that I would ask the hypocrite is this: Do you think that hypocrisy and the form of religion will bring you to heaven? I say, if you had a profession a thousand times bigger than it is, it should never bring you to heaven. I confess indeed that a profession of religion is beautiful, and that a good name is excellent; but O if you could be persuaded to pursue less after the approbation of men, and more after the approbation of God! I think that word which is spoken of Demetrius—"Demetrius hath good report of all men, and of the truth itself" (3 John 12)—I say, put these two together, to be of good report of all men and of the truth itself, and you have an excellent combination.

The third question that I would ask the hypocrite is this: Think you that you can satisfy God with a profession? O know it: the joy of the hypocrite is but for a moment. Speaking of the joy of the hypocrite, Job says, "Though his excellency mount up to the heavens, and his head reach unto the clouds.... He shall fly away as a dream, and shall not be found" (Job 20:6, 8). O know it: God is One whose eyes are as a flame of fire that can discern the secrets and intents of the heart.

---

2. Original, "feigneth."

There is this, fourth, that I would ask you, namely, what a poor advantage have you, though everyone who knows you should cry, "Hosanna, hosanna," and should be praising you in the gate, and all your acquaintance should be putting an eminent note of excellency upon you? If Christ shall say to you, "Depart from me," what a poor advantage have you? What does it matter though all men speak evil to us, if Christ speak good of us? And what does it matter though all men speak good of us, if Christ does not believe it? Christ's commendation is worth the commendation of a world of precious saints.

There is this, lastly, that I would ask you, namely, what poor beauty and excellency is in the form of religion? And what exquisite and unspeakable beauty is in the power of religion? Now, what is the reason you are so much taken up in pursuing that which is less beautiful? And neglecting to pursue that which is yet more beautiful? I shall give you these two reasons why some pursue more the form than the power of religion. First, the form of religion is much more easily gotten than the power of it, and that is the reason why many persons seek the form of religion yet seek not the power of it. It is easy to be a Christian in name, but it is not easy to be a Christian in deed. The second reason why persons seek the form of religion and not the substance of it is because some persons can discern the beauty of the form of religion who cannot discern the beauty of the substance of religion. Search your own hearts and you will find this to be the ground why many persons pursue the form of religion yet do not pursue after the reality and substance of it. I desire you, as in the sight of God who shall one day judge your hearts, that you would pursue after truth in the inward parts. I shall say no more to guard against any who may take advantage from what is not said against the mere form without the power of religion, but that they take this along with them: we have not in all this been speaking against the professions of religion. I would say these two words to such. First, you who are so grossly profane, will you be convinced of this: Must not religion be an excellent thing, that so many fall in love with the very form of it? I say, if there were no more to convince profane persons that religion is an excellent thing but this, it would be more than sufficient. O strangers to godliness, must not religion be a precious thing, seeing there are thousands in the visible church who are lovers of the very form of it? Second, I would say this: if a person who has the form of godliness come short of heaven, how much rather you who have neither the form nor the substance of godliness? I entreat the persons whom this discourse concerns that they would search their hearts, and see if this root of bitterness be in them. As likewise, you who are strangers of God, will you be provoked to give up your hearts unto Him, and make an everlasting resignation of yourselves to Him? Now unto Him who is able to persuade you, we desire to give praise.

The Great Prejudice of Slothfulness (Part 1)

"Slothfulness casteth into a deep sleep."
—Proverbs 19:15

Where is the advantage and profit of all the pains that are taken upon you? Is my preaching merely like writing on the sand and plowing upon the rock, which leaves no impression? I preach much unto you, and you hear much from day to day, and yet you do not profit. I would say this: there is no preaching that shall ever do you good till it be preached three times. I don't mean it ought to be merely *said* three times to you, but it must be *preached* three times before it does you good.

First, it must be preached from heaven to the minister's heart. Second, it must be preached from his heart unto the people. Third, the people must preach it to their own hearts over again. And the lack of some of these steps is the reason that often we have occasion to cry forth, "My leanness, my leanness, woe unto me" (Isa. 24:16). Are you not longing for the reproach of your barrenness to be taken away, that that commandment might come forth, "O barren, thou that didst not bear; break forth into singing, and cry aloud, thou that didst not travail with child" (Isa. 54:1)? This evil of slothfulness, we conceive, was a most reigning and universal evil in those days. In Proverbs 19:15, we have slothfulness painted forth in a most lively form and shape, that people may be constrained to hate it, to loathe it. There are four things to notice in this verse.

First, slothfulness, sluggishness, and neglect of duty are evils that people ought to avoid and shun. Second, slothfulness is the mother of deep security ("slothfulness casteth into a deep sleep"). Third, slothfulness is the forerunner of many sad spiritual strokes which a person shall meet. The fourth observation is made by comparing verse 15 with verse 16—"He that keepeth the commandment keepeth his own soul; but he that despiseth his ways shall die"—that slothfulness is a soul-destroying sin; it is that which is the ruin of our precious souls. Let me expand on these four observations.

That people ought to shun slothfulness, sluggishness, and neglect of duty is clear in Romans 12:11: "[Be] not slothful in business; [be] fervent in spirit; serving the Lord." The same is true for Hebrews 6:12: "Be not slothful, but followers of them who through faith and patience inherit the promises." It is likewise clear that we ought to beware of slothfulness, as shown by the constant experience of the saints who have gone before us, those who have diligently and constantly acted according to their duty. Psalm 132:4 provides an example of this: "I will not give sleep to mine eyes, or slumber to my eyelids." It is also made clear from the many disadvantages and inconveniencies that wait upon slothfulness; the truth of this is found in the Scripture. Lastly, it is clear that it is the duty of a Christian especially to avoid slothfulness, because of the many excellent commandments that are given to diligence and the many sweet advantages that wait upon the Christian who makes godliness his exercise.

Now, before I can proceed to speak any further unto this truth, I would clarify a little what slothfulness is by making these five points. First, it stands in a Christian's neglect of known duty, that notwithstanding such a thing is known to be our duty, yet we will sinfully neglect it. Second, it stands in a Christian's fleeing the opportunity that he has for going about duty. When there is an occasion sent unto you to pray, you dreadfully flee the opportunity and will not set about to do it. Third, it stands in a person's not seeking and awaiting an opportunity for the doing of duty. Some will not at all exercise themselves in this, in seeking and awaiting an opportunity in which they may go about duty. Fourth, it stands in the smallest temptation of diversion that one meets with—such a diversion will be a sufficient impediment to hinder one from duty, a woeful step of a person's slothfulness. And, lastly, which is the capstone of slothfulness, is that oftentimes people are glad when they meet with such a diversion from duty; we are more glad to embrace the temptation of the devil than he is to tempt us.

Regarding its nature, what is the rise, the origin, the fountain of the dreadful slothfulness that is among many? What are the reasons that people are such dreadful neglecters of known duty, the influences that cause this to be so? The first thing that has influence upon it is much worldly-mindedness, and those heart pursuits and engagements after and unto our idols and the things of this world. Know you not that verse, "No man can serve two masters" (Matt. 6:24)? If you make the world your master, you cannot make Christ your Master. It is good to make the world our servant, but it is a desperate iniquity to make it our master: "Every man that striveth [that is, would be diligent] for the mastery is temperate [or moderate] in all things" (1 Cor. 9:25). Compare also Isaiah 64:6–7: "Our iniquities, like the wind, have taken us away...and there is none that calleth upon [God]." Is it not known that our hearts are so bent upon the world that it is almost a burden for us to give any time to duty? I would have you take this along with you: it is a great mistake among people who say that prayer may help a Christian to comfort, prayer may help a Christian to heaven, prayer may help a minister to preach, but it will not help a merchant to sell his wares and another tradesman to exercise his calling. For I have known merchants that knew their own hearts better than some of us do who assured me that they never had the spirit of their employment better than when they prayed best and most in the morning. Now, as you would not lie under this evil of slothfulness, then stop your hearts in the pursuit of the things of the world.

The second thing that has influence upon our slothfulness is our lack of delight in God and love unto Him. Is it possible that people who have delight in the Lord, people whose hearts burn within them with love, can be so little in the exercise of duty as we are? Believe it: our little exercise of duty is a speaking evidence of the decay of delight in God and love to Him. In Isaiah 43:22, the fathers neglect their duty upon the lack of delight in God. I am sure that delight in God would make us bow more often to God than we do; delight in God would make it a weariness for us to desist from the duty of prayer. It is no wonder some of us do not pray much, and do not meditate much, and do not read the Scriptures much—because we question much if ever the fire of love was kindled in our hearts. "O sleeper...arise, call upon thy God" (Jonah 1:6). If delight in God were our mercy and our exercise, we would think it our burden to be shut out from His presence but one day.

A third thing that has influence upon it is our formality in duty when we go about it. Nothing is so much the forerunner of slothfulness as to be formal in duty when we go about it. These two sister sins are joined together. "There is none that calleth upon thy name, that stirreth up himself to take hold of thee" (Isa. 64:7). If once you come that length to go about duty in a formal and indifferent way, ere long this shall be your lot: you will be unwilling to go about any duty. I am sure if some overheard us pray when we are alone they might say, "I am sure yonder person cares not whether he be heard or no." And it is, we think, one of the most dreadful evidences of the self-seeking that reigns in many that, when they pray in company, they will hoist up all their sails and wait for the coming of the wind, and there will not be an expression that may help for the getting of liberty but they will make use of it; and, when they are alone, they will let their words fall to the ground and will not stir themselves up to take hold of God. What does this mean? It means in your public prayers you seek yourselves more than God. And I am sure if you were seeking Him in public, you would seek Him in private also.

A fourth thing that has influence upon it is this: there are three constraining fountains and principles of doing duty which are not lively upon our hearts. Know you the three things that drive Christians unto duty? Love, necessity, and fear. And if none of these be lively upon a Christian's heart, he will not pray much aright. Love unto God, and delight in Him, is that which leads a Christian to duty, and so necessities, when they are lively and apprehended, will make Christians go up to the fountain which is able to compensate and fill up the depth of their necessity. The depth of necessity leads up to the fullness of God; necessity leads a Christian to duty. I tell you what necessity is like—it is like hunger. If a man be hungry, he will dig through stone walls for meat; so necessity, if it be lively upon a Christian, he would rather go far off than want an opportunity to pray. Necessity has not a desire but to be near God. And also love, when it is lively upon a Christian's spirit, is the principle of his obedience, according to the Scriptures, "If ye love me, keep my commandments" (John 14:15). Love never knew what it was to flee and dispute a commandment. This is the great divinity of love: "God hath spoken in his holiness; I will rejoice" (Ps. 108:7). And love cries out, "All that the LORD hath spoken we will do" (Ex. 19:8). Fear is that which puts a Christian to duty: fear to offend the majesty of God, and fear of the disadvantages that attend the neglect of duty. "Thou castest off fear, and restrainest prayer before God" (Job 15:4).

Fifth, the dreadful atheism that is among many has influence upon it. Atheists do not believe there is a God, and therefore they flee that which He calls for. This is clear by reading Psalm 14:1–3. This set of verse begins, "The fool hath said in his heart, There is no God." And, in the end of the passage, there is "not one" who seeks God. That is a speaking evidence of our atheism — we do sinfully flee and neglect known duties.

Sixth, this has influence upon slothfulness, and neglect of those duties that God calls for at our hands, namely, the sweetness and beauty of duties are gone away from us. Some look upon the duties of religion as their burden, and some look upon the duties of religion as their bond and obligation, but few of us look upon the duties of religion as our honor. Now, till once you come to this understanding—to think the duties of religion as much a part of your honor as a part of your subjection—it will be much for you to be constant in the exercise of them. Is it not certain that, before we prayed sometimes, we had rather go very far off? We do not abide to subject ourselves to the yoke of Christ, and hence it is that we cry forth, "O what a weariness it is to serve the Lord!" We think it hard to subject ourselves to all those things which He calls for at our hands.

Seventh, there is this that has as much influence upon it as any other thing, though it be not much observed: there are many who have not come to believe the reality of this, that godliness is great gain. And no doubt, if the reality, the beauty, and the advantage of godliness were believed, we could not but walk in the paths of it. I think, indeed, that he who has come to believe and be persuaded in his soul of this, that godliness is a real thing, that he has come to a good length. And, if people will search themselves, they will find that many of the evils of those days, and those evils that are to be found with them, have sprung from this root of bitterness, the want of the faith of this, that godliness is great gain. I desire you to believe that godliness is no fancy or mere notion—ere long it shall be made to appear a truth.

The eighth thing that has influence upon it is that the great dominion that our idols have over us and the reigning power of our predominant lusts are that which lead us aside from the doing of duty. I tell you two great idols that are enemies to diligence, and are therefore the parents of slothfulness. There is that great idol of self-righteousness, for which people have great respect. This is clear in Song of Solomon 5:3, "I have washed my feet; how shall I defile them?" That is, "I have attained to such a length of sanctification that I need not trouble myself for more." And hence it is that "the sluggard is wiser in his own conceit than seven men that can render a reason" (Prov. 26:16). But Paul says, "This one thing I do, forgetting those things which are behind, and reaching forth unto those things which are before" (Phil. 3:13). The second idol that has much influence upon it is self-indulgence; we do not put ourselves to any toil and labor. That is oftentimes our word unto ourselves, the word of self-pity, which Peter had unto Christ (cf. Matt. 16:22). And O what cursed pity and cruel mercy we have unto ourselves! I may say, the mercy of such a cruel one is but cruelty. We do not want to lack an hour's sleep, even if we should have an hour's enjoyment of Christ.

Now I shall, second, propose some considerations to hold forth the aggravations of this sin of slothfulness. There is this first aggravation of it, that persons flee a duty though they have an opportunity to do it. They will flee and sin away a golden occasion that they have for the doing of duty. A person who has come this length may know that slothfulness has a great power and dominion over him. Is it not oftentimes so? I think that if we knew of all the times we neglected duty when we had opportunity to do it, and have been under the conviction of its being our duty, we would be ashamed of ourselves. Yea, to make this stronger, there are some, when they have the opportunity to do duty, and conviction that it is their duty, the very air of a temptation, yea, the very power of slothfulness, will make them flee that duty.

The second aggravation of slothfulness is this: when the opportunity to pray and the motions of the Spirit come together, we flee the duty. It is not certain we will sometimes have an opportunity to pray, and likewise there will be the beginnings and forerunners of an approaching enjoyment, and of the sweet breathings of the Spirit; the heart will be, as it were, all on wing. And yet, notwithstanding both of these, you will sit alone and keep silence? That is a mighty aggravation of slothfulness; it is for a person to say, "I care not for Christ." And when He sends the forerunner of His approaching presence, we close all the doors of our hearts that He may not enter in.

The third aggravation of slothfulness is this: when we have an opportunity, and when the beauty of the duty is also revealed unto us, yet we neglect it. Is it not sometimes that God will present an opportunity, and the beauty of the duty is also revealed unto us, yet we neglect it? Is it not sometimes that God will present an opportunity to pray, and He will reveal to the soul the sweetness, the beauty, and the advantage of the duty, and yet at the same time the Christian will flee the call and keep silence and not bow unto God? Now, no question—that is a great aggravation of slothfulness. It is the same as for a person to say he cares not for the doing of His commandments, even when they are adorned with all beauty.

The fourth aggravation of slothfulness is for people to neglect duty after the Lord has appeared unto them in that duty twice, after eminent discoveries of the beauty, excellency, and sweetness of Christ in such a duty. This was the aggravation of Solomon's sin: "And the LORD was angry with Solomon, because his heart was turned from the LORD God of Israel, which had appeared unto him twice" (1 Kings 11:9). Now, is not this a great aggravation of this sin, that after in prayer we have tasted of the sweetness that causes the lips of those who are asleep to speak, after in prayer we have been caught up to the third heaven, after in prayer we have tasted of that excellent inheritance, after those discoveries of God in prayer and other duties—yet the person will flee that duty? This was the aggravation of the bride, when you compare her security in Song of Solomon 5:1 with her fleeing from Christ in verses 2 and 3. In the first verse is the enjoyment she had of Christ, and yet upon the back of that she flees His invitation. This tells us that many of us do not truly care about enjoying God. Sometimes people have found so much of God in prayer that they have been forced to call the place of their praying Ebenezer, the place of living after seeing. Yet, after that they flee duty — what a dreadful offense! And how will God contend with that person, after the Lord has appeared unto him twice?

The fifth aggravation of it is for a person to flee duty after the Lord has appeared to them, while at the same time bearing convictions of the great disadvantages that do attend the neglect of that duty. It is known that sometimes God has taken pains to point out the disadvantages that come to us by the neglect of duty; yet at the same time when you have known it is an evil and a bitter thing to depart from the Lord, and to flee His commandments, you through slothfulness will cry out, "Yet a little sleep, a little slumber, a little folding of the hands to sleep" (Prov. 24:33). Is it not a great sin to flee duty, after the unanswerable convictions of the disadvantages that we have by the neglect of it?

The sixth aggravation of slothfulness is for people who have neglected their known duty, who, after strong resolutions and covenants taken upon their hearts, commit that they will not flee duty any more, but continue to do so. Did not some take on such resolutions at the last Communion in this place, such as, "I shall be more in secret duty than ever I was before"? Did not some take on that resolution, "God shall be more the delight of my soul, and the cover of my eyes, and the desire of my heart, than ever He was before"? Now, have you not fled those duties, after those bonds and resolutions were taken on upon your heart? Would you not then have written upon your foreheads, "Their heart was not right with [God], neither were they stedfast in his covenant" (Ps. 78:37)?

The seventh aggravation of it is that there are some people here today who have heard some when they were passing in through the gates of death, when the eye strings[1] had begun to break, and the shadows of death had been sitting on their eyelids, who had this complaint, "Alas, for the days that I have fled duty so much!"

---

1. "Eye strings," the system of the eye that was thought to break at death or the onset of blindness.

I think there are many who sometimes have heard such a complaint; and what a dreadful aggravation is this of your sin? I shall say of the professors of this time, it is possible some of them may be saved, but I doubt much if there be many of the professors of this time who shall be saved but so as by fire. And what is the reason that many people who die in these days (whom we, in charity, suppose to have Christ in them, the hope of glory) enter into heaven under a cloud? Is it not their neglect of exercising themselves unto godliness, and their not making it their work?

The third thing that I shall speak to, and with which I shall close, is some disadvantages that wait upon this evil of slothfulness. And the first that I shall name is a takeaway from the text: slothfulness is the mother of deep security. Some people ask, "What is the reason that they have a sleeping conscience, sleeping affections, and a sleeping judgment?" It is that they are not diligent in duty. "Slothfulness casteth into a deep sleep" (Prov. 19:5). It is like a nurse—it rocks you in the cradle of a deep sleep. Slothfulness has made many sleep a long time, and if there were no more to press you to guard against it but this, that it is the mother of security, it would be more than sufficient.

Second, the slothful Christian is the Christian who has not much communion with God, nor enjoyment of Him. Many in these days have this question, "What is the reason that God and I never meet? In preaching and prayer, and every duty that I go about, this may be written upon it, 'God is not here.' What is the reason that I go not in sometimes to the chambers of presence and am not satisfied with honey out of the rock?" It is even this—slothfulness and neglect of duty is that which draws a veil between Christ and you. "Seest thou a man diligent in his business? He shall stand before kings" (Prov. 22:29). We may take the words in a spiritual sense, that a Christian diligent in his duty and active in his work shall stand before the King and have enjoyment of God. Scripture says, "The hand of the diligent maketh rich" (Prov. 10:4) and, "The soul of the diligent shall be made fat" (Prov. 13:4). The reason that oftentimes there is a veil drawn between Christ and you is your neglect of duty.

A third disadvantage that comes by slothfulness is the rise and origin of those decays, backslidings, and ruins of the work of God which are in the hearts of many in these days. Are there not many who may write this on their foreheads, "Decay, decay, decay"? What is the reason that love, faith, tenderness, and mortification are dying around us so much? Is it the dreadful slothfulness and fleeing of duty that is with us? "By much slothfulness the building decayeth; and through idleness of the hands the house droppeth through" (Eccl. 10:18). Your slothfulness in known duty is that which makes your building decay. I suppose some make so little progress in the duties of religion, and their buildings do so little advance, that they may be put to that question, "Shall ever the copestone be put on, and I have occasion to cry, 'Grace, grace to it'?"

The fourth disadvantage that comes by slothfulness is that it impairs, darkens, and exceedingly deforms the beauty and excellency of the Christian. Slothfulness makes Christians like beggars—once, they were in an excellent estate, and now they have become exceedingly low through slothfulness. This is made clear in Proverbs 23:21, "Drowsiness shall clothe a man with rags." The beautiful robes and the change of raiment that once they were clothed with are now taken away, and they are now clothed with rags.

Fifth, it is the rise of the prevailing power our idols have over us. Some ask that question, "What is the reason my idols do so much prevail?" It is that you are slothful. This is clear in Proverbs 12:24, "The hand of the diligent shall bear rule: but the slothful shall be under tribute." The slothful Christian shall be in subjection to his lusts and idols. It is no wonder every temptation that meets us prevails over us, because we are not diligent. We who do engage ourselves in this blessed war do entangle ourselves with the vanities of this world.

The sixth disadvantage that waits upon it is this: slothfulness and neglect of duty are the mother of formality in duty. What is the reason that some, when they go to prayer, are under so many bonds? It is even this: you pray but seldom, and so you cannot have much liberty when you pray. Some pray so seldom to God that, in a manner, when they pray, they cannot get words to tell what ails them. "There is none that calleth upon thy name, that stirreth up himself to take hold of thee" (Isa. 64:7). There is no question that if a Christian would endeavor to be serious and active, he would be diligent.

The seventh disadvantage that waits upon slothfulness is that a slothful Christian is the Christian who breaks forth into debates against God's interests. It is impossible for a slothful Christian to be in much clearness concerning his peace with God. What is the reason that the consciences of some people speak such terrible things against them? It is this: they exercise not themselves unto godliness. What is the reason that some of us have not the "peace of God, which passeth all understanding, [guarding our] hearts and minds" (Phil. 4:7)? It is because we do not "in every thing by prayer and supplication with thanksgiving let [our] requests be made known unto God" (v. 6).

The last disadvantage that comes by slothfulness is this: all duties of religion become a burden unto the slothful Christian. What is the reason that preaching becomes a burden to many, and all that God requires we cannot abide? It is slothfulness. "The way of the slothful man is as an hedge of thorns"—a slothful Christian, before he would pray, would rather go through a hedge of thorns and cut himself—"but the way of the righteous is made plain"—the way of the diligent Christian is easy (Prov. 15:19). Now I say, "If you would have the duties of religion to become your delight, then be much in the exercise of Christian diligence."

I shall not stand to speak much more at this time, it not being the multiplying of words that will do it. I shall only add, that you may go away with advantage by what is said, two words by way of application. First, I would seriously desire you who flee your duties—not only in public, but when you are alone—I would desire that this day you would be engaged to set about the duty of prayer. I think there are many houses in Glasgow that are very like hell, there being nothing heard in them but the voice of cursing and sinful speaking. You do not indeed know God, and therefore you do not care for the serving of Him.

There are three great objections in the hearts of them who are acquainted with God which hinder them from the exercise of prayer. The first is this: "O what need I pray, or obey the minister, when he bids me read the Scriptures and hear preaching and think upon my own state and condition? If I be predestinate to life, I will win heaven whether I pray and read or not; and if I be predestinate to hell, though I should pray and weep all my days, I will never win heaven." That is the very old temptation of the devil. But I say this: may you not argue thus with your own hearts also, "If I be appointed to be a rich man, I shall become rich though I never put my hands to labor"? And, second, why will you not also reason thus with yourselves, "If I be appointed to live forty years, I need neither eat nor drink, for I will live that time whether I eat or drink or no"? I say this to you: God has made a sweet conjunction between the end and the means that lead unto that end; God has predestined to life through the believing on His Son, so that there is a connection between the decree of God, the end of it, and the midst that leads unto that end.

The second objection is this: "I cannot pray; I know not what to say to God." I would say this: you who say you cannot pray condemn yourselves, when you have a tongue to speak and a heart to think. A person is bound in conscience by the commandment of the Lord, though he should not pray with his heart, to pray with his tongue. I say, pray with your tongue, if it were only to say, "Lord, help me to pray," till your heart comes up to this length. It is a strange word, "Take with you words…and say…" (Hos. 14:2). Now, what do you know but what God will bring up in your heart when you cannot bring it up yourself?

And there is that third objection of some: "Alas! I sin more when I pray than when I let prayer alone." To this I answer, "Perhaps you sin not more in prayer than when you do neglect it; but oftentimes it is thus: you see your sins better when you pray than when you are not praying." This is the ground of that objection: you sin not more in prayer, but you see your sins more in prayer than when you are not praying. And I would further say you ought to pray because you sin much in it. For it is not the fault of prayer that you sin much in it, but your own fault. Is this good divinity: "I am a very sinful man, and therefore I will not go to Christ; and I am polluted, therefore I will never go to the fountain to wash me"?

Now there is this, second, that I would close with: I would give that advice to all of you who are here which the mariners gave to Jonah, "O sleeper…arise, call upon thy God" (Jonah 1:6). Since your work is great and your day is almost spent, I entreat you to be serious and stirred to duty. It would be a shame for some of us to confess how seldom we pray—nay, we have come that length—to flee prayer without a conviction. I would say to such, look at the dreadful sentence which was passed upon the servant who received one talent and went and hid it in a napkin. Be this not your lot: "Cast ye the unprofitable servant into outer darkness" (Matt. 25:30). I pray you, what account will you make of all your gifts, of all your opportunities to serve God, and of all the sermons and lectures you have heard from the Word of the Lord? There are many to whom I may give that reproof which Pharaoh gave to the children of Israel: "Ye are idle, ye are idle" (Ex. 5:17). I would give that advice to many who are here which Christ gave unto him who stood idle in the marketplace, "Why stand ye here all the day idle?" (Matt. 20:6). This is the time and occasion for you to work, and I would desire to know what you intend to do, since all day you stand idle and do not work. No doubt it holds true that a person who will not work should not eat. Some Christians are like rich merchants who have gathered much and do now sit down and spend of the stock. So some Christians feed upon their experiences and think they are far enough advanced; they say to their own hearts, as that rich man says, "Soul, thou hast much goods laid up for many years; take thine ease" (Luke 12:19). A Christian who has taken that course shall go halting to heaven. I shall say no more but this: "Awake thou that sleepest, and arise from the dead, and Christ shall give thee light" (Eph. 5:14).

The Great Prejudice of Slothfulness (Part 2)

Slothfulness casteth into a deep sleep.
—Proverbs 19:15

There are many animals which Solomon speaks of in Proverbs 30:24–36, every one of which may teach man a spiritual lesson and doctrine. First, the ants may teach a man that lesson of Christian providence, that though they be "a people not strong, yet they prepare their meat in the summer." This ought to be the duty of every Christian, to provide against the day of straits. There is a second beast commended, and that is the conies, who may teach a Christian that lesson of humanity and self-denial. They be "but a feeble folk, yet make they their houses in the rocks"—so a Christian, not being strong in himself, might flee to the Rock which is stronger than himself. The third beast that he commends is the locusts, who "have no king, yet go forth all of them by bands." Thus a Christian should march forth in order under his King when he goes out to fight. The fourth beast that he commends is the spider, which "taketh hold with her hands, and is in kings' palaces," which may teach a man the lesson of Christian diligence that he should take hold of his duty and work that he may be brought into the King's presence.

I would only say this: slothfulness is the abomination that sits uppermost in our hearts. It was an ancient observation of Solomon that "he also that is slothful in his work is brother to him that is a great waster" (Prov. 18:9). And I think, if it were the fruit and advantage of our doctrine that persons under this idol of slothfulness were wakened and stirred up to diligence, we might go away with joy. As for you who have Christ in you, the hope of glory, I would ask this question of you: Do you not think Christ as precious as ever He was? Is there not as much sweetness, as much advantage to be found in Christ, as ever was to be found in Him? Now, if it be so, what is the reason we take so little pains to correspond with Him? What is the reason that there is so little travelling of the soul between infinite emptiness and infinite fullness, infinite inability in a Christian to help himself and complete ability in Christ to help him, that the one deep is not crying unto the other deep? Many of us are likely to go down to our graves in our misery and barrenness because of our slothfulness.

At the last occasion that we spoke upon these words, I told you that there are four observations in them, the first of which was that slothfulness and neglect of duty was an evil ordinarily incident to many. This, we told you, was clear in the scope, and from this truth we have spoken to several things. There are yet three things that remain further to be spoken of from it.

The first thing that I shall speak to at this time is to propose *eight considerations to press you to guard against this evil of slothfulness and neglect of duty*. I would exhort you, since it is not a matter of small concern, and since everlasting advantage lies in the doing of duty, that you would be stirred up by these considerations, now at last to take this bond upon your heart, that you shall be exercised unto godliness.

The first consideration is this: the work that a Christian has to do is exceedingly great, and his journey is very long. Therefore awake, and be not slothful. I suppose there are some here who may take up this complaint: "There is much of my day spent, and there is not much of my work done." Yea, there are some who have spent a great part of their day and are yet to begin their work. Now, since it is certain that your work is great, then, O sleeper, awake and shake off your slothfulness. Is not faith, and believing in the name of the Son of God, a great work? Is not mortification to your idols a great work? Is not sanctification and attaining to a blessed conformity with God a great work? Is not patience a great work? Is not assurance of our being in Christ a great work? And is not heavenly-mindedness a great work? Since all these great works are before you, will you not then shake off your slothfulness and stir yourselves? This is clear from 1 Peter 1, where he presses Christians to diligence, from the greatness of their work. He sets down there all the great works of religion as if he would press them to diligence from these, that faith, meekness, patience, virtue, and brotherly love are to be done by them. Know you not that a person who has a great work to do will rise early in the morning to do it? And a person who has a long journey to go before night will rise by the breaking of the day? And do you think eternity is not approaching? What do you think, O sleepers, slothful, and neglecters of the work that is of your everlasting concern? Will you not now be provoked to shake off that laziness that now has overtaken you? I would say this to every one of us: it is high time for us to awake, for our day is far spent. "O sleeper...arise, call upon thy God" (Jonah 1:6).

I think a Christian ought to answer all his temptations as Nehemiah answered the messengers of Sanballat, "I am doing a great work, so that I cannot come down" (Neh. 6:3). I say, when a temptation assaults you, you may say this, "O temptation, I have a great work to do, and therefore I cannot obey you."

The second consideration to press you to guard against slothfulness is that as the work is great, the time and the day in which you must do the work is very short. Christ said, "Are there not twelve hours in the day? If any man walk in the day, he stumbleth not, because he seeth the light of this world" (John 11:9). I say, what know you but this is the eleventh hour of your day, and you have only one hour to work in? That is a precious word of Christ, that I must walk while it is today, for the night comes in which no man can work. What know we but this may be the last sermon we shall attend? What know we but some of us who are here, who are lusty and strong, may yet be walking upon the borders of eternity, and before night we may hear the death bell toll for them? Now, once your day is short and very uncertain, then be provoked to rise from your sleep, and fall to your work, that when your Master comes He may find you so doing. But let not this scare off any of you from religion, that the work of it is so great and the day so short. If you have a great work, comfort yourselves with this: you have also a great reward. If you accomplish your work, though your work be great, there is a great recompense of reward also. There is great help laid upon One who is mighty, who shall communicate to you for doing your work. Is your work great, and your day short? Yet be pressed to set about your work, because there is a necessity lying upon you for doing the work of this day.

The third consideration to press you to guard against slothfulness is this: the fleeing of the duties of religion has an eternal disadvantage waiting upon it. Therefore, I say, awake, and stir yourselves. If the neglect of the duties of religion were attended only with outward disadvantages, then you might with more liberty cry out, "Yet a little sleep, a little slumber" (Prov. 24:33). But since the neglect of the duties of religion have eternal disadvantages waiting upon it, then I say, "O sleeper, awake, and shake off your sluggishness." The day is approaching when the persons in Glasgow who have fled private worship, public ordinances, and the duties of religion most shall cry out, "Alas for the day that ever I fled those things so much! O for the time again, and for sermons again! I should never flee them so much as I have done." What makes us to flee the duties of religion? It is even this: we do not indeed believe there is eternal disadvantage waiting upon the fleeing of them. O you who flee Christ both when you are alone and when you are in company, let this provoke you: the fleeing of these things that are clearly pointed out to be your duty may bring eternal destruction upon you, when your poverty shall come upon you as an armed man, and as travail upon a woman with child.

The fourth consideration to press you to guard against slothfulness is this: there are eight things that slothfulness kills. First, it kills many precious and excellent convictions. Perhaps there are some who go home from sermons with this conviction, "I am a truly slothful Christian, and am truly far below my duty." Now, what becomes of all your convictions? Slothfulness, the great murderer, ruins and murders them all. There are some who are convinced, and say, "Alas, I want love." Yet slothfulness kills that conviction. Some are convinced of this idea: "I am yet a stranger to the Son of God, and unacquainted with Him." And yet slothfulness kills that conviction. Slothfulness is to conviction like Pharaoh to the male children of Israel—as soon as they are born it drowns them and puts them away. How oft have you been convinced, and yet slothfulness banishes your convictions?

Second, it kills many precious and excellent resolutions. Is it not certain that sometimes a Christian, at such a fast and at such a communion, takes on such resolutions and purposes? And what becomes of them all? Even slothfulness cuts the neck of all these resolutions and makes all our goodness to be fleeting as the early cloud and as the morning dew. Are there not any here who are not convinced that they have broken the resolutions they took on at the last communion they attended? Now, what has done it? Even slothfulness. You do not take pains to prosecute your resolutions and bring them to performance. Some of us resolve today yet break [that resolve] tomorrow.

Third, it kills many precious and excellent desires for God and Jesus Christ. Will not sometimes the soul desire for communion with God? And will it not sometimes cry forth, "When shall I come and appear before God" (Ps. 42:2)? And will it not sometimes put up that desire, "O to be near Him, and to be conformed to His image!" Slothfulness kills those desires and makes them to vanish and fly away.

Fourth, it kills many precious and excellent motions of the Spirit of God. Is it not certain that Christ will sometimes come unto your heart, and cry out, "Open to me, my sister, my love, my dove, my undefiled" (Song 5:2)? What becomes of these? Even slothfulness makes Christ to depart and kills these excellent motions of the Spirit.

Fifth, it kills many sweet and excellent enjoyments of God. What is the reason that Christians are often brought to put up this complaint, "If this were Christ whom I have found, would He not rest in His love and stay longer with me? His visits are but standing visits; He comes, and presently He is gone again." It is even slothfulness that kills many sweet and excellent enjoyments.

Sixth, slothfulness kills in a great measure (at least it brings to the very gates of spiritual death) the graces of faith and of love, so that Christ may take that complaint against them, "Thou hast left thy first love" (Rev. 2:4). And what is the reason that so many are weak in the faith? It is even this: slothfulness.

Seventh, it kills in a very great measure our hatred against sin and detestation of our idols. Believe it: slothfulness is one of the strongest and most silent protectors for our idols. What is the reason that so many persons have so little hatred and detestation of sin? Slothfulness has eaten out the hatred as it were—slothfulness is that which takes up the matter and makes peace between our idols and our hearts.

Eighth, it kills the strength that sometimes a Christian has had in refilling and wrestling against his temptations. What is the reason that not only a temptation, but the very shadow of a temptation, is able to overcome us? It is because of slothfulness. There is nothing that some people meet with but it becomes a temptation to them; affliction and poverty become their temptation, prosperity and abundance becomes their temptation, applause and approbation becomes a temptation, lack of applause and approbation becomes a temptation, liberty in prayer becomes a temptation, lack of liberty, and bonds in prayer become a temptation to them; yea, a wife becomes a temptation to her husband, and children become a temptation to parents. Almost such is the cursed frame of our hearts, that we can cast our eyes upon nothing but it becomes a temptation to us.

The fifth consideration to provoke you to guard against slothfulness is this: if a spirit is slothful in doing the work of religion, then no doubt it is most active in the work of the devil, for it is impossible to keep the spirit of man idle. Therefore, if your spirit be not active in doing the work of religion, unquestionably it will be diligent in the work of the devil. It is impossible to keep the spirit of a man not active about something. Our spirits are not idle even when we sleep. I do not question, but I am sure of it: the spirit of man may do as much sin when he is sleeping as might ruin a thousand worlds. When our eyes sleep, our spirits sleep not. This is indeed a strange thing, as it proves the immortality of the soul and the fact that there is a root of bitterness springing within us night and day.

There is this sixth consideration to press you to this: slothfulness is that which blackens the beauty and excellency of a Christian. What is the reason that Christians, who were once white as the snow, and pure as the eagle, are now become black as a raven? What is the reason that Christians are become degenerate, that we have lost the beauty that once the saints had? What is the reason that we are degenerate, that we are neither father-like nor brother-like? "I went by the field of the slothful...and, lo, it was all grown over with thorns" (Prov. 24:30–31). A Christian is called "a garden inclosed" in the Scriptures (Song 4:12) in which there ought to grow nothing but pleasant plants. And what is the reason that he who ought to be a garden trimmed is now a field of thorns? It is even our slothfulness, which makes us unpleasant in the sight of God.

The seventh consideration to provoke you to guard against slothfulness is this: that slothfulness has these three notable prejudices and disadvantages waiting on it. First, it is the mother of much senseless unbelief and formal disputing of our interest in Christ. I may allude to Psalm 14:4–5, which says, "They…call not upon the LORD. There were they in great fear." I say, slothfulness in duty is that which is the rile of many of our disputings.

I do not say that diligence would loosen many of our knots, but I am sure if the Christians of this time were more diligent, there would be fewer disputings (I mean formally) of our interest in God. If so I may speak by the way, there is a fourfold form that Christ does exceedingly hate: there is a form of religion lacking the power of it, a form of knowledge lacking the life of it, a form of duty lacking the substance of it, and a form of exercise lacking the real exercise. It is no wonder God gives some of us a dreadful exercise, for when we lack an exercise, we counterfeit an exercise. But I think a Christian need never lack an exercise; for, when you lacked an exercise, this may be an exercise to you, that you lack an exercise.

The second disadvantage that comes by slothfulness is this: it is the mother of apostasy and declining. It may provoke the justice of God to write your spot upon your forehead, that all who pass by shall cry out, "There is the person who made not the God of Jacob his refuge!" One to a hundred if a slothful Christian goes through the world without a spot; and if he goes through the world without some dispensation of the anger of God, or some wonderful exercise, I would have that person suspecting whither he is going.

And what wonder is it, since prayer is that which seeks strength from God to help him in his way? I would ask this, by the way, of the sluggards in this house, of the professors sitting up and sitting down upon the length of that which you have attained: What do you know but there may be a temptation within some days' march of you that may make you a scandal unto the gospel, and the gospel a scandal unto you? What do you know but when your spot may be written on your forehead in legible letters that all who pass by may read it? The disadvantage that waits upon it is this: a slothful Christian is a naked Christian. You know what I mean by a naked Christian. I mean this: a slothful Christian is naked because his shame appears, and he is an open bait to all temptations. The devil needs not use more than one word to a slothful Christian. Yea, if I may speak in such a grave purpose, if the devil do but wag his finger upon a slothful Christian, he will run after him. The devil needs not fight much with a slothful Christian, for a slothful Christian fights against himself. Therefore, guard against slothfulness: "Watch ye and pray, lest ye enter into temptation" (Mark 14:38).

The last consideration to move you to guard against slothfulness is this: slothfulness brings a Christian to much spiritual poverty. I mean not that poverty which is mentioned in Matthew 5:3. I mean that poverty which is accompanied with much decay. Hence that word, "He becometh poor that dealeth with a slack hand" (Prov. 10:4). What is the reason that we are decayed and become poor? It is even this: we are not fervent in spirit, diligent in business, serving the Lord.

There are three sorts of religion, none of which are right, and if we were all searched, we would be found one of those sorts. There is first the sluggard's religion, and that is a most predominant religion. The sluggard's soul desires and has nothing because "his hands refuse to labour" (Prov. 21:25). If desires could bring a soul to heaven, then Balaam would be in heaven, for he had many excellent desires. The second sort of religion which is not right is the hypocrite's religion. There is as much difference between a hypocrite and a real Christian as there is between a painted man and a real man. I confess, a hypocrite has the outside of religion, but he lacks the inward part of it. A third form of religion which is also most common and yet comes short of true religion is the conceited, presumptuous, and proud religion. Many think to win heaven by their own righteousness, but they have a better opinion[1] of themselves than God has of them.

The second thing that I shall speak to at this time is this: Are there none of you who, since we began to speak of those disadvantages

---

1. Original, "conceit."

that wait upon slothfulness, are provoked to cry out, "O how shall I get slothfulness killed and amended"? *I will now propose these nine remedies of this evil.*

First, O sluggard, would you be diligent? Then let the lively impression of that which you seek from God be engraved upon your heart. What is the reason that the Christians of this time are not diligent? It is because they know not their need. You know that phrase which we use, "Necessity makes dumb men orators"—I may add, necessity makes lame men to labor.

Second, if we saw our necessity, we would not take a refusal. If so I may speak, necessity is one of the most unmannerly things that can be, for it will not go away from God's door till He answers it. Oh, necessity would make us diligent in the things unto which He calls us! "This poor man cried, and the LORD heard him" (Ps. 34:6). It would be an excellent sight if every one of us got a sight of our necessities, for I suppose some of us are as great strangers unto our own hearts as if we were living a thousand miles away from one another.

The third thing that I would propose as a remedy of this evil is this, O sluggard: study to be much acquainted with God, and to have much knowledge of the Most High. This is clear when we compare Job 22:21 with verse 27: "Acquaint now thyself with [God]" (v. 21), and the fruit shall be that "thou shalt make thy prayer unto him" (v. 27). "If thou knewest the gift of God, and who it is that saith to thee, Give me to drink...thou wouldest have asked of him, and he would have given thee living water" (John 4:10). What is the reason we correspond so little with God? It is because we know Him not.

Sadly, O Christian, would you be diligent? Then, fourth, walk within sight of approaching death and judgment. O Christian, would you shake hands with cold earth every day, would you walk within sight of this that once you must appear before Him, it would provoke you to be diligent. "Whatsoever thy hand findeth to do, do it with thy might" (Eccl. 9:10). The argument is that eternity approaches, after which you can do nothing. I am sure that if in the morning we thought we are now a day nearer eternity than before, it would be impossible for us to be so slothful as we are.

The fifth remedy that I would propose is this: that a Christian should walk under the impression of the sweet constraining love of God, that the soul should be under the sweet impression of Christ's love. This is clear in 2 Corinthians 5:14 where Paul, letting down the principle of his obedience, says, "The love of Christ constraineth us."

The sixth remedy that I would propose is this: that a Christian should walk under the impression of the omniscience of God. "I have kept thy precepts and thy testimonies: for all my ways are before thee" (Ps. 119:168). "Would you know," says he, "why I am such a diligent Christian? Because I knew there was nothing I did but the Lord knew it."

The seventh remedy that I would prescribe is this: study to have your heart inclined and engaged to the doing of duty. This was David's practice: "I have inclined mine heart to perform thy statutes alway, even unto the end" (Ps. 119:112). It is indeed a thing most remarkable, never to be out of obedience of His commandments, and not just for a while, but always, even to the end. He goes on to say, "My soul hath kept thy testimonies" (v. 167). And what leads him to this? "I love them," he says of God's testimonies. To have your heart engaged unto the duties of religion would make you a diligent Christian.

The eighth remedy that I would propose is this: I would charge every one who is here, young and old, professors and not professors, you who know God, and you who are ignorant of Him—I desire you today, in His name, to take that bond of love upon your heart, that you may take this resolution away with you, "I shall never be such a slothful Christian anymore." This was David's practice: "I have sworn, and I will perform it, that I will keep thy righteous judgments" (Ps. 119:106). I do not press you to hold up your hands, but I press you in the sight of God the Father, the first person of the blessed Trinity, and in the sight of the Son, the second person of the blessed Trinity, and in the sight of the Holy Ghost, the third person of the blessed Trinity, and in the sight of all the angels and saints who are about the throne, and in the sight of all the people who are here, that this be the oath that you will swear, and that you will study to perform, that you will not be slothful anymore.

The ninth remedy that I would prescribe is this: if you would be above the idol of slothfulness, then study to keep yourself under high, stately, and majestic apprehensions of God. I am sure of this:

the low conceptions we have of the majesty of God are the cause why many of us bow so seldom to Him. That is a strange word of the psalmist, "I give myself unto prayer" (Ps. 109:4), or, as the word may be translated, "I prayed." He would say, "I am so much taken up in that work that they may call my name 'Prayer.'"

I shall not at this time speak much more unto you, only I would have you take these two words home with you. First, will you think, and second consider, what is the exercise of the saints who are above, of whom that word may be said? They have died in the Lord, and rest from their labors; their reward is with them, and their works follow them. I say, think what is the exercise of all those glorious thousands who are round about the throne, who have now entered into the glorious and eternal possession and enjoyment of God, to whom wisdom's ways, while they were here, were pleasant? I am sure the day is coming when the Christian who is most in the duties of religion shall not repent of it. Never a person went down to his grave without this conviction, "Woe is me that I spent so little of my time in the duties of religion." Are there not some here who have not spoken their prayers to God today? There are some who they either slight duties without conviction, or else without sorrow if they be convinced; for the neglect of duty they do not mourn. Now, do you think that heaven will be given without work? Do you not know that word, "The kingdom of heaven suffereth violence, and the violent take it by force" (Matt. 11:12)? O can such a delusion as this overtake you? Do not think to win heaven without prayer! Dare I say that word? I wish I were mistaken, but I doubt much if there was a generation since Christ was in the flesh in which there were fewer heirs of salvation than there shall be in this one. I think we have served ourselves heirs to all the evils that are common to the people of God more now than in any age before.

And there is this that I would say: I confess it is a matter of astonishment to us that, though God is taking so much pains with us, there should be so little stirring and moving of our hearts in the duties of religion. O Glasgow's ignorance of God! I may speak it to your name. I doubt not but there are some in Glasgow who by their lack of knowledge do not distinguish themselves from pagans; that, though they be thirty or forty or eighty years old, do not know that there is a God. I am afraid one of these three sad and lamentable sentences is cast upon many in this place.

First, "If any man be ignorant, let him be ignorant" (1 Cor. 14:38). If there be any person who has not the knowledge of the Most High, let him be ignorant still. Shut his eyes, that he does not see nor understand the things that belong to his peace. There is no question that I have ground to say that there may be many about whom this sentence is said.

Second, "He that is unjust, let him be unjust still" (Rev. 22:11). These words are the seal of the prophecy, as the words going before show: "He who is filthy, let him be filthy still." Hosea 4:17 is an explication of this sad truth: "Ephraim is joined to idols: let him alone."

Third, "Because I have purged thee, and thou wast not purged, thou shalt not be purged from thy filthiness any more, till I have caused my fury to rest upon thee" (Ezek. 24:13). As it were, God with His hand lifted up to heaven has sworn this with an oath, "O sluggard, you would not be purged, and you shall not be purged any more till thou die."

But some of us are under such hardness and blindness that all those dangers will not occasion one sad thought. I shall say no more (oh that I could say, "I do not desire this evil day") but I am sure there have been such pains taken upon you these several years past that, if the same pains had been taken upon the heathen, they would have brought forth more answerable fruit. And I may say this, O Glasgow, Glasgow, if the things that have been done in you had been done in Tyre and Sidon, or Sodom and Gomorrah, they would have repented long ago in dust and ashes. Now, what will you do in the day of desolation, when destruction shall come from afar? Where will you flee for rest? And where will you leave your glory? It is He who can commend this word to you, and cause you to stand up from the dead, that He may give you life. To Him be the praise.

What if Andrew Gray had a blog today?

Would you want to read it?

VISIT
ReformationScotland.org/blog/andrew-gray/

REFORMATION SCOTLAND

Reforming Yourself | Reforming Your Family | Reforming Your Church

REFORMATION SCOTLAND

Andrew Gray came from an era of great Scottish preachers and writers. The period of the Second Reformation (1638–1661) was the greatest time of radical reformation and rediscovery of biblical truth in Scotland. It was also the greatest spiritual revival that Scotland has ever experienced.

Reformation Scotland mines spiritual wisdom from Second Reformation leaders, making their profound insights into Christ and biblical truth accessible for today's church and the challenges it faces. Through film, podcasts, print, study courses, and blog articles, Reformation Scotland provides resources for engaging in reformation today. The spiritual heritage of the Second Reformation helps us make mature disciples by teaching them to observe all that Christ has commanded.